Jailhouse Journal of an OB/GYN

Bruce S. Steir, M.D.

AuthorHouse™
1663 Liberty Drive, Suite 200
Bloomington, IN 47403
www.authorhouse.com
Phone: 1-800-839-8640

© 2008 Bruce S. Steir, M.D.. All rights reserved.

No part of this book may be reproduced, stored in a retrieval system, or transmitted by any means without the written permission of the author.

First published by AuthorHouse 5/12/2008

ISBN: 978-1-4343-7460-8 (sc)
ISBN: 978-1-4343-7461-5 (hc)

Library of Congress Control Number: 2008902679

Printed in the United States of America
Bloomington, Indiana

This book is printed on acid-free paper.

Dedication

This memoir is primarily dedicated to my loving wife, Yen Aeschliman, whose patience and skills have provided me with the necessary guidance to produce this manuscript. More importantly she has comforted me through a very difficult place in my life that has allowed me to live in peace and to accept the fate of my involuntary retirement.

And to all the women who have exercised their right to reproductive choices and to their daughters and granddaughters that their rights will continue to be honored.

Acknowledgements

My noteworthy thanks to Laura Leon for her creativity and professionalism in the editing of this manuscript.

And to my tireless attorney, Doron Weinberg and his staff, who did their best to have my indictment for homicide dismissed by the court and finally had me plead down to involuntary manslaughter to avoid a trial in an inhospitable venue.

My heartfelt appreciation to my brother-in-law, Bich Nguyen, a technology wizard, who saved me from despair by retrieving and reconstructing my manuscript after I had accidentally deleted the entire text on two different occasions.

My gratitude to the many hard-working, dedicated feminists of the Women's Health Specialists Clinics in Northern California, who provided me with emotional support, legal research and a Defense Fund that enabled me to somehow survive the ordeal.

Table of Contents

Pre-Med
"Camp Miami Beach" 1942-45 29
We Are The (White) Boys From Old Florida, F-L-O-R-I-D-A! . . .41
An Ordinary Hangover 49

Medical School
My Gift To Microbiology 67
Cadavers Tell No Tales 71

Internship
Huey Long's Cement Uterus 97
Come To The Mardi Gras 109
A Rare Obstetrical Complication .117
Sex and the Crescent City 121

Residency
Saint Vincent's and a Slice of Pizza 135
The Sisters of Mercy 153
Mount Sinai Hospital (Back Home Again) 157
A New Concept in Contraception 165
I Can't Be Pregnant 169
Muchos Bandidos 175
First-Born Baby 185

US Air Force
How A Gynecologist Helped To Win the Cold War 195
Where Were You When You Heard About JFK's Assassination? 201
Where Are Those Baby Girls Today? 207
Abortion and the French Connection 211
The Guilt of Our Fathers 215

Private Practice
To Cut or Not To Cut? 223
Abortion Is a Sin unless.... I need one 233
A Larger Venue Is Needed 237
Easter Egg Hunt In Seattle 241

US Navy
The Sailor From Twenty-Nine Palms 247

Abortion Provider
The Anti-Abortion Woman and the Hired Baby Killer 263
Have Speculum, Will Travel 267
A Botched Operation for Christmas: 273

Felon
Six In A Cell, One Bad Apple 287
From Quietude to Noise from Hell 293
Written Up 301
We are Praying for You 303
Vending Machine Cuisine 311
The Spousal Visit 319
Our Weekly Sarong Party 323
My Hospital Visit as a Felon 329

Prologue

This memoir is about the events that would terminate my career of forty years as a physician and have me incarcerated as well. These are some of the milestones in my life that inspired me to become a physician, encourage me to specialize in obstetrics & gynecology and eventually to compel me to become a full time abortion provider.

Although my professional life had been filled with exciting and remarkable adventures, my experiences as a doctor terminated as the result of the tragic death of a patient. This was followed by the collaboration between the anti-abortion network, the Medical Board of California and the District Attorney's Office in Riverside County. Their combined efforts enabled them to transform a civil lawsuit of malpractice into a criminal case with the charge of homicide.

My tumble into professional oblivion and financial collapse began on Friday the thirteenth of December 1996. On that day I performed sixteen abortions at a clinic in Riverside County, California. One of the women died that day. It was the only death I had ever been responsible for. Over the course of my career I performed somewhere around 40,000 legal abortions. That was one death too many for the patient, for the Medical Board of California, for the DA from Riverside County, for the anti-abortion activists and for me.

The patient was Sharon, a 27 year old, single mother of a 5-year-old boy. Sharon was about 21 weeks gestation based on a sonogram. Sharon was seen in the clinic on two consecutive days prior to the actual abortion. Because of the lack of abortion providers in her hometown she had to travel three hours in each direction three times to have her abortion. That adds up to six hours round trip on three consecutive days. This amount of travel could not have been good for her, although it is difficult to tell whether the travel itself contributed to the downward spiral her health took after she left the clinic.

It was routine for second trimester pregnancies to have their cervix softened and dilated prior to the procedure to enhance the ease and safety of the abortion. This process was accomplished by inserting several wooden matchstick-size firm rods made from Japanese processed seaweed called *laminara*. The sterilized *laminara* are osmotic dilators that swell overnight to the diameter of a pencil. Vaginal and cervical fluids are absorbed to enhance their enlargement. The next day they are removed by pulling them out of the cervical canal with an instrument. The partially dilated cervix then has multiple laminaria inserted to further advance the cervical dilatation. I removed her second set of *laminara* at the time of her abortion. Her cervix was adequately dilated. Everything seemed completely normal.

Sharon was administered intravenous sedation and a cervical block with *lidocaine* to augment pain management. The procedure went smoothly. The entire fetus was easily removed except for the *calvarium* or skull. It is very common for the *calvarium* to detach during the abortion. I was unable to locate it with the grasping forceps. I knew from experience that probing about and searching in the uterine cavity was a blind procedure and could lead to an accidental perforation of the uterus. Instead of searching with my mind's eye, I took care to ask my assistant to bring the portable sonogram machine into the procedure room. She complied and asked me why I wanted the sonogram machine. I answered with a cavalier remark, "because I want to retrieve the *calvarium* and not the bowel". The misinterpretation of that comment would later prove to be my undoing.

With direct visualization via the sonogram I was able to remove the fetal skull quickly and finish the procedure uneventfully.

Sharon went to the recovery area where her postoperative recovery course was normal with the usual sleepiness and cramping. All of her vital signs remained within the normal range. I performed several abortion procedures on other clients after Sharon's. Before she left I spoke with her and shared a Pepsi with her and her little son. She was very nice and there was no indication of the ill-fated future that awaited her. After the usual rest period in the clinic, her mother drove her home. From what I was told they made a short stop at a fast-food place. Sharon then told her mother she was feeling tired and wanted to lie down in the back seat.

When they arrived home an hour or so later Sharon could not be aroused from the car. Paramedics arrived and were unable to revive her. She was pronounced dead at a local hospital.

The autopsy report of the San Bernardo County Medical Examiner, Doctor Frank Sheridan, stated that the cause of death was intra-abdominal bleeding from a relatively small 1.5-centimeter perforation of the uterus. In addition it was noted that the small and large intestines were intact and there was no evidence of trauma to the bowel. In his initial autopsy report he referred to her death as accidental.

However, after receiving "additional information" weeks later, the Medical Examiner, under pressure from local anti-abortion activists and the California Medical Board, amended the conclusion to reflect that the manner of death was a "homicide as a result of gross negligence". The "additional information" was later proven to be completely incorrect.

The Riverside County prosecutors charged me not merely with involuntary manslaughter, which would be an appropriate charge for a death caused by gross negligence, but they charged me with second-degree murder. To the great astonishment of the medical and legal communities, they claimed that I consciously appreciated that I had placed Sharon's life in danger and willfully disregarded that danger. The prosecution oddly alleged that I knowingly perforated Sharon's uterus and pulled bowel down into the vagina through the dilated cervix with an instrument and then performed the incredible feat of pushing it back up through a 1.5-centimeter perforation, even though the autopsy had specifically noted that the bowel was completely in tact.

I allegedly disregarded a pulse rate of 110 beats per minute, reported to me by a clinic employee, and allowed Sharon to depart the clinic an hour after her procedure when I knew that her vital signs were unstable. If even one of these allegations were true I should have been charged with homicide. The true facts of the case would not come out until Bertha, the second attendant, testified some time later. But the damage had been done and the inaccuracies were allowed to stand as fact.

The prosecution relied almost entirely on the testimony of Nancy, the medical assistant who participated in Sharon's abortion procedure. She was interviewed on several occasions by investigators from the Medical Board. A critical portion of Nancy's testimony was her reconstruction of a brief conversation with me near the end of the ill-fated abortion procedure. Based on this conversation alone that allegedly supported the unjust charge of second-degree murder. When I asked her to bring the sonogram machine into the operating room she asked me why I wanted the sonogram machine. I responded, as previously stated, that "I want to retrieve the *calvarium* and not the bowel". Weeks later she recalled my casual remark as "I think I pulled bowel". Nancy also recalled that she asked me what I would do if I did pull bowel. I told her quite simply "I would call 911 for an ambulance".

Apart from that brief conversation, Nancy's testimony established that indeed nothing else disturbing or unusual had occurred that day with respect to Sharon's procedure or recovery. Nancy noted that Sharon never indicated that she had any sudden sharp pain during the procedure, as one would almost certainly expect if the uterus were perforated with a surgical instrument. She testified that my demeanor in the operating room, both before and after my conversation with her, was completely normal and neither frantic nor agitated. In the recovery area Sharon showed no indication of distress or unusual discomfort. She had stable vital signs, no excessive bleeding and she was able to walk to the bathroom with the usual assistance. Sharon's only complaint was that she was quite sleepy. That would not have been considered unusual being that she had received intra-venous medication for sedation and that she weighed only 90 pounds. All indications were that she would recover well in the usual course of time.

THE DEFENSE'S THEORY:

Frank Sheridan, the Medical Examiner for San Bernardino County, testified that his conclusion that the manner of death was changed to homicide rather than an accident was based significantly on investigative reports from the Medical Board of California instead of on clinical records and autopsy findings.

Sheridan was unaware that the Medical Board reports were inaccurate in a number of respects, and that their reports were written before the two principal percipient witnesses had been interviewed. Sheridan conceded that his altered conclusion "might have been affected by information that was subsequently demonstrated to be erroneous". Most significantly, Sheridan was led to believe from the Medical Board reports that Sharon, at the time of her release from the clinic, was exhibiting signs of physical distress, including an elevated pulse rate, pallor, vomiting, chills, pain and abdominal distension. In fact, however, none of these signs or symptoms, aside of one episode of vomiting, were observed or reported by any of the witnesses.

With respect to the prosecution's theory that "bowel had been pulled through the uterine perforation and into the vagina and then pushed back up into the abdomen", Sheridan could not state whether this had occurred or not. He did note that the autopsy did not reveal any damage to the bowel wall. Several expert witnesses for the defense clearly stated that it would be impossible to maneuver the bowel as suggested by the prosecution without causing major damage to the wall of the grasped intestine.

Bertha, an experienced medical assistant, testified that she assisted me on several cases after the procedure on Sharon. She also stated that I did not seem agitated or preoccupied, nor did I appear to be in a hurry to leave the clinic to "catch my plane".

Bertha testified that she did not observe Sharon to be in any distress while she was in the recovery room. When Bertha asked Sharon how she was doing, Sharon replied that she was okay except that she felt drowsy.

Bertha took and recorded Sharon's final vital signs at 6:05 P.M.

Her blood pressure was 110/62 and her pulse was 92. The pulse oxymeter revealed the oxygen level to be normal.

Doctor Eugene Albright testified as an expert witness for the prosecution. Planned Parenthood in Riverside employed Dr. Eugene Albright. He admitted that he had performed only several hundred second trimester abortions but would not knowingly perform abortions beyond 16 weeks. Dr. Albright was unfamiliar with the instruments used in 20-week procedures and was not able to distinguish or name the different kinds of forceps used. Why he testified as an expert witness in my case is puzzling and troubling since he had no experience with the procedure I performed.

Dr. Albright had received the same medical reports on which Dr. Sheridan had relied. He expressed some concern when it was revealed that most of the information upon which he relied might have been erroneous. Albright additionally testified that he believed that a physician could pull the bowel through the 1.5-centimeter uterine perforation and into the vagina and then replace it into the abdominal cavity in such a way that an autopsy would not detect this occurrence. He stated further that all of that maneuvering could be accomplished without injury to the bowel and without causing severe pain to the patient. This statement amazed all those in attendance who had performed or assisted in abortion procedures. His statements simply could not be true, his credentials in no way made him an expert in the case, and yet what he stated as an "expert witness" was allowed to stand as fact.

The California Medical Association, (CMA) a non-profit professional organization representing more than 30,000 physicians throughout the state, was understandably alarmed that a physician would be charged with homicide as the result of a patient's death. Subsequently they convened a panel of physicians that were Board Certified in obstetrics and gynecology and with current experience in performing second trimester abortions. The experts practiced in different areas of the state, and were in both academic and private practice. Their services were provided without financial compensation.

Although I was not a member of the CMA, the panel reviewed the medical records, the coroner's report, and testimony from witnesses in my case. They refuted the prosecution's assertion that I should have known that Sharon was in distress following the procedure and its assertion that I had knowingly "pulled bowel" during the abortion. Had I pulled the bowel through the uterine wall, the experts stated, the bowel would have shown significant signs of trauma, which it did not; Sharon would have reacted strongly to the pain, which she did not; and it would have been extremely difficult if not impossible to push the bowel back through the small 1.5 centimeter perforation in the uterus without the attendant noticing what was happening. The CMA experts concluded: *"Based on the information reviewed and their collective experience or judgment, the conduct of Dr. Steir on December 13, 1996 cannot be characterized as criminally negligent behavior, manslaughter or any kind of criminal act"*.

At this point it became clear that criminal charges should be dismissed. Instead of dismissing the charge of homicide, the judge, who was noticeably inattentive during the hearing, claimed that "it sounded like a crime had been committed and a person had died as a result and that the People should proceed to trial". It sounded like a phrase he had used before to expedite cases with which he was visibly, exasperatingly bored. He simply refused to listen.

Soon afterwards the defense's local investigator revealed that this judge was an evangelical Christian and was known to hold bible sessions in his chambers. We dismissed the judge from the case.

From the very beginning, this case had been a part of the overall attacks on abortion providers by the Medical Board of California, which in 1997 was stacked with anti-abortion administrators and investigators. They were engaged in a concerted and well-documented campaign to harass providers of late term abortions, by placing them on probation and suspending or revoking their licenses. The strategy seemed to be to scare doctors away from becoming abortion providers. Without abortion providers there is no "choice".

It soon became apparent that the Medical Board had acted against me with extreme and unusual haste and vigor-- and with incorrect information. The Medical Board submitted its investigative report before they had interviewed the two critical witnesses. As a result, the Medical Examiner also received inaccurate information about Sharon's death when he ruled it a homicide. He subsequently testified that he would have ruled differently had he been presented with more complete and accurate information. How could such inaccuracies stand uncorrected?

Despite assertions that that their main responsibility is in regard to physicians' licenses, the Medical Board continued to work on my case with the Riverside County prosecutor's office six months after I had surrendered my medical license. A communication from the Deputy District Attorney of Riverside County to the Medical Board primary investigator urging him to "beef up" the charges against me to enable them to have the charges changed from involuntary manslaughter to second-degree murder. The Medical Board complied by summoning the so-called medical expert in the case. That was when the not-so-expert Doctor Albright came into the picture.

When my attorney was made aware of this correspondence he asserted, "Since the Board has repeatedly taken the position that its only responsibility is with regard to licenses, it is not clear why a Medical Board investigator remained active in the criminal prosecution of the defendant long after Dr. Steir had surrendered his license".

An anti-abortion activist was inappropriately involved in the Medical Board's case against me. I don't know how or why she become involved, but Janet Dreisbach, a virulent anti-abortion activist from the Palm Springs area in Riverside County, described by a former Director of the Medical Board as having a "very close liaison" with the board, somehow obtained copies of the Medical Board's investigative materials before they were available to the public. She exerted heavy pressure on the Medical Board and the District Attorney to prosecute me as a criminal.

My attorney asserts that I am the only physician ever referred by the Medical Board for criminal prosecution for a *medical error*. The Medical Board has not refuted this assertion.

Dreisbach has pressured the board to take action against doctors in California who provided abortion services. She has received special access and attention as a result. As early as 1990, Dreisbach was in contact with Vernon Leeper, then the Chief of the Medical Board's enforcement section, who sent her the names of several abortion providers with pending accusations. In a 1990 letter, she wrote, "Would you please list the active accusations against doctors based on botched abortions. I need physician's name, deputy Attorney General handling the case, filing date and nature of the accusation". Mr. Leeper provided her with information relating to four doctors and wrote: "The following information is only from my memory, and as soon as time permits, I will pull [sic] my regional staff to see if there are additional cases."

The Medical Board welcomed this "close liaison" with Dreisbach and this arrangement provided fuel to an effort that was clearly anti-abortion and politically motivated and hardly the blind justice that we expect from the legal system.

I learned many things during this ordeal. One important lesson is that our legal system is, if nothing else, chaotic. Certain types of cases like my own get rigorously investigated while others fade into oblivion. Under such circumstances, justice cannot possibly be applied equally across the board.

The Medical Board submitted their version of events in my case to the office of the Attorney General. They contended that I knew or should have known that I had perforated Sharon's uterus, that her vital signs were unstable and she was in visible physical distress after the procedure, and that I had left the clinic while she was showing signs of distress because I was in a hurry to get to the airport. Where this false information originated I have no idea.

The Attorney General at that time was Dan Lungren, an avid abortion opponent who in his subsequent unsuccessful run for governor of the state would declare that his "prosecution of doctors for botched abortions was a testament to his support for women's rights."

I did not go to trial. The practice of Medicine went on trial.

A patient's death is a devastating blow to any physician. We have taken an oath to heal and to do no harm. Based on that premise we fail when a patient dies in our care. To be charged with murder for a patient's death, however, is a situation beyond anyone's worst nightmare. I believe that doctors who provide abortion services should be held accountable and afforded the same due process as any other medical professional. To my knowledge, it is extremely rare for doctors to be brought up on murder charges for the death of a patient. While always tragic, patient deaths sometimes occur in nearly every branch of medicine, including legal abortion.

The State's highly unusual action of prosecuting me, an abortion provider, for murder would surely serve as a deterrent to doctors willing to provide this procedure as an integral part of their services to women as part of their reproductive rights. There is little doubt that this small group of vocal activists succeeds in scaring away many doctors from providing abortions. I am very sorry to see the justice system be used as a tool to attack the few doctors who perform legal but controversial procedures. To do so threatens all physicians and their patients.

From the date of Sharon's death on December 13th, 1996 until my surprise arrest in October, 1997 I had been engaged in a civil law suit based on the charges of malpractice and negligence.

The insurance carriers paid the liability claims to her young son and to his guardian grandparents. The amount of the settlement was very substantial (close to a million dollars).

In lieu of a lengthy and costly hearing with the Medical Board I decided that it would be best to surrender my medical license. A hearing, with a more than likely negative outcome, would find my license being revoked or suspended. In March 1997 I bid a sad farewell to my medical license and to my practice over the past forty years . I rationalized that at 66 years of age it was not so disastrous an end as it would have been if I were not at the age of senior retirement.

The Medical Board sent a letter acknowledging the surrendering of my license. They also advised me that I might not use the designation "M.D." after my name on cards or stationary. My frame of mind at the time understandably perceived their letter as somewhat overbearing. I responded to them by declaring that the University of Miami awarded my M.D. degree to me and only they could revoke my diploma and title. Of course I agreed that I would not practice medicine without a license. I did not receive any further communication from them.

Ten months after Sharon's tragic death, the doorbell interrupted my breakfast. The ringer communicated through the intercom that he was there to pick up my surrendered medical license certificate. I went downstairs wearing my bathrobe.

When I opened my front door six men in dark suits greeted me. I was hoping that they were evangelists from the church of the Latter Day Saints. The suit closest to my door recited that I was under arrest for murder but did not read my Miranda rights that we know so well from TV's Law and Order. They then introduced themselves, not by name but by their jurisdiction. Two were from the San Francisco County sheriff's office, two from Riverside County and a pair of aces from the Medical Board.

I was so totally surprised that instead of being speechless I uttered worthless words "You're arresting me for murder? Just wait until Diane Feinstein and Barbara Boxer get word of this!"

They told me that I could go back into my house and get dressed but two of them would accompany me. My wife was still in bed and when I returned to the bedroom I sheepishly informed her of my plight. Gallows humor did not escape me as I told her "Lenny Brisco was waiting for me to change clothes and go downtown" (Jerry Orbach's character in Law & Order). One of the detectives followed me into the bathroom and watched me shave, urinate and wash-up. They allowed me to call my attorney, Mark Merin in Sacramento. Mark told me that he did not defend criminal cases but referred me to an attorney that specialized in criminal law.

I bid adieu to my wife and told her that I would post bail and come home as soon as possible.

They accompanied me back to the front door. I was informed that ordinarily they would handcuff me for the ride downtown but they would spare me the embarrassment from neighbors seeing me hand-cuffed. When we arrived at the Hall of Justice in downtown San Francisco they placed the mandatory handcuffs on me. I covered them with my jacket as I walked from the car to the building across the street. I was formally booked, fingerprinted, photographed and placed in a holding cell.

The cell was too brightly lit and furnished with a stainless steel commode and benches fastened to the plain cement floor. It was inhabited by an assortment of scary looking disheveled drunks and accused criminals. The cell population varied from 3 to as many as 12 men at any given time. It was a revolving door for the local drunks who get picked up for disorderly conduct like urinating in public or being sprawled out unconscious on the sidewalk.

Some, like me, were waiting to post bail or to be arraigned. Others were going off to cells in the county jail in the adjoining building or awaiting transportation to a state prison having already been sentenced.

My attorney arrived and we met behind a glass partition and conversed on telephones. He informed me that Riverside County had set my bail amount at $250,000. That certainly was not an amount that I could write out a check for. It would take several working days to sell stocks and place a lien on my home for Riverside County. Doron, my attorney coordinated this activity with my stockbroker and wife.

Because of my advanced years and history of hypertension, I spent that night in a medical ward cell in the county jail. I did not sleep because of my mind working overtime and the constant noise and light in and around the cell.

The following morning, I was informed that I was being shipped to Riverside County to be arraigned on the charge of homicide.

Doron spoke with the DA's office in Riverside asking them to hold off transporting me needlessly because the bail money would be forthcoming in the next day or so. The assistant D.A. agreed to hold my departure off awaiting the cashier's check the following day. Shortly thereafter, a prison bus arrived with two marshals from Riverside. They had the necessary paper work to transfer me from San Francisco to Riverside, a distance of around 400 miles.

They would not await any negotiation between my attorney and the DA's office. I was not allowed to call my wife or attorney to tell them that I was going south.

The prison bus is not like a Greyhound coach. The seats are firm without padding and loud rock music blares away on cheap speakers without stop.

The three or four other passengers were clad in orange jumpsuits and had their legs fettered and hands cuffed, just like me.

We were told that we are going to Sacramento County jail. I tried to explain calmly that I was supposed to be transported to Riverside County. The marshal and the driver told me that they know what they are doing and if they wanted any more information regarding my itinerary they would let me know. The prison bus, it seemed, makes rounds of various county jails and state prisons in order to pick up and deposit felons being transferred from one correctional facility to another for various reasons.

I know my way to San Jose and also to Sacramento. I sat there wondering why they were heading due east towards Stockton instead of northeast toward Sacramento. One fellow inmate seated across the bus aisle suggested that they were seeking a way to avoid the "five o'clock traffic" on the U.S. 80. He apparently had not noticed that we were in snail's-pace bumper-to-bumper traffic on interstate 580. The usual 90-minute journey to Sacramento lasted four and a half deafening sleepless hours.

I was to find out later that the reason for the bus's circuitous route was to avoid, or at least diminish, the possibility of being highjacked by persons invited to free a convicted felon being transported away for a long prison stay. Such bravado and drama had never occurred to my no-rap sheet mentality.

Upon arriving at the Sacramento County jail I was informed by one of my fellow passengers, no doubt a career criminal, that we had arrived at the "Old Sac jail, not the newer one downtown". This jail, he claimed, was apparently thought of in a most negative way. It did not take long for me to see why.

I had entered a debtor's prison in Dickensian London, or so it seemed in appearance. The facility was much in need of renovation or better yet demolition.

I was in my second day of incarceration and now I was being lined up against a wall and told to strip and assume the humiliating position for my second strip search. The evening meal served on the cement floor of a holding cell was a bologna sandwich on soggy cold white bread, an orange and a container of milk.

As bedtime approached, I asked the marshal to inquire about my high blood pressure medication that was to be transported with me from San Francisco. He returned an hour later to tell me that the nurse does not have my medicine. And besides, overnight prisoners do not qualify for dispensing of medications.

My sleepless night was long and quite horrible; not unlike a bad repetitive dream. The cell contained eight double-decked beds, all inhabited by white males. There were floor to ceiling bars as in old jailhouse movies facing a dimly lit corridor. Across the narrow hall was a similar cell where all the inmates were black males. Racial slurring, some funny but mostly ugly, were hurled back and forth like verbal mortar rounds. It was as if being imprisoned had caused sudden-onset immaturity. It became so annoying and stupid that I found myself yelling from my upper bunk, "quit the god-damned N word and shut up already!" From the other end of the cell came, "Hey, old man, are you a nigger lover?" I replied that I wanted to get some sleep. When there was some silence I could hear the pitter-patter of little feet running about and the high pitched squealing sound of rats running hastily across the cement floor of the cell. I leaned over the side of my bunk and saw them scurrying about. I felt some comfort being assigned to an upper bunk.

To make the night longer and more bizarre, someone had rolled a joint in toilet paper and was passing it around. I could smell the illegal weed that has the aroma of mild skunk and the momentary whiff from a Corona cerveza as it is opened. I am familiar with this odor from living one block from Haight-Ashbury in beautiful San Francisco. Instead of refusing to take a hit and being anti-social, I feigned sleep. I pondered about the cunning ingenuity of the felon who was able to sneak weed and matches into the jail, or was it being supplied by enterprising fellows from the inside? Besides the possibility of contracting hepatitis,

I knew that marijuana produced a strange time warp for me. I wanted my stay in the Sacramento old-jailhouse to be as short and uneventful as possible.

Very early in the A.M. it was time for me to hit the road again. There would be no morning hot shower, hot coffee or anti-hypertension medications. An orange, a hard-boiled egg and milk would have to satisfy my hunger.

Before we could leave for the prison bus we had to be strip-searched. As I assumed that most degrading position I could not help but wonder, "What the hell do they think I want to take *out* of jail?"

I never realized how many prisons there are in the Central Valley of California. To just live in the Central Valley would be enough punishment let alone to be incarcerated there. Our bus stopped at every one of the correctional facilities in route to Riverside for a felon drop off or pick up.

One of the stops was at the women's prison near the town of Chowchilla. The two male marshals left the motor running while they were in the prison for one and a half hours. Lots of diesel fuel to pollute the clean desert air. That was a long lunch break. Perhaps it was a routine "nooner" at a women's prison. As at all the facilities that we visited, the bus was driven into an electrically controlled gate that essentially enclosed the vehicle within a fenced off area with razor wired tops on both sides. This surrounded the bus and rendered it inaccessible from the prison and the outside world.

At the state prison in Wasco, the marshals again left the motor running and this time the radio was left on blaring out very loud and stupid music. As they were departing the bus I asked the one that was riding "shotgun" if he could turn the music down as it was hurting my ears. He smiled and nodded, "No problem Pop". He then proceeded to the radio volume control near the dashboard and turned the volume up a little higher. He then smiled, looked me in the eye and asked, "Is that better now?"

I eyed a crumpled sheet of facial tissue on an empty seat behind me. I tore small fragments off and rolled them up to create earplugs. Inserting them proved to be a chore because of the limited reach of the waist shackle chain attached to my handcuffs.

My mouth was closer than my ears to my cuffed hands so eating dinner was a mere annoyance and self-humiliating experience.

The bus stopped at a fast-food joint in the town of Mojave where we dined on burgers, fries and soda inside the confines of the bus. I have difficulty opening those little plastic ketchup holders even without wearing handcuffs.

I kept thinking about that sadistic marshal and wondered how he got that way and how he might treat his wife and children. I suspected that if we were in Nazi Germany he would have used his revolver or club on me for asking him to lower the radio volume.

It was dark when the bus arrived at the Riverside County jail. The long wait in the cold, overly bright holding cell was followed by fingerprinting, mug shots, receiving bedding and fresh jail clothes, and of course no visit to a jail would be complete without the *de rigueur* strip search. Then came the surprise of the evening, a mandatory blood sample was drawn for future DNA studies. That act of involuntary phlebotomy bothered me. Shouldn't the implementation of a major decision like this first be subjected to a bioethics debate or a vote in a democracy?! I was in custody and at the mercy of the police. That is a scary feeling, especially when you are labeled a felon even though you are not a criminal.

My two sons and daughter arrived about ten hours after I was booked into the County jail. They carried with them a $250,000 cashier's check derived from liquidating my stock portfolio. This was given up as bail money. We then flew back home to San Francisco. I had been in three different jails in three days. I had been fingerprinted and photographed two times and strip-searched five times.

Before it was all over my entire life savings were depleted and I was no longer able to practice medicine. Medical liability insurance does not cover criminal charges that were imposed on me.

During that period, from the time of my arrest until my pleading guilty, there were seemingly endless trips to Riverside from San Francisco for my attorney and me. We were there for pre-trial hearings and various legal motions to dismiss evidence, motions to admit evidence, motion to dismiss the case based on selective prosecution. There were even legalese shenanigans like "Motion for reconsideration of orders granting in part and denying in part motion to quash subpoena Duces Tecum and motion for discovery has been taken under submission". Sure, O.K., whatever. The system seems to be set up to wear you down, tire you out and exhaust your resources until you simply don't care anymore.

The consensus of opinions from friends, family members and my attorneys was that I should plead guilty to involuntary manslaughter in lieu of standing trial for second-degree homicide. The latter, if I were found guilty, could send me to prison for as much as fifteen years. For me that would be a life sentence; my greatest fear was that the jury selection process would not exclude virulent closeted anti-abortion citizens. Also my serious depletion of financial assets convinced me to "throw in the towel". I felt I had no choice. I was emotionally and physically exhausted.

My wife joined my attorney and me into the judge's chambers in the Riverside County courthouse. We expressed our desire to plead guilty to involuntary manslaughter if there would be no jail time. The Honorable Judge Sherman made eye contact with me then turned her head to my attorney and clearly stated, "I don't want to send him to jail". She seemed pleased that we would settle this politically charged, high profile case without a lengthy and costly trial. The British born judge indicated that I would receive probation and community service. I felt like I was betraying the pro-choice people by pleading guilty to a crime that I did not commit, but I was experiencing a sense of relief that could only be perceived by putting this nightmare to rest.

The courtroom was full on the day of my formal sentencing. The Honorable Judge Vilia Sherman was presiding. The parents and son of the deceased addressed the Court as did the Deputy District Attorney, Kennis Clark. The synopsis of the Assistant D.A.'s remarks was to establish the fact that I was a well trained, experienced and Board Certified OB/GYN physician who either knew or should have known that I had caused injury to my patient. After all, she implied, I had experienced complications in the past.

A friend of the deceased spoke briefly and then lost her composure and began to scream repeatedly at me from the opposite end of the courtroom, "You should go to the graveyard to see what you have done", the Judge politely asked her to refrain from her emotional outburst.

My attorney, Doron Weinberg, presented his argument and then I addressed the Court hoping that my words would express the remorse that I had felt over the past years for Sharon's death. My only admission of guilt was that I had inadvertently broken my Hippocratic oath. As a physician I had sworn to "Do no harm". The sad fact was that I had inadvertently caused harm and she had died. Then the Judge pronounced my sentence:

- o Probation for a period of sixty months/ five years.

- o To be committed to the custody of the Riverside County jail for a period of one year, six months of which is to be suspended if I perform 1,000 community service hours.

There was an outbreak of audible dismay from my supporters in the courtroom. They must have wondered, as I did, whatever happened to the plea bargain that stated no incarceration.

The courtroom deputy marshal allowed me a quick hug goodbye with my wife. I flashed a goodbye wave to my three adult children. Then I was handcuffed and escorted out a side door to an elevator that took me down to a basement corridor that led me to the county jail.

PRE-MED

CHAPTER 1
Ninety-Day Wonders Came To Town
"Camp Miami Beach"
1942-45

The young soldiers arrived in droves. Thousands upon thousands of men of college age came to Miami Beach, Florida to train at the Officers' Candidate School (OCS). They were given the nickname "Ninety Day Wonders" because they would receive their officer's commission in only three months.

After three months of rigorous classroom studies, strenuous obstacle courses, long marching drills and vigorous exercise, they became second lieutenants of the U.S. Army or U.S. Army Air Corps.

It was 1942 and they were prepared to help put an end to World War II. They came from all over the United States and from all walks of life. As long as they had finished a minimum two years of college, passed a physical examination and had volunteered by enlisting they were qualified for OCS training.

The entire Miami Beach tourist industry--hotels, restaurants, and shops--was put on hold. Jeeps and Army trucks now replaced the Lincolns and Cadillacs that had been so prevalent on Collins Avenue and Ocean Drive, the main drags of the luxury hotels. The hotels and restaurants were leased or commandeered by the military for mess halls and barracks for the soldiers.

These young lions would leave after they received their commission and were either sent directly overseas to the theaters of war in Europe or the Pacific or to yet another state side military base for further specialized training.

My father, mother, sister, and I moved to Miami Beach in 1940. I was nine; my sister Irene was fourteen years old. My father owned a drug store and the business would soon become a family business.

Many of the OCS soldiers said that they enjoyed coming to the Cameo Pharmacy for the food, music, and for that warm feeling of being back home. The drug store also employed two young women and my sister, Irene, who was now sixteen years old. All three were very shapely and beautiful. Perhaps that was the main reason the young soldiers hung out at the drug store. Home style meat loaf and jukebox music may not have been the only reasons after all.

My sister worked at the drug store after school. She was in the tenth grade at Miami Beach Senior High School. She had fewer restrictions imposed on her for than she should have had. That is why she became pregnant in 1943. The OCS soldier that she had been seeing, from what I was told, was a twenty-one-year-old handsome lad with the Aryan looks so commonly seen in his home state of Wisconsin.

He had received his second lieutenant gold bars before my sister knew she was with child. He was shipped overseas with the Infantry shortly after being commissioned as an officer.

As you can imagine, my pregnant sister was devastated and was very afraid to tell our parents about her romance and subsequent predicament. She visited a local physician and had a pregnancy test and her first pelvic examination. The doctor told her that she was about ten weeks pregnant. My sister knew that her lover was now serving in North Africa. They had exchanged letters but she stopped hearing from him after a few months. Her last letter informed him of her pregnancy.

My sister broke the news to my mother. From all accounts and knowing my mother, she was neither comforting nor sympathetic. My mother reacted in the contrary by being very angry with my sister. My mother told my father in order to share this bad news too. The lack of empathy by my parents was not unusual for families in 1943, especially considering the turmoil and changes during WWII. A pregnancy without being married was a social disgrace beyond our imagination in the twentieth century.

Social morality and standards of right and wrong dictated that anyone in the type of "trouble" she was in should be harshly judged and shunned. But nature does not seem to agree. By every indication, the anticipated arrival of a first born should be a cause for great celebration. My sister felt betrayed by her own family and by society in general. She was in love. But her beau was in North Africa by now and could not defend her. How could the most beautiful thing that had ever happened to her be greeted with consternation, shame and judgment?! Where did these rules and preoccupations with rules come from when they clearly make no sense to the human mind, heart, or body?! Many nights she thought quietly in her room about "her little baby" and then cried herself to sleep. The truth doesn't mean much when everyone around you is living decorously rule-bound lives, or at least pretending to. The attitudes that prevailed forced my sister to have an abortion. What else was there to do? Well, she could drop out of school and have a baby and be a seventeen-year-old single mother, or she could have an illegal abortion and face the danger of dying, or she could have a baby and put it up for adoption, which would be too emotionally traumatic. It was, in that time and place, a no win situation.

My dad wanted the young man who made my sister pregnant to be aware of the situation, so he had my sister notify the Red Cross and told them to get in touch with the second lieutenant in North Africa as an emergency situation had arisen at home: a pregnancy! Surprisingly enough, after a week or so the Red Cross contacted my sister, they told her that she should call or write to his parents in Wisconsin. They furnished her with their telephone number and address. She did call them.

His mother told my sister that she was very sorry about the pregnancy. Her son, she said, was killed in action in Tunisia almost two months ago. She made no overture to meet with my sister but did wish her the best.

The sadness of her lover being killed in action added to her burdens. She considered her options and discussed them with her girl friends and our mother.

My sister decided that she would have an abortion. An abortion would "erase the problem" and then she could go back to school and get on with her life. Having an abortion appeared to be the only reasonable solution to her problem. Certainly an abortion was more of a realistic approach than dropping out of school, having a baby out of wedlock or carrying the baby for nine months and then putting it up for adoption. My sister remembered the thought of aborting her "little baby" and thus ridding herself of the last remnant of a lost romance during their short lustful relationship.

She felt strongly that abortion, especially early in her pregnancy, would be best for everyone, herself, her family, and even for the baby. Because she was still in the early stage of pregnancy, an abortion would be more like an erasure of a mistake than the killing of a human being. She rationalized so that in her mind her life would be better without a fatherless child. Her attitude was seemingly, "my future, my choice".

My father expressed strong feelings against an abortion for my sister. His adamant stance against my sister having an abortion was not based on moral or religious reasons. He told my sister straight and simple that abortion was against the law and would be too dangerous from a health standpoint.

In 1943, a few older physicians and some who were 4F (or medically disqualified to serve in the military) were still around to take care of the civilian population. Almost all of the younger physicians had been recruited to serve in the Armed Forces. My father, being a pharmacist, had learned from physician contacts and friends that women who were having abortions were going to Cuba. Havana was only a two-hour flight by commercial prop-plane. Overnight tourist cruise ships from Miami to Havana were not running during the war. This is because German U-boats prowled the Florida Straits and had sunk several cargo ships.

My father was informed that the complication rate from abortion in Cuba was quite high and that some women came back home and went into their local hospital. Some died and others needed corrective surgery, blood transfusions and some became sterile as result of abortion complications. This was probably true. The aseptic technique used in 1943 plus the lack of antibiotics made a "back-alley" abortion a perilous procedure. Whether it was done in a gynecologist's office in New York or in Havana by a mid-wife, abortion was risky.

My father expressed his disfavor for an abortion in Havana to my sister by telling her how much he loved her and would fear for her life and safety if she had an abortion. He stressed the feelings of love he had for her and that it was too bad that she had gotten pregnant but to have an abortion complication would only add to the problem. The disgrace and shame that having a baby out of wedlock would provide, plus the real life burden of raising a baby as a single mother and being a high school drop out prompted my parents to recommend an out-of-town adoption as the best solution for this problem.

At first my sister remembered that she was not comfortable with the idea of carrying her pregnancy to term and then giving her baby away to strangers. This dilemma would be easy to deal with today. The option of abortion was taken off the table by my father because of his rightful fear of the dangers of illegal abortion. That left the only legal options being having the baby and raising it or having the baby and adopting it out. My sister's decision then became not an easy choice, but a pragmatic one at best.

The arrangement was made in a private and confidential manner. My sister went packing off to New York City, the place of her birth. She was taken into a home for Jewish women both married and unwed who were to give birth and adopt out their newborn. Through their list of couples awaiting an adoption of a newborn the home was well funded and very selective of both adopting parents and the women who were relinquishing their babies. All the expenses—medical, living and legal—were paid in full by the adopting family. During her stay in New York City, I was led to believe that my sister was enrolled in a private school for girls. My parents told me that Irene needed to be in a school that provided the necessary disciplines and it would be a chance for her to receive higher education away from Miami Beach with all those wild Army boys.

After an uneventful delivery, my sister gave birth to a beautiful and healthy baby boy. He was whisked away immediately out of the delivery room and into the hospital nursery while she was still "asleep" (under general anesthesia). This, of course, was the custom of the day. It was thought that not seeing nor holding the baby and then going through the anguish and emotional stress of relinquishment would minimize psychological trauma.

Some experts still believe that to avoid bonding was a better approach then how it is practiced today. Most of the women adopting their babies out now are awake during the delivery. They not only can see the baby but also can hold the baby in their arms. Some women choose to bond for the short duration of "to have and to hold" and a few choose the extreme to even breast-feed or at least put the baby to the breast. But these days the hospital stay is so short for maternity admissions that there is little time for adequate lactation to set in. Perhaps it is important to acknowledge that the mother and child have already been bonding during the entire pregnancy, and that the entire birthing experience is set up at the scientific level by nature to insure that the mother does not abandon her child. Nothing can change this fact or mitigate the pain and tremendous sense of loss of having one's child ripped from them, whether the loss occurs during pregnancy (miscarriage or abortion) or at birth (adoption). It is odd to be pro-choice and to recognize the rights of a woman to not keep her child, and yet simultaneously recognize that human biology and human emotions perceive this as a loss, whether the woman is sensitive or callous to the fact.

The loss was compounded in my sister's case by the fact that her lover had been killed in battle. How she would have loved to watch the child grow—it was all she had left of him. Didn't he deserve to have a well-born son? But these were thoughts she barely dared admit to herself, and they were soon drowned in a cacophony of shame and guilt.

Soon after my sister left the hospital without her baby, she was told to come to an attorney's office in Manhattan to sign the adoption papers. She responded to this request with a heavy heart. The pain of delivering the baby and the ensuing postpartum discomfort are pale in comparison to the sadness of most mothers who adopt out their babies. For some reason, perhaps because of the finality of it, abortion seems to be easier to deal with than giving one's baby away.

My sister related that she received instructions regarding her legal rights and the waiver of other rights as a mother who was relinquishing her newborn. While doing so the attorney was interrupted by his secretary. He excused himself from the office and left my sister sitting beside his desk. While the attorney was absent from the room, my sister noted that the adoption papers were on the lawyer's desk just in front of her. She peered over the desk and noticed one page had names and addresses typed. She could not resist the temptation to read the names so she turned the paper around. She noted the place for her signature, the relinquisher of a baby boy still unnamed. The adoption parents were Charles & Lillian Preiser. Their address was in Manhattan. After she learned of this, she turned the paper back to its original position on the desk. It was just in time too for the lawyer had just returned. Irene signed her name and glanced once again to read the names of the people who were to take and raise her son.

My sister returned to Miami Beach. She was seventeen years old and could not imagine going back to school to begin the eleventh grade.

Some time after the war ended in the mid 1940s, my sister met her future husband. The family was vacationing in a Catskill mountain resort. Paul's Hotel was one of the better resorts in the "Borscht Belt". Julie Karson was the Master of Ceremonies (MC) at the Paul's Hotel. To be a master of ceremonies, one must possess a tuxedo, good looks, a pleasant personality, and charm and wit. Julie as the MC had the job of overseeing rehearsals and was responsible for the stage, sound, and lighting to be properly set for the evening and that the entertainers were introduced in an articulate and professional manner.

Julie fell madly in love with my gorgeous eighteen-year-old sister. My parents were likewise delighted with their perspective future son-in-law. He was quite handsome and charming and had all the qualities of the potential rising star.

Top named hotels in the Catskill Mountains vied for Julie's talent for the position of MC. He finally accepted the position offered by the Grossinger's Hotel. Soon after, Irene and Julie were married. At first, they enjoyed basking in the sun, playing golf and tennis in the summer and skiing in the winter. Irene also enjoyed dancing at the nightclub after the entertainment in the casino. She also reveled in the pleasure and exhilaration of being around the celebrities that visited and entertained at the Grossinger's Resort. The likes of Milton Berle, Sandy Koufax, Rocky Marciano and Jerry Lewis were frequenters and Irene often mingled with them, joining them for drinks or dinner and plenty of conversation. She had always been a charming person, and now she was thoroughly enjoying being Julie's wife.

During my summers of college and medical school, I too worked at the Grossinger Hotel. The bellboys were kept extremely busy. I earned my supplemental income this way and learned how to carry four suitcases at a time and place the string of a hatbox between my teeth.

One summer, after my first year of medical school, for a period of about three weeks I had a personal task assigned to me that would become a treasured memory. Every evening at around 8:00 PM I delivered a chocolate milkshake and a comic book to Rocky Marciano's room at the hotel. The undefeated heavyweight champ of the world answered my knock and tucked the comic book under his left arm, took the milkshake with his left hand and gave me a man's handshake with his deadly right hand. He never failed to thank me with a crisp Bostonian accent. Rocky Marciano was one sweet man and a class act. There was never a foul word from his mouth and never a woman in his room.

One evening, while delivering his bedtime snack, I asked the champ how he had felt when he knocked out Joe Louis well after the Brown Bomber's prime. He thought for a moment and then told me that was a sad moment for him. Louis had been a boxing role model and a hero for him when he was a youngster. That was when he had given thought about retiring undefeated and with dignity, while he was still the world's champ.

Rocky Marciano was at the Grossinger's Hotel in training for a fight to defend his title against Archie Moore. Marciano did retire undefeated. His ring record was an amazing forty-nine wins and no defeats. Forty-three of his victories were knockouts. Marciano ended Joe Louis's long career with an eight round KO in 1951. He then won the heavyweight championship with a startling thirteenth round knockout of Jersey Joe Walcott one year later. Marciano defended his title six times before retiring in 1956. He had the shortest reach, sixty-eight inches, of any heavyweight champ ever. He took pride in being the only undefeated heavyweight champion in history. Rocky died in a plane crash shortly after his retirement.

My sister Irene had time on her hands so she went to work at the Grossinger. She became a dance teacher during the Mambo & Cha-Cha-Cha days and later worked as a receptionist at the Grossinger's beauty salon. Julie and Irene wanted to have a baby but it never happened. As I recall, there were some type of infertility problems. They often dined in the lavish main dining room of the hotel. They had a place of honor at the table with the owner and founder, Jenny Grossinger who was the most luminous and celebrated hostess in the Catskills.

Jenny was an elegant elderly woman. She was the daughter of Austrian-Jewish immigrants who settled in the Catskills at the turn of the century. Originally, to make ends meet on their small farm, the Grossinger family rented a room for travelers. Soon they converted the barn into a rooming house and the rest is, as you can imagine, history—a history shared with so many hard-working immigrants with imagination, foresight, and luck.

One summer day in 1962, a woman and a fellow Grossingers employee approached my sister and engaged in casual conversation about life in general. Then she mentioned to my sister "Irene, if I did not know that you did not have any children, I would have sworn that a young man I saw playing tennis today was your son. He has your face." My sister responded with more than curiosity. She went straight away to the telephone switchboard room. There the busy operators had at their side an updated list of Grossinger's guests. The list was by room number and in alphabetical order. She thumbed through the index file. To her amazement, her eyes fell on a line she gazed at for some time: "Charles & Lillian Preiser & Son".

Nineteen years had passed since the birth of her son, but she had remembered the name of the adopting parents. The names were tattooed in her brain. Having her son appear serendipitously in her midst was a bittersweet feeling. It would be difficult for her not to at least have a glimpse of her offspring. Certainly it would appear to be a harmless adventure at best to satisfy her maternal instinct and curiosity. The guest names printed in the cardex indicated the Preiser's room number and their dining room table assignment. My sister had their table number. As she walked past their table down the center aisle, she glanced sideways and stole a glimpse. The table seated eight persons. There was only one young man among the others. She noted a young fair-haired handsome youth with an oval shaped face and striking blue eyes. Their eyes did not meet and she calmly proceeded down the aisle to her table. Irene was so overwhelmed with the experience that she could barely eat her dinner. She described this experience as that of an adventure of a spy. It was almost as if looking into the past; a lost chapter of her life that had somehow now found its way back to her.

That evening there was entertainment at the theater-casino. Julie, Irene's husband presided as Master of Ceremony. Irene usually dolled up for weekend night shows and after the festivities Irene would accompany her husband to the nearby nightclub in the hotel. There the guests would dance to the beat of Latin music that was all the rage at the time.

Irene usually stood at the end of the long nightclub bar. The advantage for Irene at the end of the bar was for the sweeping view of the entire club. As she remembered it, her favorite bartender Duke mixed the best martini that she had ever imbibed.

She spotted the Preiser boy at the middle of the bar. He appeared to be alone. With drink in hand, Irene walked up to where he was standing. He was listening to the Cuban beats and watching couples showing off their fine feathers and their newly learned dance steps.

She had wondered what to say to him without being intrusive or making him think that she was flirting with him. Many women vacationed in the Catskills without their husbands who were busy working in New York City. It was well known that some of these women were in search for romance and sexual adventure with young staff workers or guests at the resort.

My sister made eye contact with this young man and was responded with a sly smile and a head nod. Small conversation ensued as normal dialogue about the music, the show in the casino, and the vacation, etc. Then she asked the Preiser boy how often he comes to the Grossinger. She also inquired about where he lived and whether he was working or attending college. He replied that this was his first visit to Grossinger's and that he was born and raised and lived in Manhattan. He told her that he was attending Windemere College in Vermont. "I am studying Art History," he elaborated. She then inquired whether he had any brothers or sisters. He candidly responded saying that he was the only child and had been adopted at birth. Irene told him that she loved living and working at Grossinger's and that she was the wife of Julie Carson, the master of ceremony. With that, the Preiser boy excused himself with the polite "It was nice meeting you, Mrs. Carson". She responded with a smile and said "Please, next time if we should meet again, call me Irene." The Preiser family checked out the next day.

Two years later life had taken some dramatic changes for my sister. She and Julie were divorced. She left Grossingers and moved back home to Miami Beach. She found work as a cigarette girl at the "Poodle Room" nightclub at the Fontainebleau Hotel.

One evening, while home alone in her apartment, feeling depressed after a few martinis, she decided that she needed to speak to her son. She had directory assistance obtain the telephone number of his college in Vermont. The small school had a switchboard that connected to his dormitory room. He was by chance in his room that early evening thus she was able to speak with him. Irene told him that she had met him at the bar in the Terrace Room of the Grossinger's hotel two years ago. "I was the wife of the master of ceremony", she stated. Without hesitating or acknowledging her comment, he simply said, "You are my mother, aren't you?" Although she wasn't totally surprised, she nevertheless experienced an emotional chill followed by a sense of an epiphany for a new beginning from her lost chapter of life. She admitted that she indeed was his biological mother and that she had given him up for adoption at birth. She told him she would be delighted if he would visit her in Miami Beach over the Christmas holidays. She assured him that she would not interfere with or have any contact with his parents. She also told him that she would send him a round trip paid airfare if he should decide to visit with her.

Although he told her that he would like to meet with her, he did not know whether he could go and he would have to get back to her about that. He returned her call a week later and told my sister that he would indeed come south for a visit during the Christmas holiday. .

Irene and her son, Fred spent about five days together in Miami Beach. She took him around like a mother would a son visiting a tourist town. But alas she was only his biological mother. Love must be nurtured over a period of time. He adored his adopted mother who he had known all of his life. He would not want to make her feel sad and upset. He vowed never to tell his parents that he had met and visited with his "real" mother.

A few days into his Miami Beach vacation, Fred decided that he could not and would not betray the women who adopted him back in New York City. He felt that Irene wanted to be his instant mother. She offered motherly advice too soon in their relationship. A natural thing to do, I suppose, but in this strange context it only served to repel Fred who was by now a grown young man and certainly was not looking for motherly advice.

Fred told Irene that he would like to meet her brother. I was his only uncle. When my sister approached me regarding such a visit, I was enthusiastic to meet a long-lost blood relative. My newly found nephew came to visit me in 1967. He was 24 years old and recently wed. I was living at Travis Air Force Base in California where I was serving as an OB/GYN medical officer.

Fred eventually moved to California. He married and they had a son born in 1981. His adopting parents were by now deceased. His biologic mother, my sister Irene, was a retired hotel casino worker, lived in Las Vegas and suffered from arthritis and failed hip replacement surgery. Fred saw her on occasion when she would visit me in California. She died at age 79 never having remarried. Fred and I have remained close over the years and we often bond at baseball games and family holidays.

Chapter 2

We Are The (White) Boys
From Old Florida, F-L-O-R-I-D-A!
1949-1953

In 1949, the year that I graduated high school, most of my friends were going to attend the University of Florida in Gainesville. I had not been a particularly good student at Miami Beach High School and I thought that going off to college would be a waste of time, money and would probably be an academic disaster.

I had not realized at that time that in order to be admitted to the University of Florida in 1949, the entrance requirements were both easy and impossible, depending on who you were. You only needed three things:

1) A high school diploma

2) White skin

3) Fifty dollars tuition per semester

And therein lies the reason why I achieved such high grades and made the Dean's List at the University of Florida, the home of the Fighting Gators. I was virtually competing with a large number of semi-literate freshmen. Many were from small citrus growing communities and from the Florida Panhandle (also known as Baja Alabama.) Grades were on a curve and the flunk out or dropout rate was somewhere around forty percent in the first year. I soon realized that by attending class, taking notes, studying a few hours a night and reviewing legal copies of past exams that were available I could continue to earn a startlingly number of A's.

The freshman and sophomore subjects were primarily comprehensive and required courses. The electives that I signed up for were preparing me for a career in the U.S. Foreign Service. I took courses in political science, geography, history, economics, and tackled the Russian language. The Cold War was starting up. Some of my fraternity brothers called me *Pushkin* and some believed me to be a KGB agent.

Near the end of my sophomore year a recruiting representative from the Foreign Service came to the campus to interview and consult with interested students. I eagerly signed up.

The government personate looked like a Dean Acheson sort of fellow. He was tall, handsome, articulate, well groomed and quite patronizing to me. He did comment that he was pleased that I was studying the Russian language, geography and history.

We spent about thirty minutes together. We discussed the opportunities in the Foreign Service and he inquired about my family background and extra curricular activities. His final advice to me was well intended, I think, but quite a let down for my youthful enthusiasm. He suggested that I forego my Foreign Service aspirations and look into another professional field that would be more suitable for me. Of course I was taken back by his quick determination that I was not cut out to be a future diplomat. I asked him why so? He looked down squarely in my eyes and said "please do not take this as a derogatory statement, but the simple fact is that you are a short Jew". His statement was more fatherly than anti-Semitic. I felt what I perceived as his embarrassment and reassured him that I was not offended. But I was. He explained the workings of the mostly white male "good old boy's club" in Washington D.C. and the preferential treatment given by them to those people that looked like him.

This, of course, was before the days of Secretary-of-State Henry Kissinger, Madeline Albright and Condoleeza Rice. So what does the future hold for a short Jew with a 3.7 grade point average?

I took the Foreign Service rep's advice and turned my interest to pre-med. I should not have succumbed to his advice so readily.

Wouldn't my old high school chemistry teacher, Miss Carlin, be surprised that I was going to major in chemistry. Such irony, I thought. I did not like chemistry and could only tolerate biology with little enthusiasm. My passion was geography, history and the humanities.

They were subject areas that were not a major part of pre-med curricula as they are today. I compensated somewhat in biology and comparative anatomy by convincing myself that anatomy was the geography of species, be it a frog, cat or human.

During my junior year at the university two events occurred that are worth mentioning. These incidents impressed me in a negative way but gave me enlightenment for the future.

In addition to a myriad of required college courses, the applicant for medical school must also take an all day exam. The obvious name of this test is the Medical Aptitude Test (MAT). Its name speaks for itself. Most premed courses are not valuable for medical school per se except perhaps comparative anatomy and maybe organic chemistry. It is my opinion that liberal arts, literature and humanities would best serve the educational needs of a future physician. But it is the wisdom of the medical school admission people to weed out those premed students who cannot sit on their butts for hours and memorize. There is no understanding to the branches of the rat's carotid artery or to the molecular structure of cholesterol. It must be painstakingly memorized and spewed out for examinations.

If a premed student cannot make A's or B's they will probably not get through the first or second year of medical school. The student's grade point average plus his/her extra -curricular activities and score from the MAT is used to evaluate the applicant before an interview is granted. The MAT is given on the same day all over the country at selected colleges.

When I entered the large university auditorium I could not help notice that several rows in the very back were roped off. The rope appeared to be ordinary clothesline. There was a hand printed sign attached to the rope. It said in bold black letters, "COLORED ONLY".

There were no black students at the University of Florida in 1952. No Negroes. No colored people at all.

I took my seat toward the middle of the auditorium. After awhile, looking behind me, I noticed a contingent of black students entering the rear of the auditorium. I counted eleven of them. All young males. They saw the sign. They lifted the rope up one at a time and ducked under it and took their seats.

I remember clearly that the visiting black students all wore white dress shirts and neckties. In the meantime the postwar dress for the white boys was khaki pants with a military web belt, a white T-shirt without a logo and white buck shoes. The latter, by necessity, was to be scuffed up and somewhat soiled in order to look cool.

The MAT was a series of several one-hour tests. Each was designed to ascertain the speed and comprehension of the examinee. If you were foolish enough to ponder one particular question too long then you would not be able to finish the entire test. After the second test there was a ten-minute break. I walked to the rear exit in order to get some fresh air and to approach the black students. One of them, a tall young man with horn-rimmed glasses was standing by the rope near the aisle. I spoke to him as if I was a spokesperson for the upcoming civil rights movement.

"Hello and welcome to the U of F campus. Sorry about those stupid ropes". His shy voice retorted, "That's OK we're glad to be here" I asked him where they were from. He told me that they were all students at Florida A&M in Tallahassee. They had driven down in two cars that very morning. They left Tallahassee at three A.M. in order to be in Gainesville on time for the exam. Florida A&M was an all black school then and is probably a predominately black school today. The University of Florida's all-white student body integrated sometime after I graduated in 1953. That is why the Gators have done so well in intercollegiate sports over the past decades. (Think Steve Spurrier and Emmit Smith)

Following the third exam there was a one and a half-hour lunch break. One of my fraternity brothers was taking the exams that day. The two of us invited the eleven black students to follow us to the on campus Student Union cafeteria. It was close by and they served what we now call "fast-food".

Shortly after we entered the building and proceeded to the cafeteria line the manager approached the black students and told them, in a polite southern way, that they must leave and would not be served. The students offered no argument and filed out at once. I told them to wait outside the auditorium and that we would bring their lunches to them. We ordered thirteen hamburgers with ketchup and onions and thirteen Cokes to go.

Between the two of us we were six dollars short. I spotted a physics classmate that I also knew from the track team. He was a long distance runner from Peru. He loaned me a ten-dollar bill.

Each hamburger was wrapped individually and placed in an open carton. The lid of the carton was used to carry the Cokes.

We met them back at the auditorium. I announced that there was a cluster of benches under some old trees with Spanish moss not too far away. We walked over, sat down and handed out the lunches. I collected one dollar and ten cents from each of them. That was the 1952 cost of a hamburger and a large Coke.

One of the students apologized for the group for not being smart enough to have "brown bagged" their lunch. He admitted that the idea of not being able to eat on campus never entered his mind.

He was correct. Blacks were barred from becoming students and were not allowed to be on campus.

Within five minutes a very large campus police officer approached our benches. I knew who he was. Dwayne Douglas was a huge Gator football lineman from Kissimmee, Florida. It was a small country town then but today it is a suburb of Orlando. Athletes on scholarship received jobs on campus to help them earn at least pocket money.

"Sorry boys", he said in a non-threatening voice, "y'all can't be eating on campus." I explained to him that they were on campus taking exams to go to medical school. "This", he explained, "is an all white state university and they should not be sitting here let alone be eating lunch on our benches." The burley blonde cop looked around then checked his wristwatch. "OK, finish up your lunch and pick up all your litter. I'll pretend that I never saw y'all. Goodbye and good luck." Then he walked away. Now it was time to return to the auditorium.

I do not know how those eleven black premed students did on the MAT but I imagine most of them ended up in medical school. But I do know that if they were accepted to medical school it would most likely have been to Meharry University in Nashville or Howard University in Washington D.C. In 1952 these were both "Negro schools".

The Deep South was not admitting blacks. Perhaps they could have matriculated in an integrated Northern school or a medical school in the West.

During that same year I applied to several medical schools, twelve to be exact. The state of Florida did not have a medical school. The reason, I was told, was because there was an anti-vivisection law on the state books that made it illegal to dissect a living animal even though it was anesthetized. This was a fundamental exercise in learning about the basic physiology of the human body (i.e., circulation, respiration, digestion, etc.) and performing the exercises in the laboratory on mice, rabbits and dogs were a crucial part of a medical education.

There were plans underway to open a medical school at the University of Miami in the near future. Most white pre-med students from Florida went to medical school at Tulane University in New Orleans, Emory University in Atlanta or Duke University in North Carolina.

Emory University School of Medicine in Atlanta sent a letter to me stating that they had interest in me as a candidate for their freshmen class. I responded immediately requesting an appointment for an interview. Soon afterward I received a date and time for my interview and a list of nearby hotels.

Emory also invited one of my premed classmates for an interview. His date was the same as mine and we decided to drive up together in my 1949 powder blue Chevy ragtop.

Archie was a pleasant and soft-spoken man that was several years older than most college students. At least he appeared to be older. He was prematurely balding, had a protuberant lower abdomen and usually had an unlit cigar protruding from his mouth. Archie brought along a wooden crate of Florida oranges that were destined for Atlanta. The citrus was from his family groves in the Tampa area. Archie told me that his Dad wanted him to present the crate to one of the members of the Admissions Committee. His father knew this member from way back in undergraduate days at Emory University. I believe that Archie's Dad was a physician.

On our drive up to Atlanta we talked about our future dreams of being physicians and about some of the premed courses that we were enrolled in. Archie announced that his grade point average (GPA) was 2.7. That would amount to less than a "B" average. It was a rather anemic GPA for a premed student with serious hopes of being admitted to medical school. You do not apply to Harvard College or Stanford unless you have a 4.0 GPA or damn close to that. My GPA was 3.65 at that time. I had mostly A's and B's.

When I entered the conference room for my interview at Emory University I was cordially introduced to the six men sitting around a large wooden table. All that I can remember about them was that they were white elderly men in seersucker suits with white shirts and striped neckties.

The suited gentleman at the head of the table indicated that they had invited me here because they were impressed with my grades, elective subjects and extra-curricular activities. He wanted to know why I had chosen Russian as my foreign language. "Most premeds", he pointed out, "study French or German".

I explained that before I decided on premed I chose Russian because I was a Political Science major. The next question was unrelated to the topic of foreign language. The distinguished looking board member sitting across the table from me asked "How do you pronounce your last name, is it *STEER* or is it *STYER* or is it *STEIN*? " It is pronounced *STEER*, just like a castrated bull", I responded with a slight attempt to make it humorous". Not even a small chuckle emanated from any of the six. He retorted without looking up from his folder, "how *was your name spelled in the old-country? Was it Steerski or Steerowitz?*" I knew at that moment that I was not welcome and what game he was playing. I also figured that I would not be attending medical school in Atlanta.

I explained to the crew that when my grandfather emigrated from what was then Hungary in 1898 he landed at Ellis Island. There the immigration officer asked my grandfather *"vas is der namen?"*

My grandfather replied that his name was pronounced *SHTIYER* and spelled it *STIER* on paper. The Officer told my grandfather that the English language does not have that SHTI sound. That was a Germanic guttural sound. He suggested that my grandfather should change his name to *STEIR* and pronounce it in an English tone as *STEER*.

Then I said nothing else. The headman thanked me for coming to see them. I thanked them for their invitation and then I left the room. I was annoyed and embarrassed for them. During our drive back to Gainesville I did not tell Archie about my interview. Besides I was not in the mood to tell Archie that he was in a Chevy with a Jew. (Although he probably already knew that).

Two weeks later I ran into Archie in one of our classes. He told me that he had received an acceptance letter from Emory. I told him that I had accepted an admission to the University of Miami School of Medicine for the class of 1957 and that I would be in their second graduating class.

I did not bother to mention to Archie that I had received a rejection letter from Emory University.

Chapter 3

An Ordinary Hangover

After three noisy, hell-raising semesters in the *Tau Epsilon Phi* fraternity house I decided that my commitment to achieving high grades would take priority over the raucous fraternity house life that was a full-time pursuit for many of my fraternity brothers. Pre-med courses were challenging and required a great deal of memorization. This would require long hours of study in a quiet atmosphere.

Our fraternity house was inhabited primarily by an assortment of carefree and wild guys who had little interest in studying or making honorable grade point averages.

Not infrequently a friendly, lonely, non-studious fraternity brother would enter my room, oblivious to my open book and illumination of the study lamp on my desk. This would usually lead to conversation that was for the most part, to quote Bob Dylan, "Worthless foam from the mouth."

After three semesters it became clear that I would have to move out of the fraternity house if I wanted to make schoolwork a priority. I looked forward to the change in living space and the quietude and privacy it would offer me. I would otherwise remain active in fraternity life for the duration of my college days.

I rented an apartment in a converted old family house just a few blocks away from the TEP house. Now I could study and nap whenever it suited me without being bothered at all hours. I rarely hit the books on Saturday night except during demanding final exams week. It was a perfect arrangement that left me free to enjoy the fraternity house parties that were frequently held on Saturday evenings.

The University of Florida had only become coed a few years back shortly after World War II. Prior to that time the women attended Florida State University in Tallahassee and the men were in Gainesville. The return of WWII veterans and their well-earned GI Bill of Rights gave impetus to this change to coed status. Some of the veterans brought their wives and family to campus and the state and federal government were obliged to provide low cost off-campus housing. The married Florida veterans lived in a village with the imaginative name of FLAVETS. I'm sure this cultural change of suddenly having more women around campus also helped to open the door for women veterans and vets' wives who wanted to attend school.

The WWII veterans not only brought coeds to Gainesville but also illegal booze and a multitude of ways to consume it. The University is in Alachua County, which was "dry" during my undergrad days. All we needed to do to get the stuff was to drive south about twenty miles away to the next county. There in the town of Micanopy was a liquor store that catered to the party crowd in Gainesville.

These hard drinking, Camel-smoking vets added a new dimension in booze drinking. I do not remember anyone buying or drinking wine. A keg of beer on ice was always available but mixed drinks were the in-thing. The vets were our heroes and so we watched and listened to what they were imbibing at the fraternity parties. We, of course, assumed that these older warriors who had defeated the Wermacht and pushed the Japanese back to Tokyo were more than qualified to teach us about the manly art of drinking.

If bourbon and ginger ale or seven and seven (7up and Seagrams7) were their drinks of choice, they most certainly would be suitable for the freshman novice. And so they were for me.

Our fraternity parties frequently became drinking orgies. The shortage of available women added to this rowdiness. I began regularly guzzling Jim Beam bourbon and ginger ale, not fully realizing that this is a lot of sugar to consume. The ice cubes diluted the sugar and surely kept us from becoming juvenile diabetics. In addition to this nauseating choice and its equally sickeningly sweet taste, we also naturally smoked too many cigarettes. But we were young and these things didn't deter us from enjoying ourselves.

During most of the school year it was hot and humid in Gainesville. This awful sticky heat encouraged an increase in fluid intake. Of course alcohol will dehydrate you since it also works as a diuretic. The reason that we did not succumb to dehydration and hyperglycemia was that we also indulged in on-the-rocks drinks. The ice cubes saved us from dehydration and hyperglycemia.

On a beautiful Sunday springtime morning I woke up with a class-A hangover. Without thinking of the logical outcome, I drank a cup of coffee in my small kitchen. Shortly thereafter I visited the commode to vomit. Next I heated up a can of Campbell's cream of mushroom soup. I actually rented it for about ten minutes before it left me with projectile force. I decided to err on the side of caution and go to the Student Health Center on campus to get some medication to settle my stomach. I should have gone to the local Piggly-Wiggly market and bought a bottle of pink Pepto-Bismol. That would have solved the problem quickly and inexpensively and would have spared me my first adventure of note into the realm of medicine. But instead I trudged a weary mile to the University Infirmary, naïve of the consequences of such a trusting decision.

After the usual filling out of forms I was moved to an examining room where my vital signs were taken and recorded by a female medical assistant. I remember an elderly man coming into the examination room. He wore a white coat so I knew he was a doctor before he casually introduced himself as the physician on duty. I told him that I was ashamed to admit that I had a rip-roaring hangover and had vomited several times. Because I had not ingested any food or drink since I left my apartment I was actually feeling blissfully better. My nausea had subsided and the vomiting had ceased. At that point I should have walked out of there while I still had the chance.

The soft-spoken doctor examined my abdomen by palpating both lower quadrants below the navel. His deep palpation did not elicit any pain or tenderness. He then ausculated my heart, lungs and lower abdomen with his cold stethoscope. He spoke at last in a low mumbling voice. "Your bowel sounds are gurgling up a storm young man," he informed me. I told him it was probably because my stomach was empty and I was beginning to feel hungry. Thus ended his exam. He proceeded to pick up my chart and a wall telephone with the other hand and asked someone to connect him with some other doctor. Shortly after he introduced himself in a familiar tone using his first name and asked the listener to come over to the infirmary as soon as possible. Turning to me he said with a paternalistic air, "I just want to get another opinion before I decide what to do with you." I put my clothes back on and picked up a magazine while I waited.

A tall middle-aged man with gray hair entered the examining room and introduced himself as Doctor Maynard. He wore a light khaki-colored poplin cotton suit and spoke with an authoritative Florida Cracker accent. He proceeded to mash down on my abdomen and then listened to my lower abdomen just like the older infirmary doctor had done just an hour ago. He spoke to me while he continued to gently poke my tummy. I remember that his exam did not elicit any pain, and that my abdomen did not seem to be the focus of his attention.

"Where you from, son?"

"Miami sir," I responded.

"What part of Miami son?"

"Miami Beach, sir."

"What's your daddy do son?"

"He is a pharmacist sir."

"Works in a drug store?" He asked.

"Yes, sir, he does. He owns a drug store."

The dialogue ended abruptly at this point and so did the examination. The consulting physician turned to the older infirmary doctor who was standing in the doorway of the examining room and announced: "Your boy has acute appendicitis."

"I have appendicitis?" I groaned. His diagnostic pronouncement was still ringing in my ears. "Yes, I'm afraid so son," he said with serious authority. "We need to get some lab work but first I need to call your folks and let them know about their son." I gave him the drug store number and my home number as well (only five digits in 1951, 50657).

Doctor Maynard repeated the pronouncement for my mother on the phone: I had acute appendicitis, but not to worry. He assured her that my condition was not critical because he had caught it early and it had not ruptured yet. My mother knew that a ruptured appendix was a disaster awaiting certain death. He went on to explain that he was a board certified surgeon and a member of the American College of Surgeons. My worried mother, of course, gave Doctor Maynard permission over the telephone to operate on me. I did not consider myself a minor at age twenty because I was a member of the United States Naval Reserve. To perform surgery on me without parental notification and permission would have been then, as now, unprofessional. Parental permission would also enhance financial responsibility to the hospital and physician.

I spoke with my Mom and Dad. I knew even then without formal medical education that I did not have a serious problem like appendicitis. I knew for sure that I had a rip-roaring hangover. I knew I did not have any abdominal pain, that my vomiting had ceased and that I did not feel the least bit feverish. I mentioned the lack of all these important symptoms to Doctor Maynard and to my parents. I wanted to run out of the infirmary and back to my little student hovel and sleep off my hangover and then get up and study. It was too close to final exams to have an unnecessary operation, but what did I know? Decorum and respect for authority mandated that I sit there like a sheep to the slaughter even though I knew I was already recovering and didn't really have anything wrong with me.

My dear mother was even more convincing and cautious than the surgeon. "Do what the doctor says. He is smarter than you. He wants to remove your appendix before it ruptures and spreads pus into your belly. So don't be afraid, son. You'll be ok. My niece, Blanche, almost died when she was a kid with a ruptured appendix." "Ok mom", I reassured her. My dad echoed my mother's sentiments. He recommended that I do as my mother and the doctor suggested because they knew what was best. My father was a good man, a *mensch*, as we would say. He was very kind and helpful to family, friends, employees and even strangers.

So off I went, not quite kicking and screaming but not willingly either, to Alachua General Hospital. I think it must have been the only hospital in Gainesville. The medical school and teaching facility would not be built for several more years.

To my chagrin I went directly to the operating room. There was the anesthesiologist all set to say hello and start an intravenous drip in my arm vein. He then sat me up on the OR table to administer a spinal anesthetic. I became numb from the waist down. Then my abdomen was prepped with an antiseptic and white drapes were placed over my body. The surgeon made a small incision through the skin of the right lower quadrant of my abdomen. After entering the abdominal cavity they found and removed my appendix. I did not suffer any postoperative complications except that I was unable to sleep very well in the hospital.

They placed me in an open six-bed ward across the room from an alcoholic having delirium tremors. I can still recall the smell of paraldehyde, a drug used to treat his "D.T.'s". His intermittent nightmarish screams kept me on edge and frightened. I told Doctor Maynard that I wanted to go home to get some rest. He discharged me on the second post op day.

My appendix was probably placed in a specimen jar with formaldehyde as a preservative. The hospital pathologist is to examine the tissue specimen and describe the gross and microscopic appearance of the appendix. The final diagnosis would be dependent on his findings and dictation. The surgeon makes the preoperative diagnosis but the postoperative diagnosis is confirmed or disputed by the pathologist. No one ever contacted me about the postoperative diagnosis of my appendix and I never inquired further.

Four years later when I was a second year medical student studying "Physical Diagnosis," I became convinced that my removed appendix was probably normal. I thought, but mostly fantasized, about going back to the Alachua General Hospital and demanding to see the pathology report describing my innocent and very normal appendix. In the years to come, as a physician, I would occasionally encounter such arrogant, unnecessary surgical procedures.

Medical School

Chapter 4

BACK ALLEY ABORTION

I attended medical school twenty-three years before Roe vs. Wade became the law of the land. The only position that I had about abortion back then was that my sister should have been allowed to have the choice to have a safe, legal abortion instead of having to go through the heartbreak of giving birth and then giving her baby up for adoption to another family.

As a medical student I lived two blocks away from my parent's apartment in Miami Beach. I rented a room in a residential hotel away from the tourist hotels near the ocean. This arrangement worked out well for my parents and me. I had my privacy and quietude to study at all hours of the night or to socialize as I wished.

The close proximity to my parents allowed me to have dinner with them and to view some post-prandial TV with my dad. I made my mother happy by taking snacks and clean laundry back to my hotel room.

My strange study habits evolved during the first few months of my freshman year. The textbooks were very large, expensive and quite boring for the most part. I usually hit the books around seven thirty P.M. After about two hours of anatomy or physiology I would begin to realize that I was reading the same paragraph six times or more and was beginning to hallucinate into a dreamlike state. I would then turn off the light and indulge myself with a delicious half-hour nap. This invariably would clear the cobwebs from my twenty-three year old brain.

The Parada Hotel was an affordable second-rate abode for transients or blue-collar workers. I was of course the only unemployed medical student inhabitant. I enjoyed the not so sophisticated atmosphere and "ma and pa" management. Most of the guests were long term: bellhops, cocktail waitresses, retirees on small pensions, and a few nice-looking hookers.

Joni was a precious-looking young waitress that I found very attractive. She was not slutty or flirtatious but came across as sweet and petite and with a Chicago accent. Unfortunately for me, Joni had a live-in scoundrel of a boyfriend. The two of them lived across the hall from my room. I would frequently hear them argue and at times the loud bickering would become down right combative. I could hear screams emanating from Joni. There were sounds of smacking, crying and frequent use of the 'f' word. When these clashes occurred I would leave my door open to enhance the sound. It frightened me somewhat but it also had a libidinous effect. The chaos within their room was, I suppose, for me, a form of auditory voyeurism. At that time in my life I was too naïve to know very much about sexual sadomasochism relationships. But theirs was a textbook case, I am sure.

I never heard any complaints of pain from Joni's boyfriend. He did the hitting and cursing and she was the recipient of the beatings. He was a young, husky, and handsome fellow who was undoubtedly enjoying the S and M ecstasy. I wanted to come to her rescue and be her knight in shining armor but I knew better. Twice over the first month of this frequent nighttime distraction I knocked on their door to inquire, "Joni are you alright?" Her yelling was never the "Oh baby!" sound that one expects from sexual passion. Each time her response was a polite but timid "Oh yes, I'm OK, thanks, I'm OK."

One evening while I was studying, the boyfriend, who I had grown to envy and dislike, knocked on my door. When I opened it I found him in his underwear and t-shirt. He had blood on both garments. He urgently requested that I come to their room. "Can you come over, Doc? Joni is sick and is looking very bad." I walked across the hall to their room. The aroma of fresh blood filled my nostrils. As a second year medical student the odor of fresh blood was experienced every time I walked into or through the Emergency Room at Jackson Memorial Hospital.

Joni was in the bathroom and sitting on the commode. She invited me to come in although she was completely nude. She told me that she was passing huge clots, the size of her fists. "I'm cramping like hell" she sobbed. I noticed that the empty bathtub had a red colored ring around it. I asked Joni if she had just bathed. Joni nodded yes that she had a hot bath hoping to relieve some of the horrible cramps. She went on to say that was when she began passing huge clots and the vaginal bleeding and cramps increased. The boyfriend uttered the same in agreement. I asked Joni if her periods were ever like this in the past. Joni looked up at me. She was shockingly pallid and merely nodded no.

I told the boyfriend to pick Joni up, put her in bed and cover her up with a blanket. Physiology 101 from the previous year clicked right in. The basic primary treatment for shock is to keep the patient warm and stop the bleeding. The boyfriend lifted her frail looking nude body and followed my advice. I took her pulse for thirty seconds and counted sixty beats. That meant that her pulse rate was elevated to one hundred and twenty beats per minute. The normal pulse rate at rest is in the sixty to ninety beats per minute range. I went across the hall to my room and retrieved my brand new sphygmomanometer and stethoscope from my black leather doctor's bag. My parents had bought the bag for me from a medical supply store and presented it to me as a gift when I began my second year of medical school. As was the custom, my name was engraved in gold letters below the zippered top. Every medical student had to have a doctor's bag to carry his or her basic diagnostic tools. I still have mine in my garage among my memorabilia.

Now my heart rate was racing too. I knew from Joni's pallid looks and rapid pulse rate that she was in trouble from blood loss. I placed the gray colored cuff around her petite arm and secured it snuggly in place with the small chrome fasteners. We did not have Velcro cuffs in 1954. Her blood pressure measured out at 80/40 or perhaps zero. The diastolic sound was so faint that I could not be sure when it disappeared. I deflated the cuff and took her blood pressure once again. I inflated the cuff by squeezing the small rubber bulb until the needle reached 140 millimeters. Then I slowly let the manometer needle down until the first pulse sound became audible at 80 millimeters of pressure. That is the systolic pressure or the "upper number" which is the pressure within the heart chamber as it contracts to eject blood to the rest of the body. The sound then faded away and vanished when the needle reached forty millimeters. That is the "lower number" or diastolic reading that measures the pressure inside the heart chambers when it is at momentary rest between contractions.

We were facing a medical emergency. As a second year medical student this was my first such encounter. My visceral feeling then, as I remember it today, was that I very much wanted to be a physician to help people and that I must not let Joni die. This young woman was slowly going into shock from blood loss. The cause was obvious and the signs and symptoms were classic: low blood pressure, a rapid pulse and a sheet-white complexion. She urgently needed an intravenous lifeline for fluids, but it was simply not available.

I urged Joni that she must go to the hospital straight away. I told her that she was going into shock from blood loss. The hot tub bath had dilated her pelvic blood vessels and increased the blood flow to the uterus. Joni shook her head no and insisted that she would be all right. She said, "I need to get some rest. I am so sleepy." I pulled back the blanket that covered Joni. The underlying sheet was soaked with blood as were the inner aspects of her thighs.

I told her boyfriend that I was going to call for an ambulance to rush Joni to the hospital. He agreed with my decision and asked me what he could do. I told him that he should put a robe or housecoat on her and ask her if she prefers Mount Sinai Hospital or Saint Francis Hospital. Both were equal-distant from the hotel.

I called an ambulance from the number in the yellow pages in the phonebook in my room and explained the nature of the emergency to the dispatcher. After repeating the address and directions they indicated that they would arrive in about five minutes. I then called the desk clerk downstairs to alert him of the imminent arrival of the ambulance and suggested that they secure the elevator for them. Every moment would be crucial in determining her fate.

The boyfriend informed me that Joni wanted to go to Saint Francis Hospital because she knew a doctor that worked in the emergency room there. He indicated that she hoped that he would be there or come into the hospital to see her. She knew him from the coffee shop where she waitressed on Lincoln Road.

Joni lifted her tired looking head off the pillow, looked directly at me and said softly, "Bruce, should I tell the doctors that I had an abortion yesterday or just tell them that I'm having a miscarriage? Will they know the difference?"

"Oh!" I exclaimed, "So it isn't a heavy period after all!"

Joni began to sob gently and her boyfriend sat down on the bed beside her and placed his arm around her shoulder.

I made it known to Joni that the doctors would probably know the difference between an illegal abortion procedure and a spontaneous abortion or miscarriage.

For an abortion procedure the operator would pinch the cervix with an instrument called a *tenaculum* in order to hold the pregnant uterus in place so that the cervix could then be easily dilated. I had observed a "D&C" in the operating room as part of my student rotation in OB/GYN. The tissue-grasping instrument would leave two small puncture wounds that would be visible on the cervix. (Not unlike a snakebite).

I asked Joni how far along her pregnancy had been. The boyfriend interceded and said that they thought she was seven weeks but the doctor told that she was more like eleven weeks pregnant.

He went on to say that the doctor, at Joni's request, referred her to an abortion provider, a refugee from Havana. There being a month of discrepancy would not be unusual especially if the menstrual periods were not regular or the actual dates not memorialized on a calendar.

I strongly urged them not to go to Saint Francis Hospital. I explained, with a note of authority, that if the E.R. people discover that you had an abortion they may not behave professionally and might "throw you out the window and into Indian Creek below." I reminded her that Saint Francis was a Catholic hospital. They would, by Florida law, be required to report your abortion to the local police. Abortion was, after all, illegal.

Joni's boyfriend agreed that she had better head for Mount Sinai Hospital. "We don't want any trouble with priests, nuns or cops."

Being extra careful not to sound judgmental, I asked Joni where she had obtained her abortion. She informed me that a Cuban woman doctor had performed the abortion. She was, according to Joni, a naturopathic doctor who had an office in her house in Opa Locka, a poor section of Miami near the airport. Joni did not wish to go to Cuba for her abortion. She had heard rumors that many women died from complications after having an abortion in Havana. The truth was that the complication rate for life-threatening infection leading to fatal toxic shock was high enough to occupy many hospitals beds throughout the United States in any community where illegal abortions were performed.

Joni was given the name of the Cuban woman naturopath by a woman who owned the coffee shop where she worked. Joni told me that the naturopath had reassured her after the painful procedure that all had gone well and she would not have any problems.

I too tried to reassure her that she was going to be in good hands at the hospital and everything would be OK.

I suggested to Joni that it might be better, if anyone should ask, to say that your abortion was performed in Havana and not in Miami. If they knew that the abortion was done here in Miami they may, by law, report this to the police. Then you would be involved with identifying the abortion provider and maybe required to testify in court. Joni said that she would not want the naturopath to get into trouble.

The ambulance arrived and three paramedic attendants came up to the room with a gurney and several bags with medical emergency paraphernalia. They spoke with Joni and told her what they would be doing. I informed them of Joni's last blood pressure reading and elevated pulse. They ignored my report and placed her on the gurney. They checked her vital signs and told me that her blood pressure was similar to my findings. That made me feel useful and skilled. Then they proceeded to start an IV in her forearm and they placed a mask over her mouth and nose to deliver oxygen to her from a tank on a shelf below the gurney.

The boyfriend and Joni went off to Mount Sinai Hospital in the ambulance. Several residents from the hotel came out to the sidewalk to see what was going on and to gossip. One hotel guest, an overweight barmaid who lived on the same floor as Joni and me, quipped to me that she knew that "son-of-a-bitch would eventually kill that poor little girl." She asked me what had happened to Joni. I placed my hand on her shoulder and told her to relax and assured her that Joni was OK. I told her that Joni was having a miscarriage.

When I first heard the word "abortion" stated by Joni, I recall feeling queasy and uncomfortable. The thought of dirty instruments being held by unwashed hands and being inserted into Joni's pelvic organs was quite repugnant. Mental images of back alley abortions were tattooed in my brain from the anecdotal comments, true or imagined, exchanged over a beer or from a student nurse who trusted me in confidence.

I wanted to ask Joni and the boyfriend why they would want to end a pregnancy when they love each other so passionately and would procreate such a gorgeous kid together.

It was later that it dawned on me that they were not ready for parenthood. Why, I wondered, didn't they keep the pregnancy and put the baby up for adoption. I pondered all of these choices as I sat at the desk in my hotel room. The answer was becoming clear. Most couples that do not wish to have a baby were not planning on a pregnancy. The act of abortion is to remove an unplanned and unwanted pregnancy. The abortion is to erase the mistake they have made together and to get on with their lives. That is why there will always be abortion, be it legal or illegal, in this imperfect world that we breed in.

The next day during lunch break at medical school I called Mount Sinai Hospital. The operator connected me to the Charity Service ward. It's astonishing today to realize that almost half of the beds at the hospital were set aside for the indigent who were without adequate income or medical insurance. This was before the days of Medicaid and Medicare, back when hospitals existed for the sake of helping people in need rather than making money like a business.

The charge nurse told me that Joni was in a room without a phone but her boyfriend had been there all night and was still there at her bedside. She called the boyfriend to the phone by the nurse's station. My worst fear had vanished. Joni was alive.

He told me of the events that took place throughout the long night. Joni needed four or five units of blood to stabilize her vital signs. The E.R. doctor told him that was a lot of blood loss for such a little woman. They called in a "woman's doctor." He came in quite promptly at about 2:00 AM. The boyfriend went on to tell me that the doctor spoke to Joni and took her behind a curtained off examining area to assess her progress. Then he checked out her chart and laboratory work findings. He then called the operating room crew on call. The doctor told them to set up for an emergency operation and call in anesthesia. I asked the boyfriend what kind of operation was performed. Ma Bell interrupted us. After I inserted another dime into the payphone, he went on to tell me that the doctor's name is Danny Stone and he was real nice. He did a "clean out" or a D and C. He told me that he had found pieces of pregnancy and lots of blood clots.

Doctor Stone told him that he knew that Joni had had an abortion and that this was not a natural miscarriage. The boyfriend asked Doctor Stone if he had to report this to anyone. He told me that the doctor was "real cool." He reassured him, "Relax. I'm a gynecologist, not a detective".

Joni came back to her hotel room three days later. I visited her briefly in her room. Her face once again had a healthy glow and her Irish smile had reappeared. She thanked me for "taking charge" and calling an ambulance for her. I presented her with a bunch of red grapes that my mother had given to me that evening. As I was leaving her room I walked past the dresser and noticed a prescription sitting on top of a phone book. Without asking her permission I picked it up to take a closer look. It was an order from the naturopathic physician, an Elizabeth Fernandez, for a medication called *Methergine* to be taken three times a day. I knew what these tablets were taken for. I was able to decipher the prescription because one of my courses in my second year of medical school was pharmacology.

Joni took note of my spying her unfilled prescription and volunteered a confession. They did not take it to the pharmacy to get it filled. Then she asked me if I knew what the medicine was for.

Without hesitation I informed her that *Methergine* was prescribed to contract down the uterus to decrease bleeding and to help expel blood clots after the abortion. Holding the neglected prescription in my outstretched hand, I asked Joni why she had not gotten it filled. "We just did not have any money left after paying for the abortion," she replied.

As I left the room I noticed a bottle of Seagram's whiskey and a new carton of Old Gold smokes on the dresser top. I placed the prescription down next to them.

Chapter 5

My Gift To Microbiology

Down the hall on my floor at the Parada Hotel was a saucy brunette named Sophia. I had seen her on several occasions in the small hotel lobby where she usually sat waiting for a taxi to take her to work. Sophia was the type of woman that I felt comfortable flirting with. She flirted back in the elevator one day and invited me to her room for a drink. Not wanting to appear to be too anxious, although I was, I thanked her for the invite and told her that I had to prepare for a pathology quiz scheduled for tomorrow. I suggested that I would call her in her room that evening.

Sophia was of a Greek father and a Lebanese mother. She immigrated to the USA from Greece with her American G.I. husband and settled in a small town in Ohio. After her divorce, like many others, she moved to Miami. Sophia did some exotic dancing for a while and landed a more lucrative job as a cocktail waitress at the swanky Beachcomber nightclub in Miami Beach.

Back in my room, it was hard to concentrate on the diseases of the liver in Doctor W.A.D. Anderson's textbook "Synopsis of Pathology." My mind was really on Sophia. She came to my rescue by knocking on my door. She had in her hand a bottle of Ouzo and two glasses. She had these items perched on a small brown plastic tray, the same type I had in my room under the ice bucket, the kind you would find in an inexpensive hotel. Sophia was wearing a silky looking nylon robe. The back of the robe had a machine-embroidered green dragon. "You called for room service, Monsieur?" she joked.

I wanted to mouth out a clever repartee but nothing would come out except "entrez vous!" Sophia suggested that the doctor needed a drink and a smoke to relax before studying at night. I agreed to that.

Sophia only stayed about two hours. I was too inebriated and too pleased to study pathology. I went to sleep with a smile on my face. I knew full well that I would cram for the pathology exam in the morning and the quiz would go okay.

While studying Clinical Diagnosis in my room one night, about ten days after my encounter with Sophia, I noticed an itch in my pubic hair region. I had no problem scratching the area because I studied in my under-shorts in my not-air-conditioned room. The scratching did not seem to relieve the itch very long. I decided that the perceived *pruritis* was psychological because I was reading about viral childhood diseases like chicken pox *(varicella)*. There was a picture of a *varicella* victim's inflamed chest full of bumpy blisters in my textbook. The book described these lesions as "tears drop on a rose petal." Very poetic for a medical text, I thought, as I started scratching again. Now the itch might have been psychic in nature, but I decided to take a peek anyhow. Observation, we are told in medical school, is the key to rapid and accurate diagnosis. There, attached to the skin around the shafts of my pubic hair, were little brown beasts about the size of a single piece of wild-bird seed. I had crabs.

In Parisitology, one of the areas of Microbiology, we called these pesty crabs *Pediculosis Pubis*. They are referred to as crabs because under a magnifying lens they look like the crab that we order at fine seafood restaurants like Joe's Stone Crab in Miami Beach. They are complete with a small body and legs and pinchers just like their larger brother crustaceans of the deep sea. But when they inhabit your pubic hair region they are disgusting and cause intolerable itching. How awful! How humiliating! In my mind the only people who had crabs were Merchant Marine seamen that visited the squalid brothels of Marseilles or New Orleans.

I called Sophia to tell her about my recently acquired infestation. I had assumed that she had presented me with another gift besides Ouzo and the pleasure of her company that evening that we were together ten days or so ago. Sophia was not in her room. She usually returned home from work at the nightclub at about 4 AM. I decided to take a hot bath hoping so foolishly to drown my uninvited guests. It was too late at night to go to the pharmacy; I thought that I would be too embarrassed to ask for a bottle of *Cuprex,* a commonly used medication popular in 1958 to rid oneself of *pediculosis pubis.* Then I realized that I could always say to the pharmacist that the medicine was for my roommate.

While trying to fall asleep that night, I imagined that those little crabs were crawling around my bed. It was then that I began to recall the funny cure for crabs that I had heard about as a U.S. Naval Reserve Pharmacist Mate (this title was the predecessor for the present term "Corpsman").

Many legends circulated the world over about how to cure crabs. The "French Cure" is to pour wine on the infested area, then one hour later, pour in a handful of sand. The crabs would become inebriated and hostile thus have a rock fight and kill each other. The "German method" is to pour kerosene over the infested area, and then set it on fire. When the crabs flee the inferno, you stab them with an ice pick. The "Negro method" is to pour white flour over the infested area; the crabs will see each other as ghosts and die from cardiac arrest. Lastly, the "Irish method" was to hold a mirror over the entire pubic hair area. The crabs would jump out because the grass is always greener in the yard next door.

The next day while on the way to the medical school in the car pool with my classmates, I told Bill, Arthur, Joan, and Nardo about my predicament. They thought it was quite disgusting but funny as well. Nardo promptly moved a few inches from me and laughed. The conversation seemed to exacerbate my condition. I itched.

That very afternoon in microbiology laboratory we were busy viewing parasites that were embedded on slides. The timing was uncanny. We examined them under the microscope. We each had our own box of slides containing roundworm, pinworm, and even the exotic and rare *paragonius westermanni* worm, which I learned is found mainly in the lungs of the Bengal tiger. A syllabus accompanied the slides that describe the liver fluke, *schistosomiasis* and the common *pediculosis pubis.* No slides were available for these two creatures; photos of these parasites would have to suffice.

Nardo changed all that, much for the benefit of future medical students at the University of Miami. Before I knew what was happening,

Nardo got the attention of, the much-feared perfectionist, Professor Bennett Saltsman. "Dr. Saltsman!" Nardo shouted indiscreetly, "Brucie Steir can donate *pediculosis pubis* specimen for the lab." Nardo, with his cherubic face and Desi Arnez's Cuban-American accent was not the type of man that you could be angry with. I was so embarrassed that I could hardly speak. Dr. Saltsman was known for asking essay questions on exams that could only be answered if you knew to memorize some rather obscure footnotes in the microbiology textbook. Dr. Saltsman was, unlike Nardo, very diplomatic as he approached me in the laboratory. He had sensed the location of the specimen and asked me if I would come to his office. I did so eagerly just to get myself out of the lab and away from the snickering classmates (all thirty six of them). I was hoping not only to bequeath these crabs to Dr. Saltsman but also I was hoping that he would reward me somehow when he was recording our final grades.

Dr. Saltsman and I walked down the hall to the Gross Anatomy lab. There he borrowed a pair of blunt-nose pickups, which are a type of tweezers. We then proceeded to the Medical Supply Office. There he procured a small specimen jar filled with formaldehyde, an acrid preserving fluid. Dr. Salsman thanked me for my being "a good sport" and directed me to his own laboratory adjacent to his office. "Don't spill any formaldehyde on yourself," he suggested, without a hint of a smile.

I retrieved fourteen of those tiny pests, which measured about 0.3 millimeter or so. Some of them were quite tenacious and clung to my skin while others did not put up much of a struggle. That day they all perished in the jar for the sake of medical science. I also added some little black eggs that they had laid, half the size of a grain of sand. When fixed on a slide and viewed under the microscope, they would reveal various stages of development. The slides were made available for the next year class.

Perhaps Sophia's and my contribution to medicine may still be found somewhere at the Microbiology laboratory at the School of Medicine of the University of Miami.

Chapter 6

Cadavers Tell No Tales
(The True-life Medical School Adventures)

Only twice before had I ever viewed a dead person. When I was but six years of age an elderly man jumped to his death from his sixth floor apartment window. He had fallen through the tree directly below. The branches tore off some of his pajamas and the ripped cloth clung to the leafless tree in the dead of winter.

Playmates my age urged me to come and look down the street in the cement courtyard. He was almost nude, lying in a pool of his blood. An adult covered his face and upper torso with a towel.

I left as the ambulance attendants arrived to take him away forever. All I remember thinking about was how much it must have hurt when he hit the cement.

The following summer I saw a dead boy about my age. He had drowned in the ocean not too far from the safety of the beach.

There was a crowd of bathing-suit-clad people that formed a circle around the victim and the would-be lifesaver. I joined the ring of over lookers. I watched the lifeguard as he pushed water out of the boy's lungs and throat by pressing on his lower back with both of his hands. The boy was dead. His face had taken on a bluish hue. With each push by the lifeguard the boy's eyes seem to bulge through the closed lids. The air around me began to smell like iodine so I left the crowd. Poor kid, I thought, he awoke this morning, ate breakfast and came to the beach for a swim just as I did. Now he will never be going home.

I did not contemplate that that could have been me. At that time I was invincible—I believed that I could and would swim out of any undertow. I had always done so in the past.

Fifteen years later as a twenty-two-year-old freshman medical student I was about to see several dead people. This was to be on the very first day of classes. My God, I thought, these medical school professors are fiendish. They do not waste any time in shocking us with reality. We were about to meet our Gross Anatomy cadavers.

Our small class of thirty-six students was divided into groups of four. My alphabetical mates were Margaret Smotrilla, David Small, and Wesley Southerland. We introduced ourselves to each other. We were all decked out in sparkling white clothes on a hot and humid September day in Miami.

We were quickly ordered to the rear of the Gross Anatomy classroom. Through an opened double door I could see a large wooden tank resting on the floor below us. The large vat had several ropes protruding from its upper lip and it was filled with a pungent formaldehyde solution.

Each group of four was given a number affixed to the end of the rope. We were to pull up an embalmed cadaver from the vat and carry it to an assigned stainless steel table.

When it was my group's turn three of us were ghastly silent. The looks on our faces betrayed our squeamishness, not unlike condemned men facing certain execution. Only Margaret was able to direct us like a leader in combat. Margaret Smotrilla was a tough and seasoned nurse who had gotten her hands dirty more than once on hospital wards. Smitty, as we soon would call her, was no stranger to a dead body. She pulled on the rope and scolded the three of us for our meek effort in helping her hoist up the cadaver. Smitty chastised us for being cowardly and demanded that we carry the nude male cadaver to our table at the far side of the anatomy laboratory. The dissection table would be his final resting place.

Gross Anatomy tested my ability to memorize to the point of mental exhaustion. It was an entire year of lectures and lab; very detailed and intense and left us in constant fear of pop quizzes and difficult, tricky and taxing exams. I was so immersed in every element of human anatomy that when I fell off to sleep at night the odor of formaldehyde and decaying flesh lingered in my nostrils. My hands were frequently cleansed but the now familiar odor seemed to linger on for the rest of the year. It was imbedded in the olfactory area of my brain.

We studied the cadaver by systems such as cardiopulmonary for dissection of the thoracic cavity and gastrointestinal, renal and hepatic for the abdominal cavity. The muscles, nervous innervations and blood supply of the limbs and neck were meticulously dissected out and identified. We used surgical dissecting instruments with varying degrees of skill among us. All of our dissections needed final approval by Doctor George Paff. He was a beloved and feared professor. We were all terrified of him and we all loved him. For me he made anatomy like studying advanced geography. There was no better an instructor than Doctor Paff. He was our Mister Chips.

To illustrate how intricate and detailed Gross Anatomy was, we spent one month each on the neck and on the hand. As for the brain and spinal cord, that was a whole different yearlong course called Neuroanatomy. What a nightmare that was for most of us. It was vague and taught by a boring and rigid professor that made it most difficult to grasp. I suppose it would be like comprehending the inner workings of the computer.

By the middle of the school year the cadaver and I were almost inseparable. We spent many hours together even after classes preparing for anatomy exams.

Doctor Paff fiendishly placed little baggage tags with strings attached to a structure that had been dissected out on the cadaver. The string could be affixed to an artery, a tendon, a joint part, etc. We would rotate around the eerie lab until we had visited each cadaver and identified the tagged objects. On each tag there were several questions regarding that anatomical structure. After a while we began to know the cadavers quite well. We knew their nicknames given by each group. Their birth names were never divulged to us. Naming him George in homage to Doctor Paff honored my cadaver.

The cadavers came to the medical school anonymously from the county morgue and from the main county hospital. Their procurement was vital for the anatomy lab. As you can imagine, most of these cadaver were paupers who died alone and whose remains were unclaimed or unwanted. Instead of cremation or an unceremonious burial their remains served the advancement of medical education. Some people, I've been told, donate their bodies for such a purpose in their will. These days with organ transplantation being so common a procedure and so lucrative a business I imagine most of these donors would prefer to have their organs harvested instead.

Cadavers who had experienced multiple surgical procedures with removal of vital organs or those that succumbed to malignant metastatic cancers were not eligible for donation. Among our ten cadavers there were two females. One of them, Lucille, had undergone a *hysterectomy and a bilateral salpingo-oophorectomy* (the surgical removal of her uterus, tubes, and ovaries). She was useful for the rest of her anatomy which was the same as that of a male cadaver's except that Lucille had a vagina and labia and not a penis and scrotum. Viva la difference!

Speaking of the male phallus, I must confess, that at the end of the Gross Anatomy class, I succumbed to my inherent rakishness and pocketed George's penis. When the year of anatomy nears its grueling end we are told to gather up the left over parts of the now dismembered cadaver for disposal. They had served their purpose and now they were to be collected and cremated without ceremony.

I had respect for my cadaver, almost a feeling of awe, as if it were he teaching me anatomy with Doctor Paff's assistance. It was during this ghoulish and gruesome clean up that I confiscated George's penis. I did not have any plan in mind as to what I would do with it. It seemed like a shame to just cremate it.

I informed my high school and medical school classmate and friend, Arthur Gilbert, about my unholy deed. Arthur was at first somewhat piously scornful of my action and then quickly suggested that I place the penis under Joan Osheroff's windshield wiper. "Give her a parking ticket that she will not soon forget", he chuckled fiendishly. Joan was part of our five-person carpool from Miami Beach to the medical school. Arthur reminded me that today's commute was in Joan's car. I agreed that such a clever prank could not be overlooked. Joan was our soon-to-be- married classmate and we would tell her that was our wedding present to her. I rationalized that Joan was an anatomy lab veteran and would not be horrified by the grotesque gift on her windshield. I went to her car and placed it under the windshield wiper in front of the driver's side.

I told Nardo and Bill, the other two members of our carpool, what a naughty deed had just transpired at Arthur's suggestion.

The four of us made sure that Joan would go to her car before us so we could watch her reaction to her wedding gift. We watched Joan get into her car then almost immediately got out of her car. She went to the windshield, removed the penis, returned to her car and waited for us. When we arrived and entered her vehicle she took on the air that nothing unusual had occurred. In fact, she took on an almost lyrical and nonchalant coolness in her conversation all the way home. Joan did not even give us a hint about the strange parking ticket she had received. She had virtually spoiled our adolescent prank. Joan and George had had the last laugh.

The next afternoon the carpool gang struck again. The route from school to Miami Beach took us over the Venetian Causeway over Biscayne Bay. There was a twenty-cent toll crossing back in 1954. Now I do not know what the statue of limitations is for scaring a person to death. Therefore I will not divulge the identity of the perpetuator of the crime of that day. The two dimes were readied and then placed in the palm of a decaying and partially dissected cadaver's hand. As the car slowed down, the driver-of-the-day timed the handoff (no pun intended) to the toll taker perfectly and then we sped away.

We gazed back to see him leave his booth, peer at the ground, throw his hands up in the air and hastily return to his tollbooth.

The police or the Florida Highway Patrol did not intercept us, as we had feared. If we would have been apprehended the authorities could not have charged us with not paying the required toll.

Such sophomoric pranks did not follow me into the last two years of medical school at the county hospital. There it was serious business. No cadavers, just sick people.

THE INEXPLICABLE

Sylvester Glee had been admitted to the hospital in a coma three weeks prior to my rotation to the Neurology service as a junior medical student.

Sylvester was a twenty-eight year old black, male, Haitian immigrant. He had an extensive coma work-up to no avail. He underwent a spinal tap, many X-rays, and every available laboratory test that was indicated. His electroencephalogram (EEG) was normal showing a "sleeping pattern" brain wave.

Mr. Glee received life-sustaining nourishment by way of intravenous fluids containing glucose, electrolytes and vitamins. In addition, his diet was supplemented with Sustagen, a liquid protein, through a nasogastric feeding tube. He also wore an indwelling catheter in his bladder to keep his bed linens and skin dry and free of urine. The catheter also served to monitor Sylvester's urinary output.

Each week the hospital held a CPC or Clinical Pathological Conference in the hospital auditorium. The most interesting and perplexing cases are presented to the attending physicians, the house staff and medical students. The chief resident assigned to the patient's care usually presented the case summary. That was followed by a discussion of the various possibilities that could account for a diagnosis most consistent with the clinical and laboratory findings. The many possibilities are referred to as the "differential diagnosis." I always looked forward to the weekly CPC. It was entertaining and stimulating. It was fun---like trying to solve a mystery. Instead of "who done it", the question was "what is it." All of the attendees were allowed to write their diagnosis on a piece of paper and turn it in to the moderator for consideration.

In most cases the actual etiology, pathology and definitive diagnosis was soon revealed by way of autopsy findings or biopsy specimen reports including slides of the microscopic pathology. This would be followed by a brief but scholarly synopsis of the aforementioned condition.

In the matter of Sylvester Glee, his case was discussed each week with an updated progress report…to no apparent avail. His was a tough case. The doctors had no idea what had caused him to fall into a coma, and certainly did not know how to help bring him out of it. Since Sylvester had not died there was no autopsy report available!

The eminent professor and chairman of the Department of Neurology, Doctor Peritz Scheinberg, wanted the input of the hospital staff for this most baffling case. The ultimate diagnosis of course awaited the demise of comatose patient Sylvester Glee and the subsequent autopsy findings.

One day as I was writing a daily progress note in Mr. Glee's medical chart, the hospital visitors were staggering in nearby. One of them, an elderly black man walked up to the nurse's station and told the ward clerk that he wished to speak to the physician that was assigned to

Sylvester Glee. Having overheard his request, I announced that I was the medical student on the neurology ward and would be pleased to discuss the case with him. I assured him that I was well informed of Sylvester's comatose condition.

The elderly black man introduced himself as Sylvester's uncle. He too was a Haitian and spoke with that charming Afro-Francophone accent. "May I ask a favor of you doctor?" "Sure, what is it?" I replied. He informed me that he had immigrated to Miami from Haiti with his nephew over two years ago. We walked to the bedside of his comatose nephew. The uncle then recounted this dark and mysterious encounter that Sylvester had before he slipped into his present "dead state". A Haitian friend visited Sylvester at their apartment. They argued about a gambling debt that he alleged was owed to him by Sylvester. The uncle then went on to explain, much to my astonishment, "I believe he cast a bad voodoo spell on Sylvester". He related that his nephew slowly slipped into a sleep like state over a period of two or three days before being admitted to the hospital. The comatose condition was preceded by, what sounded by his Uncle's description, as a short state of catatonic behavior.

I inquired, somewhat amused, "Are you telling me that Sylvester's coma could have been caused by some damned voodoo spell?" Without hesitation he replied, "I think so doctor." He recounted that he knew people back in Haiti and here in Miami that had died from "bad voodoo spells".

"Now doctor", he whispered, "There is a voodoo doctor in the waiting room that is a friend of mine and he knows the man who cast the evil spell on my nephew. He wants to help Sylvester to wake up before he dies. I don't have to pay him any money until his voodoo works."

He pleaded to allow this voodoo guy to go to his nephew's bedside. I was excited with this non-conventional approach to coma but felt certain that it was mumbo-jumbo superstitious nonsense. I told the uncle that his friend could go to Sylvester's bedside as a visitor only. He must not give any medicine or touch him or the tubes inside his body. I stressed that he must do no harm to his nephew. The uncle assured me that no harm would come to my patient.

"Oh! One more favor," the uncle requested. "This voodoo man will need about three hours at the bedside. Will that be possible?" I mused over that for a moment, thinking about the strict rules of visiting hours. As a clinical clerk (as medical students were called) I had almost no authority to bend any hospital rules. I called the hospital operator and requested that she page the neurology resident on call.

There were no wireless beeper pagers in 1956. The operator paged the hospital staff over a speaker system that told the doctor whom to call. Another quieter way was to flash the doctor's assigned number on display panels mounted on every floor and room in the hospital. When you saw your number being signaled you telephoned the operator to find out who wants you. This was advanced technology. My number was 856. Even clinical clerks were assigned numbers. I was usually pleased deep down to see my number flashing. It made me feel like I was part of a team. Even today as an old man when I see the number 856 it gives me a bittersweet moment of remembering yesteryear.

The resident on call answered his page and called me at the ward nurse's station. He was a very British sounding gentleman whose name I cannot remember. I do recall that he was an intellect and sported a bow tie and a white handlebar moustache. After I told him the unusual narrative that had transpired he said that he would be coming over straightaway.

I introduced the Jamaican born neurology resident to Sylvester's uncle. They were both seemingly respectful towards each other and set out to fetch this voodoo doctor from the waiting room. The three of them had a hallway conference while I eavesdropped.

We then proceeded to Sylvester Glee's bedside where he lay in a coma the past 5 weeks.

I was running late for an Internal Medicine lecture to be given by the department chairman, Doctor Ralph Jones. Besides being an outstanding educator he was notorious for taking class roll. So I ran off wondering what would transpire in my absence. After a didactic and slide presentation on pancreatitis I hurried back to the neurology ward.

The voodoo doctor was sitting at Sylvester's bedside. He was speaking quietly in a language that sounded like French but I could not be certain. He had been at the bedside for over two hours. Seeing no reason to hang around and watch this silliness I drove home for a night of reading and rest. I did not deep down believe in voodoo other than as a theatrical form of hypnosis.

The following morning, as soon as time would allow, I rushed over to the neurology ward. The mustachioed senior resident was down the hall at the nurse's station. As I walked by him on my way to see Sylvester, he registered a smile above his polka-dotted bowtie and beckoned to me, "Oh, please go and say hello to Mr. Glee." I entered the room. Sylvester's bed was empty. The mattress was folded in half exposing half of the hospital bed's springs. This was an ominous sign of a patient's recent demise.

The damned voodoo doctor had somehow killed Sylvester, I judged, as the adrenaline clicked in. My mood went downhill as I turned around to confront the resident. "My God, what the hell happened to Mr. Glee?" I asked excitedly.

"Sylvester had a normal looking EEG right after he finished breakfast. I wanted to present his case to Doctor Scheinberg during grand rounds but Sylvester became so anxious to go home after I told him that he had been in the hospital for thirty-six days. He went on to state that Sylvester had left after being discharged about two hours ago. The senior resident confessed that he was at a loss to know how to sign the chart out with an appropriate diagnosis or to compose a discharge summary.

The following day, Doctor Ralph Jones, knowing of this weird case, told the medical students at rounds that Mr. Glee's rapid recovery would be best explained by a "coincidental spontaneous remission of a viral meningitis."

Later that week Doctor Scheinberg, a wise and intellectual being, informed his residents that he believed otherwise. He left us with a never-to-be-forgotten message: Even the science of medicine has its mystery and inexplicable events.

THE AUTOPSY

Autopsy call was a grim rotation for third year medical students. Whenever the hospital morgue scheduled an autopsy, the pathology resident would call up a medical student from an on-call roster sheet. If that student could not be reached in the hospital or at home then the next on the schedule list would be called. Unlike obstetrics, autopsies are not scheduled at three in the morning and they are certainly not emergencies.

Watching an autopsy is not at all like viewing an embalmed cadaver in the anatomy lab. A fresh naked corpse has the eerie and inescapable appearance of a sleeping person lying on a cold stainless steel table. Medical students observe autopsies to gain first hand knowledge of gross pathology. As second year medical students that observation was limited to textbook descriptions and slides accompanied by a didactic lecture. Now we had the opportunity to see a cirrhotic liver or a lung with advanced cancer or follow the trajectory of a bullet through the corpse to its deadly end. Even more intriguing was to watch the unfolding of a diagnosis before your eyes of a death that has occurred without a known etiology.

The pathologist, at work in the morgue, makes an incision with a large kitchen-like knife. The incision extends from the lower edge of the sternum downward, with very little effort to the pubic bone at the top of the pelvis. The first time I saw that bold cut, my toes curled up in my shoes and I swallowed deeply.

I expected that blood would squirt out and hit the pathologist and the overhead light. There was no spillage of blood. Dead people do not bleed.

Bill Kandel, one of my classmates and car-pooler, did not own a car. He was therefore teamed up with me for autopsy call since I was his closest medical school classmate neighbor. We went to the morgue together for our first autopsy call.

The pathologist removed a white sheet that covered the corpse. There on the cold stainless steel table laid a young woman with raven black hair: A sleeping beauty.

The nerdy looking pathology resident began dictating into a nearby recording device. "This is a fourteen year old Cuban-American female who died today after a ten-day hospitalization."

I was tempted to pick up the white sheet and cover her young nude body. I dared not to. I was there to observe. Bill and I were in the morgue to learn about disease and how it killed a lovely looking young woman.

The cause of her demise was "congestive heart failure" as recorded in her discharge summary in her chart.

Two months prior to her hospital admission the young woman had her ears pierced by a relative. Both of her ear lobes developed an infection within a few days. She received home treatment at first with hot soaks and an antibiotic ointment. Soon after she was seen at a local clinic and had the pus cultured and the earrings removed. The culture grew out both streptococcus and staphylococcus bacteria. This was initially treated with penicillin injections.

The resident continued his monotonic dictation, "The patient's past medical history includes the usual childhood diseases plus a diagnosis of rheumatic fever at age six following bouts of strep throat". Bill and I nodded to each other to acknowledge our recently acquired knowledge regarding this sad case. We knew of the conspiracy between "strep throats" and rheumatic heart disease.

The resident opened her chest with an electric buzz saw across the full length of her sternum. My toes curled up again. The sensation that someone gets when a prankster rubs his fingernails across a blackboard visited me briefly. The split sternum and ribs were then manually displaced laterally so as to expose the heart, lungs and great vessels. The heart was severed with long scissors from the aorta and pulmonary vessels and the vena cava and removed from the thoracic cavity. The heart was then cut open in a longitudinal manner so as to expose the aortic and mitral valves.

Our four-chambered heart has sets of valves that open and close each time our heart beats. Heart valves are very small, thin, membranous, and very durable parts of our heart. We never get to see them. I am seventy-seven years young and my heart and its valves have been working nonstop since my days as an embryo in my mother's uterus. My calculator tells me that those valves in my heart have opened and closed to regulate the flow of blood over three billion times! (Rolls Royce and Mercedes-Benz-- eat your heart out!) The sounds of our heartbeat are the valves opening and closing. Our heart is just like a finely tuned engine. Even a minor part that malfunctions can keep the engine from running properly or to fail entirely.

The young woman's earlobe infection with bacteria became blood borne. The microbes rapidly traveled to her heart valves. Because she had rheumatic fever as a young child the heart valves were already damaged by the bacterial infection. There they cause vegetation to accumulate on the surface of the valves. Listening to the heart and hearing the telltale murmur confirm this previous heart valve damage. From the recent infection she developed sub-acute bacterial endocarditis. Her damaged heart valves could no longer function properly. Heart transplantation unfortunately had not arrived in 1956, so she died.

How fragile life can be. It is so good to be alive I thought. We take every day for granted as if we are immune to death. Bill and I left the morgue and drove home. We smoked in silence most of the way.

THE E.R.

Another medical student rotation assignment was to hang on to the white coat tails of a resident in the hospital emergency room. Looking back at that experience it was very similar to the current TV program "E.R." except that you can be sure that primetime TV cannot capture the smell of booze and blood.

A big city hospital E.R. is a wondrous place full of noisy chaos followed by moments of dull silence. Then suddenly it seems another wave of humanity in dire need of help hits the fatigued workers once again. The drama and excitement commingle with the mundane and annoying. Every crammed space with or without a curtain awaits their urgent care.

When I was a medical student there weren't any residents in training for Emergency Room Medicine. Full-time nurses manned the E.R. and the physicians were from the various specialties that rotated on call for the E.R.

Today the staff physicians are capable of skillfully triaging the patients and work as a team. Most E.R.s, I have been assured, are safe places to visit now.

My classmate, Arthur Gilbert, and I were on E.R. call together one weekend night. We mostly stood back and watched the drama unfold. We walked around the various rooms and cubicles. We observed a possible heart attack, a drunk with a deep facial laceration, a baby that could not stop vomiting, vaginal bleeding so heavy that the woman's bare feet were stained, an old man brought in as a DOA awaiting a physician to "pronounce" him, a belligerent psychopath loudly demanding morphine for pain real or imagined.

The waiting room was crowded and boisterous and we marveled at the residents in action as they attempted to triage the assemblage. The seasoned orderlies provided the initial screening for the young resident physicians. For the most part I was impressed with their clinical skills and bedside manners. Some of the E.R. doctors were sleepy and fatigued from the psychopathic hours: thirty-six hours on and twelve hours off. Many survived on strong Cuban coffee that made them jittery and grouchy. Imagine yourself being kind and sensitive to a smelly drunk cursing, vomiting and thrashing about while you are attempting to suture together his gaping scalp laceration under local anesthesia. E.R. work is not glamorous.

The E.R. clerks are obligated by law, then as now, to allow all those who wished to be seen to be processed through. After evaluation they are seen in the order of urgency as decided by the triage. This is the reason that you hear or read about some people waiting five hours or so before being seen. Many people, then and now, use and often abuse the emergency room as their primary source for medical care. Our health care system, unfortunately, fosters this misuse.

Arthur Gilbert and I took turns suturing up the abundance of lacerations that deluge the E.R. on weekend nights. Some are from auto windshields, but the overwhelming majority of the lacerations are from bottles or knives and most are brandished by young and middle-aged men with a beef with the world.. The residents are pleased to have us help out.

We, of course, were delighted to gain the experience and confidence from suturing relatively minor lacerations. The residents checked out the closures for good surgical approximation before the clients were discharged. Lacerated and detached tendons were repaired by surgical residents and not by medical students for medical and legal reasons.

Plastic surgery residents mended facial lacerations on boys and girls and young women. This was, we were told, an unwritten protocol. I was pleased to learn that this practice crossed color lines.

I needed some fresh air from the peculiar odors in a busy E.R. I went outside on to the ramp where the ambulances arrive. It was about 1:00 A.M. and I had just lit up a much-needed smoke when an ambulance pulled up to the entrance. It had been racing down the street with lights flashing and sirens wailing. I knew that it was coming in with someone worth watching.

In a flash a black male was carried out of the ambulance and quickly transferred to a waiting gurney cart that was wheeled into the E.R. They knew where to bring him as a critical emergency. No stopping for paperwork and questions. Two surgical residents pulled back the cubicle curtain just as Arthur and I stepped into the space.

The patient's shirt had been ripped open and he had an intravenous drip running in his forearm. There was a white square of gauze dressing taped to his chest. This was removed to reveal a small hole in his chest just below his left nipple.

The ambulance attendant informed the residents that the call they had received was to go to the Sir John nightclub in Liberty City. (In 1956 that was the name given to the downtown "colored town.") Spectators at the club said that the victim was stabbed once in the chest with an ice pick. The police were told that the assailant was a "friend" and that he fled the scene.

The victim was a thin well-developed nineteen-year-old black male. He was unresponsive to questioning. His eyes were rolled back and his mouth was wide open and he was gasping for air.

As I looked at this tragic drama I could not help but think that this young man looked like a fish that had just been caught, a fish out of the water. This vision was enhanced when he suddenly lifted his head and shoulders and let out a loud gasp. He had just died. I had been witness to a man's death throe.

As the resident listened in vain for any sign of life I took notice of the deceased's black and white dress shoes. His shoelaces were not the standard ones from the shoe store. They were white and the two ends had a pair of dice attached. The resident doctor asked the ambulance driver if he had obtained the name of the victim. The attendant replied, "Yeah, doctor, the people at the club said that he went by the name of Lucky".

I suddenly felt a wave of nausea and quickly departed again for fresh air. I soon vomited.

It was 2:00 A.M. and Arthur and I drove home. I told Big Art, as he was named in school, that we had a man die right in front of us.

Arthur shook his head and admitted that he had gotten sick too. Two of the most important events in our life are being born and dying and we are not aware of either one of them.

OBSTETRICS: WHERE LIFE BEGINS

The event of seeing a young man dying in the E.R. had a profound effect on me. Shortly after seeing a man called Lucky die I rotated to the obstetrical service. I was glad to leave the E.R. behind that was where death often happened. OB was about life.

In our junior year on the OB rotation we mostly watched the senior medical students and interns manage the uncomplicated deliveries. We learned the art and science of OB by following a woman in labor and by observing the activities of the delivery room nurses.

I slowly gained confidence in my ascertaining the amount of cervical dilatation of the cervix. After my vaginal or rectal exam the labor room nurse would repeat the exam and compare my findings with hers. The nurse's findings were considered the correct measure.

I learned how to deliver a baby mostly by watching in the delivery room, but I also went through a mock delivery with a nude, life size dummy baby. This silly looking rag-doll even had an umbilical cord made of hemp and a round cloth placenta attached at the other end. The maternal aspect was a mannequin mold of the female pelvic cavity and the external genitalia was made of soft rubber. This teaching dummy was a valuable tool for medical students to experience a *dry run* obstetrical delivery.

I learned of the three stages of labor. The first stage is from the onset of true labor until complete dilatation of the cervix.

We simulated the power of the uterine contraction and the awesome force of the mother's pushing by a fellow classmate exerting downward pressure on the dummy baby from above as it lay in the maternal pelvis. I learned how to control the delivery of the head as it emerges out of the vagina and to prevent a sudden exit that could cause lacerations of the perineum, vulvae and vagina.

The second stage of labor is from complete dilatation of the cervix until the complete delivery of the baby. I learned how to allow the baby's upper shoulder to slide down slowly below the pubic bone. Then the lower shoulder is delivered by gently elevating the baby's head. The almost newborn's head is cradled between my two open palms. Now the torso and buttocks are delivered by slowly sliding the baby outward with one hand across its back while the index finger and thumb of the other hand support the neck of the newborn. Then the feet are grasped with my fingers and the baby is placed head down on my lap. A bulb syringe is used to gently suction make-believe mucous from the nose and mouth. The umbilical cord is doubly clamped and cut between the imaginary clamps and scissors. I then pretend to collect blood from the umbilical cord to be sent to the lab. The dummy baby is placed in a make-believe bassinet. The simulated delivery is completed with all the possible reality except the cry of the baby, the presence of blood and the moaning or screaming of the mother. After I finished my "dry-run" delivery the faculty instructor told me that I neglected to check for any coil of umbilical cord that could be looped around the baby's neck. So I was told to repeat the mock delivery. Afterwards we watched each other deliver the rag-doll dummy until all four of us performed a perfect mock delivery.

I soon realized that you can watch a hundred deliveries but you must deliver one unassisted to really "know how". You do not learn to ride a motorcycle by reading the manual.

At that time if a student wanted to deliver a baby --and I did-- it was necessary to bother or bribe an intern with the hope that you could "catch one" in a labor room as a precipitated delivery was underway. I spent a good deal of my off duty time "hanging out" in the OB suite area hoping to catch a "precip".

Doctor Howard Novell was a talented obstetrician and a decent lecturer. In my senior year he told my OB rotation group that he wanted us to ask the first two women that we delivered how it felt when the baby was being delivered. We were to record their words on tape or in writing as close to verbatim as possible. He explained that the object of the assignment was for we students to appreciate what delivering a baby was like for the mother so that we could gain empathy and sensitivity for them as patients. It sounded like an enjoyable assignment to me.

As my luck would have it, my very first patient in labor was a deaf and mute woman. I delivered her third baby. It was easy. Those repetitive mannequin sessions paid off. The delivery room nurse gave me a pat on the back even before she congratulated the mother.

My second delivery was but a few hours later. This also went smoothly except this patient, having her fourth baby, kept scaring me by yelling with each contraction," Oh Lordy Jesus please help me. Where are you Jesus when I need you?" I urged her to breathe in and out of her mouth with each contraction. She stared at me and smiled as best she could, "doctor you calls it a contraption but I calls it a pain".

With these two uncomplicated deliveries under my belt I presented my oral narratives to my OB rotation group and Doctor Novell the following week. I reported that my first patient answered my written question by opening her mouth wide, sticking out her tongue and rolling her eyes around. "That is how she described how it felt to push out her baby. She is a deaf mute mother." Doctor Novell laughed and my classmates then snickered along too. He agreed, "That was a fine description albeit unusual". I went on to patient number two by quoting from my pocket notes, "Doctor it feel just like a watermelon come out your ass". Howard Novell smiled and puffed on his always-lit cigarette and thanked me. My classmate, redheaded Sarah Lou Wells was next up for her patient narratives. Sarah began by stating, "My mommas were not as descriptive as Bruce's were". It was about that time in my senior year that I knew full well that I preferred being around young women having babies than amongst men dying from stab wounds to the chest.

THE SECRET BIOPSY

This desire for OB/GYN grew, by comparison, with each service that I rotated through. For example, when I was on the internal medicine rotation I was assigned to a ward full of sick old white men. Twenty some beds were inhabited by patients with terminal lung and colon cancer, stroke victims, liver failure from cirrhosis, diabetics with irreversible acidosis or renal failure, and one fifty-ish holocaust survivor with "intractable pneumonia".

I felt rather like part of a medical team trying to salvage the hopelessly unsalvageable. I was beginning to realize that it was more important to allow patients to pass away without severe pain and with dignity then to subject them to hopeless heroic measures when their condition was irreversible and death was inescapable. I thought that those moralistic decisions should be left up to other physicians who wish to deal with terminal conditions. So I decided that OB/GYN was for me. Ironically I chose this specialty to avoid dealing with death.

The man with pneumonia was in his late fifties whose lungs were not functioning properly to allow adequate breathing. His X-rays demonstrated evidence of bilateral densities and fluid in all of the lobes of the lungs. The good news was that there was no evidence of lung cancer on X-ray. The bad news was his pulmonary function was getting worse and he was not responding to the usual ameliorative therapy. The pulmonary specialists were puzzled even up to the time that the patient expired from respiratory failure.

The grieving widow was at her husband's bedside when he died. The senior resident who had been in charge of the deceased patient did his best to comfort her. I purposely observed his approach, as I was not well acquainted with consoling the bereaved.

He went on to tell her that the house staff did not have a definitive diagnosis as to the cause of her husband's pulmonary failure. The diagnosis could be obtained, he informed her, by having an autopsy performed. I watched her wipe her eyes, blow her nose and tell us, "We cannot allow an autopsy because we are Orthodox Jews".

"Talmudic law forbids an alteration of the body except for the ritual circumcision. Even tattoos are taboo", I quickly added trying to sound scholarly although I had just thought it up but knew it would sound authentic.

The resident placed his hand on the new widow's shoulder and indicated that he understood her religious concerns but would still appreciate a limited autopsy to include only an examination of his lungs. She apologized again and reiterated that she could not allow that to be done to her husband.

The medical ward clerk, also quite familiar with death, asked the widow to accompany her downstairs to some administrative office that deals with mortuary services as a precursor to releasing the body to a funeral home for burial or cremation.

Behind the closed curtains surrounding the deceased patient the senior resident told me to go to Central Supply for a large syringe, an 18 gauge long spinal needle and a small jar with a formalin solution. He then informed me that he wanted me to obtain a postmortem biopsy from each lung before the deceased patient is sent to the morgue. He went on to explain that no one would know the difference and we would be all the wiser for it. He was determined to find out what the hell had killed his patient. This was, I knew, not a mischievous act but an intellectually honest attempt to gain knowledge. He was certainly not a miscreant, even if he mistakenly believed anything could be gained by violating the beliefs of the deceased.

I nodded to him that I understood but I also suggested that perhaps it would be wiser if he were to obtain the biopsy since I had never placed a needle in a person's chest before. He promptly told me, as he walked away, that he was needed in the ER and that I would gain the experience of obtaining a "blind biopsy" and the patient would not feel any pain.

I obtained the necessary supplies and returned to the bedside of the deceased. I attached the long spinal needle to the 50cc glass syringe and without hesitation pushed it through the skin and deep into the chest cavity. My thrust was unobstructed and was introduced between two ribs in the lower anterior chest wall. I repeated the same procedure on the opposite side. Each time, by pulling up on the plunger of the syringe, I obtained a blood-tinged straw colored fluid with some pieces of tissue floating freely in the syringe. I transferred the contents into two separate formalin specimen jars. I labeled each jar as either left or right lung tissue.

In all, the entire lung biopsy took about two minutes to complete. I was pleased with my apparent success. I carried the specimen jars to the pathology lab just as the morgue people were arriving for the deceased gentleman.

The following afternoon I returned to the medical ward to make rounds on my assigned patients. The senior resident who had ordered me to obtain the unauthorized postmortem lung biopsy approached me.

"Hey Steir", he chuckled, "We've got the report back from the path lab on your lung biopsy." He removed the folded paper from the pocket of his white coat. He handed the report to me. I read the one sentence typed results of my biopsy. "Both specimens are labeled lung tissue and contain what microscopically appear to be normal kidney tissue." My astonishment was tempered somewhat by the resident. "Well you did try, you just went too deep or too low."

My embarrassment was comforted later as I thought about my direction of the needle and the anatomical proximity of the lung and kidney. Then I realized that the Talmud had prevailed over our deceitful cunningness.

BOTCHED ABORTION DAYS

During my senior year of medical school I chose an extra month of OB/GYN as an elective. I was feeling strongly drawn to this specialty. Perhaps it was the over-riding impression that OB/GYN encompassed almost all the fields of medicine to some degree. There was gynecological surgery, oncology, psychology, anesthesiology, endocrinology some urology and of course obstetrics including family planning.

Also, as previously mentioned, the thought of not having to deal with death, or hardly ever, was very appealing to me. The thought of spending my professional working life caring for geriatric patients with infirmities of age was not what I wished to do. More appealing was providing assistance to young women throughout their pregnancy and the delivery of a healthy baby.

On the gynecology wards I assisted, listened and learned about the care of a myriad of gynecological conditions. There were postoperative hysterectomies, ectopic pregnancies, ovarian tumors, pelvic inflammatory infections, cervical and uterine cancer and the ever-present post-abortion complications.

Abortion in 1957 was still almost two decades away from being legalized in this country. Abortion, although a medical procedure, had evolved over the years into a morality issue.

"Abortion, like prostitution and betting will always be around and so it should be legal" has been the mantra of many pro-choice activists. I do not equate abortion with prostitution as an arena of controversy in both politics and religion. There should be no stigmata associated with abortion. Abortion should be thought of in medical and not moral terms. Abortion is the voluntary treatment for an unwanted and unplanned pregnancy.

I mention this because abortion was thought of as a criminal act in 1957, during my senior year in medical school. A bank robber having been wounded by the police and hospitalized would receive more dignity and sensitivity from the hospital staff then would a post-abortion patient. The medical care however would be as good as possible and void of a punitive nature. At least I would like to believe so.

Terms such as "botched abortion' and "baby killer" still stain the patient and abortion provider today as it did almost fifty years ago. The language implies bad intentions on the part of a heartless abortionist. Have you ever-heard reference to a "botched coronary by-pass"? Of course you haven't! The patient died from a "complication arising from heart surgery". The implication is of an innocent and unavoidable complication.

A thirty-two year old white female was admitted to the gynecology ward from the E.R. with the diagnosis of pelvic abscess. On admission she had a temperature of 104.4F. That is a lot of fever, especially for an adult. The resident's note from the E.R. stated that there was exquisite tenderness on abdominal and pelvic examination. There was a pelvic mass palpable in the lower abdomen. Her blood pressure was recorded as 80/40 and she had an elevated pulse of 112 beats per minute. These vital signs raised the suspicion for impending septic shock. I did not repeat the pelvic exam as the Chief Resident explained that doing so would increase the chance of rupturing a pelvic abscess and cause the needless spread of the infection. As a medical student my assignment was to obtain a detailed medical history.

Her recent significant past medical history was that she was recently divorced and had an abortion one week ago by a doctor in downtown Miami. She had been twelve or thirteen weeks pregnant. She stated that the abortion was painful and took a "long time". Her sister had driven her home and put her to bed.

She had severe cramps all through the night. Codeine tablets did not seem to help relieve the pain. Two days later she was still having cramps but no bleeding. She called the doctor who had performed the abortion. He told her to go to the nearest emergency room to be seen as soon as possible. She went to Mercy Hospital. After she arrived there she realized that this was a Catholic hospital. She therefore wisely decided it would be prudent not to tell the E.R. physician about her recent illegal abortion. The E.R. doctor examined her and treated her for a common occurrence called "P.I.D." or pelvic inflammatory disease. He sent her home with antibiotic capsules after administering an intra-muscular injection of the same medication. He was treating her for gonorrhea, the most common cause of P.I.D. in 1957. The primary culprit today is probably an organism named *chlamydia*. The E.R. doctor also told her to take hot baths and not to have sexual intercourse and to see her regular physician or a gynecologist in a week. She went home, followed his course of treatment and slowly got worse.

On the day of admission she felt feverish (though no temperature was taken) and her pelvic and abdominal pain increased. She was unable to get out of bed because of the pain and weakness. An ambulance was summoned and she was brought to our E.R. We X-rayed her pelvis and abdomen. There was, as expected, a density in the pelvic area consistent with a pelvic mass behind her uterus. This was presumed to be an abscess. A secondary find, pointed out by the radiologist, was that there was free air beneath her diaphragm below each lung. The attending physician, Doctor Harvey Lozman; Doctor Abe Gurinsky the Chief Resident in OB/GYN and I all knew immediately what had occurred.

She had suffered a perforation of her uterus during the abortion procedure. Bacteria enter the pelvic cavity from the vagina and an abscess begins to grow. Very often, when there is a uterine perforation, injury to the surrounding bowel may occur. (The intestines coil about freely around the uterus.) This of course will spill fecal matter into the pelvic cavity causing peritonitis. The perforation may also sever blood vessels to add to the gravity of the complication.

When the wall of the uterus is inadvertently perforated with an instrument, air from the vagina goes into the pelvic cavity and travels upward until it is trapped under the diaphragm. The radiologist knew to take an X-ray with the patient in an upright position to demonstrate the trapped air.

Doctors Lozman and Gurinsky outlined the course of treatment and the urgent care our very sick patient would need. Her diagnosis of septic shock was one that the gynecology service treated frequently and so we knew that her prognosis was poor.

In spite of all the heroic efforts to stabilize her she gradually deteriorated and was deemed not to be a candidate for the operating room. Her blood pressure began to drop and she was administered an intravenous drip of Levophed. We called this now defunct medication "Holy Water" because it kept the blood pressure up artificially and was a last resort attempt to prolong the inevitable for patients who were moribund.

The next morning when I arrived on the gynecology ward she was breathing laboriously and was on oxygen. A new type of "wonder drug" antibiotic was being administered along with the Levophed. There were tubes and machines all about her bedside. That is usually a poor prognostic sign for recovering.

My thoughts turned to my sister and her predicament fourteen years prior when she was sixteen years old and wanted an abortion. I was experiencing a pleasure knowing that my sister did not have a botched abortion. I could not understand why abortion was not a legal surgical procedure.

Abe Gurinsky, the Chief Resident, arrived on the ward to make morning rounds. He made sure that he had the attention of his staff of four including me. He pulled up a chair to the patient's bedside. He leaned over toward her pillow and peered into her lethargic half-closed eyes. He held her hand and whispered, "Madeline, you may be dying soon. Please tell us who did your abortion". I was shocked at his candor. I felt the hair on my forearms tingle and held back a sudden urge to cry.

I knew that Abe Gurinsky was a good doctor, a family man, and a refugee from Castro's Cuba. He possessed a friendly easygoing bedside manner that put the patients at ease. This time he was serious, soft spoken and sadness clung to his words.

Madeline was too ill to answer even if she had comprehended his startling question. Abe Gurinsky was correct. Within a few hours Madeline would die that afternoon. I brought the news to him as he was dictating an operation in the surgeon's lounge. He wasn't surprised of the news. He said to me, with a tone of indignation, "Damn this horrible stupid mess with these abortions. They need to make it legal and make it safe." Abe was right.

Internship

Chapter 7

Huey Long's Cement Uterus

If at all possible, it is best not to be admitted as a patient to a teaching hospital during the month of July. During that time of year you would be more vulnerable to the chaos and medical mishaps made by the new house staff of residents and interns.

Historically in the U.S.A. we graduate our students in June. The same holds true for medical students. Future physicians begin their training in hospitals on the first day of July. The rotations of residents from Junior to Senior or Chief commence at this time as well. These young doctors-in-training perform most of the choirs and hospital duties in a regulated and disciplined manner. But many learn by their mistakes.

So it was with me. I graduated medical school in June and began my internship in July.

My mother packed a shoebox full of home-cooked southern fried chicken and a bowl of summer fruit for my drive to New Orleans. This along with a few medical books and some clothes were placed in my "new" two-year-old 88-Olds Hydromatic; my parent's gift to me for my graduation present.

I kissed and hugged them both goodbye and headed out for my new adventure in life. I had a sense of sadness as I drove away, especially regarding my father who was ill. I couldn't have known it then, but I would never see him again. He died twenty-four days later at age 59.

That year I was fortunate to secure an internship at Charity Hospital of Louisiana. This enormous structure of around 2,000 beds was comparable in size, volume of patients and number of deliveries by hospitals such as L.A. County, Cook County in Chicago, and Grady in Atlanta, Philadelphia General and Jackson Memorial in Miami.

Charity Hospital was one of many edifices that were built during the reign of Governor Huey "Kingfish" Long. Like all powerful and charismatic rulers, he was loved by the masses but also had those constituents not in his good graces that feared and despised him. Eventually, a friend and physician assassinated Huey Long. He was gunned down on the capitol steps in Baton Rouge.

Sadly, today the "rotating internship" has gone the way of the typewriter and the pay phone. I say sadly because it was the last bastion of opportunity for a young doctor to be exposed to all areas of medicine and surgery. Today a medical student commits to a specialty prior to graduation and their "internship" is in reality a first year of residency. So be it, for better or worse.

My internship allowed me exposure in pediatrics, psychiatry, OB/GYN, medicine, urology, emergency room, and surgery. Each lasted one or two months. It was a last chance to "get your hands dirty" and to see for yourself what specialties suited you and which you could live without.

Each new rotation was an exciting opportunity to learn about that specialty. I was filled with enthusiasm, especially at the beginning of the rotation, and then it did not take long to realize that I did not want to spend the rest of my life working in an area that was not my cup of tea. A perfect example of this was my pediatrics rotation when I was assigned to a thirty-two bed open ward of sick little people with hemophilia or leukemia.

Hemophilia, a hereditary bleeding disorder, was fairly common in Louisiana because of the common intermarriage within families especially in the backwater bayous. This social phenomenon allowed the chromosome defect to produce carriers that could pass on the disorder. These unions allowed the gene pool to pass on the hemophilia gene from mama, the carrier, to baby boys.

It was an ordeal and a half to arise at 5:00 in the A.M. to start intravenous blood transfusions into small veins. That was just to get the day started. As soon as I entered the dismal and foul-smelling ward and the little people saw me wearing my white coat, their screaming and crying would commence and not cease until I left the ward for a smoke or lunch. These poor little kids did not comprehend that I was there to help them "get better". I wonder whether things would have gone a lot smoother if someone had taken the time to explain to them step by step what was happening and how they could benefit from it. But by now the hysteria had a momentum of its own that was impossible to undo. Most of the children needed to be physically restrained by a student nurse in order for me to start an I.V. Some were so pitifully ill that they could not resist or move about.

Every morning when I entered the ward, I was greeted by at least one rolled up mattress and an empty bed or crib, a sad and unceremonious marker of a death that had occurred during the night and yet it signified nothing more than that there was one less patient to see. I wanted to mourn; someone should, I thought. Their short and sad life was just the reality of an incurable illness. So much for pediatrics, I thought.

Psychiatry, on the other hand, was interesting and at times amusing. The rotation afforded me some much-needed sleep. There were not too many emergencies and no deaths. That aspect was favorable to me but not too many patients seemed to get well either. Do I want to spend the rest of my life with crazy people? I thought not, especially after noticing that the staff psychiatrists, the psychology workers and even the psych-ward nurses seemed to act strange too, at times even bizarre. Their peculiar behavior was mostly inexplicable.

Although I had difficulty in opening boxes of cereal and Pepperidge cookie packages, I thought that the operating room was a very special drama that appealed to me. Surgery usually corrects an acute problem and the patient improves quickly or is cured. The aspect of a "quick fix" was appealing to me. Perhaps that is why abortion services attracted me later in my professional years. Abortion provided the client an almost instant relief of her problem.

As an intern the surgery rotation mostly involved getting the patient ready for the operating room and providing routine postoperative care on the open ward. If we were lucky, had all our scut work completed, and had a generous resident for our ward boss, we might be invited to watch an operation as a third assistant. That title meant that you would hold a stainless steel retractor placed inside the abdominal cavity to enhance exposure for the surgeon. Holding a retractor can be a prolonged, tiring, boring, and severely under-appreciated activity. If problems arise during the operation the surgeon usually blames the low man on the totem pole: the intern holding the retractor. Perhaps that is why they call the retractor an "idiot stick".

During a difficult *gastrectomy* for stomach cancer in an obese patient, I retracted without moving for over two hours. Deprived of sleep big time, I dozed off while on my feet and was rudely awakened by a grumpy surgical resident.

During an emergency *laparotomy* for a ruptured appendix, I had a memorable experience. Suddenly I could feel my surgical scrub pants sliding down from my waist toward my upper thighs. Apparently I failed to tie the bow in front properly. To maintain a sterile surgical field the operating personnel may not place their sterile gloved hand below the operating table. Thus I was unable to reach for my sliding breeches. Besides that, holding the retractor usually requires two hands, so I couldn't do anything about it anyway. The surgical gown, worn over the scrub suit, is tied in the back so the rear is exposed. I did not wear underwear in the operating room because of the frequent bloodstains that ensued. My scrub pants continued to fall down. To prevent the trousers from reaching my ankles and exposing my derriere, I pushed my torso up against the operating table. That maneuver helped but only for a short time. The surgical resident ordered me to the opposite side of the table in order for him to rotate to the other side. This maneuver would enhance his ability in closing the abdomen by improving his angle of exposure. I promptly released the retractors and slowly walked around the operating table trying to keep my pants up by walking with my feet apart as much as possible.

In the surgical world of sterile technique your back is not sterile just as below your waist is also considered a contaminated area. For that reason I could not turn my back to the table. That would have been considered a "contaminated field" and I would receive holy hell from the resident, anesthetist and scrub nurse. Everyone yells at interns except patients. If I had contaminated the surgical field, they would have to quickly re-drape that area of the table.

My pants fell to my ankles exposing my naked buns inside the opened back gown, but I obediently resumed my task with the "idiot sticks".

The circulating nurse that day was a Sister of Charity nun. She caught sight of my plight and quietly came to my rescue. As the circulator she is not "scrubbed in," and because she is not sterile she could reach down and lift up my pants. She then, bless her, clamped a towel clip around the waist to secure my breeches. When the operation was completed I thanked the Sister as I was leaving. She responded coquettishly, under her surgical mask, "Doctor, your pants should only come down when you are not on duty."

As an intern, staying awake and alert was for the most part an ever-present ordeal. The work hours for the lowly intern at Charity Hospital were typically 36 hours on duty and 12 hours off. We were on duty every other weekend, which was from early Saturday morning until Monday evening. We made rounds on our assigned ward at 7:00A.M.on Monday, and then we were on call Monday night and worked all day Tuesday. Interns do whatever the residents tell us to do, which is usually a task that is beneath their dignity or level of expertise. We did most of the basic lab work (blood counts and urinalysis), paper work, start I.V.s, obtain lab and X-ray reports, check on the status of pathology results, talk to family members and a never ending checklist of "things to do today."

Most nights being on call meant no sleep. If you were lucky you perhaps got an hour or three of shut-eye between phone calls to the "on call" room. Psychiatry was the only rotation that usually allowed a decent night of sleep.

All this work was in a non-air-conditioned hospital. We did get a dormitory type room across the street and meals in the staff dining room. The salary for the intern at Charity Hospital in 1957 was $75 per month. After taxes my paycheck was $71.70. If our medical records were not completed the Medical Record tyrants had a way of having your paycheck held hostage until you begrudgingly did your paper work and dictations. It was the married house staff that raised hell about that Draconian policy.

Every other night and weekend we were free to sleep, cavort about, mostly drink inexpensive local brewed beer and swap "war" stories with fellow interns and pretty student nurses. Then we were back to the slavish grind.

Surgery took a back seat for me one hot Louisiana Saturday night. The E.R. sent a 22-year-old white male directly to the O.R. This individual had smacked another man across the head with a cue stick in a pool-hall. The cue stick victim disappeared for a while and returned with a handgun. He then proceeded to empty all six rounds into the alleged assailant's abdomen.

The O.R. team-on-call was summoned to the surgical suite for an emergency *laparotomy*. For me that meant scribbling down a history and physical exam into the chart and then holding the "idiot sticks" as third assistant in the O.R.

Upon opening his abdomen we were at once overcome by the wretched and noxious odor of beer and feces. The multiple gunshot wounds had pierced his stomach, liver, and spleen and perforated his intestines. Because the elongated intestines coil about freely in the abdominal cavity, it was subject to multiple puncture wounds.

The surgeons were obliged to "run the bowel", a necessary mechanical chore to inspect the entire bowel to determine the location of damage and to surgically close all bullet hole perforations. After several units of blood were transfused we were informed that the hospital's blood bank had exhausted its supply of White "A-negative" blood. The surgeons requested that "O-negative" blood, the "Universal Donor" should be utilized. The Black blood bank was off limits for the White patient.

After six horrendous hours of surgery under general anesthesia, the young man died. What a sad waste of a young life and six hours of three surgeons and a tired intern's time that had been. Saturday night mayhems were not for me, I thought.

Before I arrived in New Orleans, the Crescent City as it is called held a romantic fascination for me. The history of the War of 1812 and Andrew Jackson, the French Quarter and Mardi Gras, Creole and Cajun cuisine, Louis Armstrong and jazz were all now a reality for me. I strolled down Canal Street towards the Mississippi and to the Café Du Monde in the French market for my morning coffee and beignet. I was a tourist for a day before reporting to duty at the hospital.

When I checked in at the hospital administration office I was told to pick out four months of elective services that I wished to rotate through for my year of internship. Charity Hospital is so large that it served as the primary teaching facility for two medical schools: Tulane and Louisiana State University (L.S.U). The local medical students that graduated a month before had the advantage of signing up for electives before we out-of towners arrived. For my elective months I chose psychiatry, urology, and gynecologic pathology. The E.R. was not an elective rotation but we were allowed to select a month.

I was forewarned that the E.R. service fills up quickly and that it might not be available to me. I was pleased to find several openings in February; the rest of the year was filled. How lucky I was, so I thought. So I signed up not thinking about the medical nightmare that is called Fat Tuesday or Mardi Gras! That was quite a rotation. It was there that I learned the art and science of medical combat triage and how to deep breathe and stay calm in an ambulance that is running red lights at high speeds...usually without the need to do so.

I was given my schedule for the year. My assignments were written as follows:

July--LSU, white male urology

August/ September--Tulane, colored OB/GYN

October--LSU, white female psychiatry

November/December--Tulane, colored male medicine

January--LSU, gynecological pathology and LSU white OB

February--E.R.

March/April--LSU, white pediatrics

May/June--- LSU, white male surgery

As I remember, at that time, Charity Hospital had two cement towers each about eighteen stories high and a central building about five stories connecting both towers. Each had its own entrance: one for blacks and the other for whites. Patients and visitors entered and stayed on their respective sides.

Patients were segregated by race, but that is easier done than done accurately. If patients had any known colored blood they would be hospitalized on the colored side of the hospital. Every so often an apparently white patient would be visited by an unmistakably colored family member, causing an involuntarily and unceremonious transfer to the colored side following their visit.

Miscegenation was quite common over the centuries in Louisiana between French, Spanish, Creole and African people. And yet the hospital authorities seemed to know who had "colored blood" and needed to be on the colored side, even regarding those patients who appeared to be and thought of themselves as white. I had wondered how they knew. Who were the "informants"? It was reminiscent of the Nazi beast's relentless pursuit for the illusive idea of "racial purity." The final solution was to impose laws that would identify, segregate, and then either murder or force into slave labor any person with as little as 1/8 Jewish blood, even if they were raised as Christians. In New Orleans in the middle of the 20th century in the freest country on earth the beast was satisfied to simply identify and segregate anyone with even one drop of known colored blood.

I found out that the "informants" were the security police who were stationed at the visitor's entrances at each mirror image tower. Their job was to obey state racial laws by enforcing segregation. As in Nazi Germany, the treacherous actions taken against their own citizens in the name of racial purity were perfectly legal and were in fact decreed by law.

By the way, there were no black doctors or medical students there at that time. And among the hundreds of student nurses not one was black. There were some black nurses on the colored side of the hospital. On the other side of the equation, about 70% of the patients and newborns that were at Charity Hospital were black. This is a recipe for problems. Racism and ageism are potentially huge problems in medicine, the only place where clients are anonymously identified by race and age: "white male, 88 years old."

There was only one area in the hospital that was not segregated. Can you guess where that was? The E.R.? No, there was a white side and a colored side. The E.R. staff percolated around depending where they were needed. It was probably the blood bank? No, they were segregated too. If there was a shortage of O- negative white blood we could not borrow from the black blood bank and visa versa. I imagined that in a dire medical emergency a reasonable blood bank worker would sneak a unit or two of blood in either direction to save a life. Maybe. You are thinking that surely the newborn nursery was integrated. No, segregation began very early in life. There were two "separate but equal" newborn nursery facilities at Charity Hospital. Integrated business office cashier perhaps? No, there were no bills to pay for either inpatient or outpatient medical services. Charity was as the name implied. The free services included prescription medicine as well. That is why the Louisiana taxpayers referred to Charity Hospital as the "Concrete Uterus". It was free care from "womb to tomb".

Segregation reigned from birth until death. But at that point, death was at last the Great Emancipator of segregation. You guessed it, the morgue was integrated.

Sarah's Memorable Wait

Forty-five years has a way of dimming the memory for some details. I cannot remember how I met Sarah or the color of her large beautiful eyes. Sarah was a recent graduate of the Sophie-Newcomb College. That, I believe, was the women's branch of Tulane University. On our first date I mixed medical business with the pleasure of her sweet southern company. Interns were encouraged to drive out of town on an off duty day to visit a place called Carville. It was there that the last Leper colony in the continental U.S.A. was still functioning. There were a few patients still living there. We did not see them. That was not part of our visit and their privacy was respected. There was a small museum that explained the history of the sanatorium and a scientific exhibit about leprosy, which is now called Hansen's disease.

Sarah packed a picnic basket and the groundskeeper directed us to a lovely idyllic spot adjacent to a pond and beneath a weeping willow tree. Sarah was intelligent, articulate, beautiful and shapely and she was raised in a loving kosher home in New Orleans. Best of all she had a keen sense of humor. My fondness for her was significantly elevated when she told me that when I smiled I looked like Paul Newman. Paul and I, after all, were both at one point in time twenty-six years old.

During my month on psychiatry I was assigned to the white female LSU service. When a patient was admitted it was either through the E.R. after a psychiatry consultation, from the local jail or from a psychiatric facility transferring an inpatient for medical care in addition to continued psychiatric needs. The intern's duty was to evaluate the patient, outline a treatment protocol and then present the case to an attending psychiatry professor or to the resident assigned to the service.

I invited Sarah to lunch at the Charity Hospital doctor's dining room. I wished to see her and at the same time I wanted to show her off to fellow interns Jim Roda and Bill Wetta, my two beer-drinking pals.

They had been playing the same sophomoric game with me for some time by escorting lovely student nurses to Raviotto's bar down the street whenever they had the chance, and now it was my turn.

Before I was to meet Sarah outside the doctor's dining room I spoke to Russell. Russ was the husky and amiable orderly on duty that day. He was the first contact for a new patient arriving on the female psych ward. I told Russ that I was going to lunch and would return soon. I informed him that I was expecting a new admission from the E.R. and that her name is Sarah. "She will tell you that she is my girlfriend and that she is here to visit with me." I told Russ to put her in a holding area. "She is harmless, just somewhat delusional and disturbed." Russ said he would page me when she arrived.

Sarah and I had a nice lunch considering it was institutional food with a Creole accent. I had some trepidation about my forthcoming prank but decided that it was too well planned to not go forward.

I also rationalized that Sarah possessed a good sense of humor and besides she would have the experience of seeing the inside of a psych ward. No bodily harm would come to her. It was just a practical joke.

After lunch I told Sarah that I had to go pick up some X-ray reports from radiology. I asked her to meet me at the LSU white female psychiatry unit and to ring the outside bell and ask for Russell. I went up on the next elevator after Sarah, about four minutes later. When I entered the unit Russell greeted me with his usual smile and informed me, "Hey Doc, your girlfriend, just as you said, is here and is annoyed that I think she is a patient and I placed her in a holding room." Russ went on to say, "She is a sweet looking young lady," I told Russ to let me into the room to see Sarah. Russ opened the locked door. Sarah starred out at Russell and me with a bright smile and said, "Bruce you tell this nice man that I am not a crazy patient but your friend," I told Russell that I was going to discharge Sarah on admission "before she does harm to both of us".

I placed my arm around Sarah and was pleased and relieved that she had laughed. I was hoping that she would be a good sport, and she was. I introduced her to Russ. He shook her hand, looked over at me and admonished me in a friendly tone saying, "You're something else, Doc, treating this nice lady so bad." Sarah left the hospital and then I went back to work. The remainder of the day was not as adventurous.

Sacred Tissues

The Sisters of Charity wore those starched stiff, snow-white winged headpieces that have now been relegated to the pages of fashion history. I had never seen them before, except in movies. I would estimate that their wingspan was three feet across. Come to think of it, nurses also used to wear strangely starched and distinctive hats with their uniforms. It would be interesting to find out who designed those things and with what purpose in mind.

My first close-up encounter with a sister was while assisting an OB/GYN resident in the O.R. The procedure was an exploratory laparotomy for a ruptured tubular pregnancy.

Fertilization of the ovum takes place in the fallopian tube and then tumbles down slowly to the uterus where it implants into the wall or lining of the womb. The growing gestational sac can become implanted in the tube especially if the tube is narrowed from infection. Then the embryo might abort in the tube or it might continue to grow and stretch the tube causing severe pain.

Worse scenario is that the tube may tear and rupture causing pain and internal bleeding which can be fatal. Tubal or ectopic pregnancy is not rare. Because of a relatively high incidence of gonorrhea in New Orleans, which may cause scarring of the tube, this was a common gynecological diagnosis. My personal discipline learned as a medical student in Miami was that any woman in the childbearing age with a missed menstrual period and lower abdominal pain was an ectopic pregnancy until proven otherwise.

In this particular case the pregnancy had ruptured through the fallopian tube. There was bleeding from the tube into the pelvic cavity.

The extruded gestational sac and attached tissue was lifted out of the pelvic cavity from the cul-de-sac behind the uterus. It was half the size of the palm of my hand. I placed it on the Mayo stand tray next to the instruments. While the resident was removing the damaged Fallopian tube, a Sister of Charity entered the O.R. Beneath her white winged starched habit she wore a surgical mask and entered with an aristocratic gait that denoted authority. She whispered to the scrub nurse who then turned to the Mayo stand. The scrub nurse lifted the ectopic pregnancy tissue off the tray and placed it in a small stainless steel bowl and dutifully handed it to the Sister in white. No discernable conversation had taken place so I asked the resident why the surgical specimen was carted away so quickly to go to the pathology laboratory. The resident, Doctor Hebert, a native Louisianan Cajun, was quick to inform me that the tissue was not being taken straight away to the pathologists. First the pregnancy tissue would be blessed and baptized. That was a powerful message, one that that I would never forget.

My initial thought was that they would be baptizing a glob of expelled tissue. Later it dawned on my secular mind that the conception had aborted because of some imperfection. The blighted ovum may have suffered a chromosome anomaly or the woman's pituitary gland may have produced insufficient hormone stimulation to nurture a fertilized ovum. Perhaps it became obstructed in the tube due to past infections. Whatever the etiology, I never believed that it was destined to become a future human being. However I was impressed with the ritualistic philosophy of the Catholic Church's sanctity for what they believed and perceived as life. To me it was love's labor lost.

My last contact with the Sisters of Charity was in a hospital elevator. Two of the nuns were on board with me. Their "flying nun" headgear took up most of the elevator space. As I bid them good morning, I noticed that both nuns had black smudge marks on their foreheads just below their white habits. How strange, I thought, that both sisters would managed to get black blemishes on precisely the same spot in the middle of their foreheads. I quickly theorized that they had both made the same move and brushed across a dusty bookshelf or leaned over a wet paint area. "Sister", I said to the nun closest to me, "excuse me but you and the other sister have smudge marks on your foreheads." She smiled at me and turned to her companion to pass on this information to her. They both exited one floor before I did. As they departed I was greeted with, "Have a prayerful and good Ash Wednesday, doctor." Later that day, my fellow intern Jim Roda explained to me the significance of Fat Tuesday or Mardi Gras, Ash Wednesday and Good Friday. In return I threw light on Jim as to why the Last Supper and Easter coincide with the Jewish Passover.

Chapter 8

Come To The Mardi Gras

Soon after I arrived at Charity Hospital in the Crescent City for my twelve months of internship I was told to report to the hospital emergency room administrative office.

They had a calendar spread sheet (no computers in 1957) and wanted to know what month I wished to rotate through the E.R. This was a required rotation and not an elective assignment. I asked what month was available. The ER secretary informed me that the LSU and Tulane University medical school graduates get first crack at the schedule and all the slots are filled except for February. No problem with February I thought so I signed my name in the schedule not realizing that was Mardi Gras time.

This turned out to be a blessing in Mardi Gras disguise. For the local interns riding the ambulance was old hat as they participated in that adventure as senior medical students rotating through the "concrete uterus" as Charity Hospital was nicknamed.

The interns on the month-long ER duty were on duty for twenty-four hours and off for twelve hours. That was enough time for a few hours of shuteye, a hot shower and a dinner date or a few beers at the local tavern with other interns and student nurses.

We were designated as "first ambulance, second or third ambulance or ER floater on the white side or the colored side. First ambulance was out on a run almost continuously. Second and third ambulances were out frequently but when not out on a run we could nap in an on-call room near the ambulance parking area adjacent to the ER or hang out in the ER and learn by watching or doing what young doctors in training do. The floater was to triage the cases as they came into the ER.

February in New Orleans is cold and damp. The poor people with asthma lined up on benches near the entrance to the ER awaiting the intravenous cocktail drawn up for them in a non-disposable glass syringe. If my memory serves me back to 1957, we infused Sparine (a tranquilizer), Benadryl (an antihistamine) and Aminophylline (a bronchodilator) and personalized the dosage according to a protocol based on age and weight.

This was remarkably effective in reducing the wheezing, air hunger and the accompanying anxiety of asthma. Those that did not respond were usually admitted for further care and observation.

Women in labor were not screened in the ER. They were sent to an elevator area where they would be taken to the tenth floor. That is where the labor and delivery area was located. They would await the elevator sitting in old wooden wheel chairs for five to twenty minutes. I had learned that the elevator operator, apparently an old time fixture, had delivered more babies then most of the interns did on their OB rotation. It was rumored that he had a set of twins and a few breech deliveries to his credit. He even boasted of his emergency baby delivering skills and claimed that he learned from the patients that many of them named their baby Otis or Alfred (his name) or the feminine counterpart, Alfreda.

When I rode first ambulance it was one run after the other. After awhile I got to know which drivers were crazy and ran red lights with the siren screaming even when it wasn't necessary. Many of the runs were not emergencies. Frequently we went out on a DOA run; that was to pronounce some poor soul "dead". New Orleans relied on the Charity Hospital ambulances to transport a physician to an assumed deceased person's home or site to verify their death and thus allow a mortuary service to pick up the corpse. The deceased were not transported in the ambulance. Some of the drivers were experienced and savvy enough to save several DOAs and catch them all in one run to save time for all concerned. On one occasion, when I was riding second ambulance, we went out to pronounce four DOAs. In a way these runs were not a learning experience but it was a welcome relief when I was tired because

I did not have to decide on a diagnosis, treatment or disposition. It did, however, provide the sad experience for dealing with death and at times the bereaved family. These events, ironically, pushed me ever so close to choosing OB/GYN as my future specialty.

The first DOA was a "floater", a drowned woman in a small estuary of the Mississippi River. Two firemen had pulled her out of the water and placed her body on the nearby sandy bank. A police officer, an expert on floaters, told me that the victim appeared to have been in the cold February water for only two or three days. She was young, maybe 25 or so and quite naked. I pronounced her very dead. She was taken to the city morgue for evaluation by the coroner's office to determine the cause of death and to rule out foul play.

The ambulance driver informed me that it was not unusual to find prostitutes who had been raped, murdered and then dumped into the river.

Number two DOA was an elderly man who had apparently died some days before at home and alone. His neighbors in the small apartment house called the police when they saw several newspapers outside his doorway. They had also detected a foul odor emanating from a partially opened bedroom window. The wise driver offered me a cloth surgical mask to wear over my nose.

He strongly suggested that I place my stethoscope at the ready and take a deep breath and listen to his absent heart beat as quickly as possible and then exhale and pronounce him dead. Taking his advice and taking advantage of my youthful speed, I hurried to his bedside, placed my stethoscope on his bare chest, listened for a heartbeat and then raced out of the bedroom to the back door. All in twelve seconds and on one breathe.

The third of the DOAs was that of an elderly woman who had died suddenly, apparently of a heart attack while driving her car. She was slumped over the steering wheel. In order to listen for a heartbeat the ambulance driver positioned her head and upper torso away from the wheel to rest against the seat. She had vomited and dislodged her upper denture plate. As I listened for a heartbeat my thoughts were that this was not a bad way to go. Her wedding ring told me she was probably married and the Cadillac she was driving announced her affluence. Here I was, a perfect stranger to her, yet I was confirming her death, a very important event in her life. She had pulled the auto to the curb in an upscale neighborhood across the street from a row of small stores. The gray-blue hairdo lady had signaled to a passerby and told him that she was having chest pain and urged him to call an ambulance. A nearby fire station arrived as a backup and notified the ambulance dispatcher that the woman was dead and not to run out with sirens through traffic. They requested an ambulance and doctor to pronounce her. That is where we came into the scenario.

The last of the four DOAs was similar in nature. This call was from a neighborhood bar. A middle-aged white male had been shooting pool and drinking beer when he complained to his friend that he was having chest pain and nausea. He went to his car parked out in front with the idea of driving to the nearby Touro Infirmary E.R.

He didn't make it. The phone call stated that he was not breathing and his face had turned blue. That was enough for the veteran dispatcher to consider it a DOA and not a crash call. When we arrived we noted that the deceased was in the driver seat with his head fully extended over the back of the seat. The engine was not running and the front windows were rolled down only three inches. In the back seat was a snarling, teeth bearing Doberman Pinscher. She darted back and forth from front seat to rear seat as we moved about outside the vehicle. Her bark was ferocious and frightening.

The ambulance driver informed me that the door was not locked but we were not going to open it. He told me, "Doc, if you open that door to pronounce him I'll be putting you into the ambulance as a patient." He then called the hospital and related the drama to them. They advised us that they would call Animal Control and the City Morgue and to "head on back home."

On the return trip we received a call to proceed to an address across town for a catheter change for a homebound paraplegic. Yes, indeed, Charity Hospital, providing care from womb to tomb.

Please do not think that all of the Charity Hospital ambulance runs were for DOAs and catheter changes. Too many of the calls were for the casualties of armed combat. There was much violence in New Orleans, especially during Mardi Gras time. Nine years after I left the Big Easy I found use for the science of triage that I had learned as an intern.

On two occasions I was assigned the duty of triage officer at Tan Son Nhut Military Hospital outside Saigon. I was visiting there as a rotating Air Force medical officer from Travis Air Force Base in California. I had been sent to a base in Texas for a crash course for Flight Surgeons and was on loan from the OB/GYN department. I would then return to Travis on an air-evacuation flight with either wounded soldiers or on a dreadful mortuary flight full of hermetically sealed aluminum caskets.

Triage was mostly needed on Friday and Saturday nights and during the Mardi Gras. Stabbings and gunshot wounds were given priorities based on trauma location. Chest, abdomen and head wounds were triaged for the first available screening area. Traumatized extremities and buttocks waited their turn accordingly.

One busy weekend night when I was floating around the ER, an ambulance brought in two adult males who had stabbed each other in a bar room brawl. This was not an unusual occurrence. What caused such a stir to long be remembered was that one of the victim-assailants removed himself from the examining table in his cubicle, while alone and awaiting medical care, and rushed to the next cubicle to his recent antagonist. A pair of bandage scissors attached to a chain secured to the examining table was used to stab the already wounded man into his chest. His scream preceded his demise.

For me, Mardi Gras was a battle zone. One busy evening the second ambulance was dispatched to join the first ambulance already at the scene. They needed backup. There had been an exchange of gunfire at a bar off Saint Charles. Six men were down from gunshot wounds. Another two were dead and awaiting to be pronounced. The six wounded warriors were loaded into the two ambulances. We raced back to Charity with sirens wailing. It was scary running red lights at fifty miles an hour. As short as I am my head frequently hit the ambulance overhead as we raced over potholes. We had already triaged the wounded at the scene. The number two ambulance driver called into the ER and announced a chest wound with poor vital signs for the first priority of care. Number two and three were both abdominal wounds and five and six were struck in the leg and shoulder. They would be seen as least urgent by triage. The two DOAs we left behind for a mortuary pickup had both suffered fatal head shots. No triage necessary.

For everyone working in the ER at that time Mardi Gras was a battlefield, not a celebration. Senseless mayhem and tragedy was rampant. Scores of people came to the ER because of deep and painful lacerations over the tibia bone. It seemed that angry hoodlums had placed single edged razor blades under the soles of the tips of their shoes. This enabled these sadistic punks to take advantage of the crowds and kick unsuspecting merrymakers in the shins.

An angry ER nurse notified the NOPD about the nature of this savagery. Security police told us later that the NOPD had rounded up and arrested several teenaged boys. The ER had treated almost eighty of these vicious and senseless attacks. Many of the victims were tourists.

During one of my twelve hours off I missed a Mardi Gras tragedy of horrific proportion. One of the many colorful floats heavily decorated with crepe paper had caught on fire during the parade. The fire spread rapidly.

On this float was a mock cage. Inside the cage were four men dressed as gorillas. As the fire raged, they were trapped in the cage and for some reason they could not get out. They suffered from massive burns and smoke inhalation; the ambulance had a difficult time forcing their way through the crowds. The burning float was on Tulane Avenue, just a few blocks from the hospital.

Two of the burn victims were brought to the hospital Burn Unit. The other two were DOA when they were brought into the ER. Both two men in the burn unit succumbed to their extensive third-degree burns and lung damage several days later.

On a lighter Mardi Gras note I recall an ambulance run to pick up a middle-aged man who was drunk and in pain. While celebrating and being inebriated he decided to urinate in the street. He caught the foreskin of his penis in the zipper of his trousers and could not free it loose. Someone came to his aid by calling for an ambulance. His pain seemed to be almost tolerable when he did not move his legs about. We covered him with a blanket and brought him to the ER. Just looking at his trapped member made me wince and hold my crotch. The ER resident attempted to move the zipper but it would not budge.

An ER nurse heard about this interesting patient and came over to his cubicle. She looked over the situation and proceeded with some maneuver to quickly move the zipper and free the redundant, imprisoned foreskin. She accomplished this in all of five or so painless seconds. I asked the Creole nurse what she had done so quickly to free him of the zipper. She laughed and told me that it was a top secret and she wanted to keep it that way. She smiled and confessed that she had performed this emergency maneuver before. "You see, doctor, I have five boys at home and only one bathroom."

CHAPTER 9

A Rare Obstetrical Complication

Towards the end of my rotating internship I served two months on the busy, chaotic, noisy and at times humorous OB service, I ran into a rare obstetrical complication. I was attending the labor of a fifteen year old that had been sedated to diminish her apparent apprehension. Under the influence of "twilight sleep"*(Scopolamine and Demerol)* she still thrashed about and moaned and groaned even between contractions. A restraining strap was placed about her mid torso and the side rails of the gurney cart were raised to lessen the chance of her falling off.

It was to be for me to have the honor to deliver this young woman. The medical students were to deliver women who had a previous vaginal delivery.

We interns were delegated to manage the women having their first baby *(primiparas)*. The residents cared for the high-risk patients and fought over the occasional Caesarian section.

Today the C-section rate in the United States is between 20 and 30% and seems to be increasing each year. In 1958 the rate of C-sections was less than 5%. This low rate was in spite of the now obsolete axiom of "once a C-section always a C-section" being adhered to.

A primary C-section required at least one "second opinion" or consultation except in an extreme emergency that threatened the life of the mother or her unborn baby. As is the case today, some patients-- especially in L.A.--have an elective C-section scheduled and performed simply because they do not wish to endure the perceived pain of labor or have stitching and/or stretching of their vagina.

When my teenage patient was ready to deliver I wheeled the gurney into an available delivery room and placed it next to the delivery room table. The nurse removed the restraining strap and I lowered the side rails and attempted to help her move over from the gurney. As I placed my left hand on her shoulder she suddenly grabbed the fingers of my left hand and placed my fourth finger firmly in her mouth. Her teeth clamped down on my finger just a centimeter from the knuckle. I let out a huge yell and tried to remove my finger from her clamped down jaw. The pain was so overwhelming that my knees buckled. The delivery room nurse rushed to my rescue. She quickly and calmly placed her fingers over the patient's nostrils so as to clamp the nose closed. Within two seconds the sedated patient opened her mouth with a snort and released my finger. Her incisor teeth had penetrated through the skin and the soft tissue on the upper side of my left ring finger. (I was and still am a total southpaw). When I clenched my fist I could see the open wound and the underlying surface of the finger's bone.

I washed and irrigated it promptly with a soapy antiseptic called *Phisohex*. The OB nurse who had saved my finger from being completely bitten off placed sterile gauze dressing on my wounded finger. I left her delivery chore to another intern.

Three days later I had the dressing changed by a surgical resident in the white male LSU surgical clinic. The wound was open and had developed a raised and reddened appearance. My finger throbbed with pain and was three times the size of my other fingers. The resident changed my dressing and started me on oral penicillin after an initial intramuscular injection into my buttocks. He told me to soak my finger in hot water three times a day. I was presented with dressing changes and a stainless steel bowl. My instructions were to return in five days.

My finger did not wait five days. During a dressing change the next day I noted that the opened wound in my finger had closed up. The redness had spread under the skin of my finger over and beyond the knuckle. My painful, swollen digit had developed a cellulitis or infection of the soft tissues. We all know how dirty a human bite can be. The culture that had been taken earlier from the wound drainage grew out a virulent bacteria named *staphylococcus* that was resistant to penicillin.

The chief surgical resident was called over to examine my finger. When he learned of the culture report and glimpsed at my infected finger he immediately had me admitted to the doctor's infirmary on the 19th floor of Charity Hospital.

The following morning, bright and early, the LSU resident came in to see me. Two other residents and the Chief of the LSU surgical service accompanied him. I have forgotten his name but I do recall that he was revered by all his colleagues and had an outstanding national reputation as a medical educator. He was renowned in the surgical community. He wore a starched white coat and sported a striped silk tie. His stethoscope was neatly coiled in his lab coat pocket. (This was before the days that every doctor, nurse, and assistant began to wear their stethoscope around their neck as if it were an icon of medicine that demanded respect.) He introduced himself and then quickly assessed my very red finger. I was certain that he would recommend partial amputation of this wounded and infected finger. Instead he told me that the infection was trapped and it needed to be drained. This, of course, is a no-brainer basic surgical principal. Without proper drainage the infection would spread out into the soft tissues and eventually become blood-borne septicemia (so-called blood poisoning).

The residents scurried about to obtain the necessary equipment and instruments for a local nerve block and a sterile incision and drainage tray. I reminded all present that I was left-handed and that they should not amputate my finger if at all possible.

The esteemed professor injected the digital nerves to anesthetize the finger. He then held my infected finger with his gloved hand and made a one and a half centimeter incision with his scalpel into the area where the bite wound had closed. He packed the underlying area with narrow iodoform gauze followed by a loose bulky dressing. I thanked him for performing painless surgery and not amputating my sick finger.

After two days I returned to work as an intern with limited dexterity for two weeks or so. I had missed two chaotic weeks of the OB service and thus many deliveries. This, however, had been a rare OB complication at Charity Hospital and a chance to switch roles and become a patient for a while." When I gaze at the scar on my wedding ring finger it brings back fond memories of my days as a young single intern.

CHAPTER 10

Sex and the Crescent City

Raviotto's bar was a favorite after-hours hangout of the overworked, under-hydrated interns. Only three short thirsty blocks away from the hospital, the jukebox was a nickel a hit and the salty nuts were on the house, as was the shuttle board game. A locally brewed Falstaff or Jax beer was only fifty cents.

Frequently some friendly student nurses would come down to Raviotto's when off duty. Drinking alcohol, especially at a bar, was against the rules imposed by the Sisters of Charity. The student nurses were mostly underage as well. These young "probies," as student nurses were called then, were mostly between 17 and 20 years old. As luck would have it, three student nurses came traipsing into Raviotto's. Tom Campbell, a fellow intern and native New Orleander pretended to know them and invited them to our booth. That was the night I met Joy.

Joy was a second-year student nurse and a twenty-year-old blonde cutie pie from a small town in the Florida Panhandle. We hit it off straight away. Both being University of Florida Fighting Gator fans we had some common ground aside from the usual doctor and nurse talk.

On our first outing, the two of us drove up river to Baton Rouge, the state capitol and home of the L.S.U. Tigers. We watched the Tigers thrash the Gators. That was the year that L.S.U. had an infamously stingy defensive line that was aptly called the Chinese Bandits. We spent the night in Baton Rouge.

It was 1958 and we were living large. I even had the good fortune that year to have access to a boat, a thirty-footer with a cabin down below. Five interns including myself, mostly buddies from Raviotto's bar, rented an old sailboat for $250, or $50 apiece for the year. She was seaworthy enough to take her out in Lake Pontchartrain for a keg party but she would not have done well in the open sea with rough water.

Whenever two or three of us were off from work on the same night and had the weekend free we would take her out. The nighttime skinny-dipping off the sides into the cool lake water was refreshing in the warm and humid Louisiana night. Joy and two of her classmates joined us on our "maiden voyage."

In fact, there was only one part of my life that wasn't quite in place at that time. The intern's quarters across the street from the huge hospital were convenient and free, but afforded no privacy. There were four to a room and it was not possible to obtain a good night sleep even on a night that I was not on call. The phone would ring so often for one or more of us during the night followed by conversation with the hospital caller. It was not a good place for sleeping at all.

Just down the street from Pat O'Brien's bar in the French Quarter was an old historic landmark occupied by a touristy restaurant. It was the Court of Two Sisters. (Or was it three sisters?) Walking by there one evening on Saint Peter's Street, I spied a handwritten sign on the wall of the adjacent building that stated "studio apartment for rent" and a telephone number to call. The court was enclosed with the typical wrought iron gate. I jotted down the phone number.

When I called the next day I was invited to come back to the French Quarter to see the apartment. The rent was $80 per month and $100 damage deposit. Utilities were included and a telephone would not be needed. The small studio was ancient, the flooring sagged and squeaked and the overhead was probably only six and a half feet. The rent would be $5 more than my gross monthly salary. I enticed a fellow intern and friend into sharing the apartment with me. It seemed that our work schedule had us rotating weekend duties. Weekends off would be the only time I would stay there overnight because during the week it was much more convenient to be across the street from the hospital for a 6:30 A.M. workday start.

I owned several War Bonds that I received as gifts for my Bar Mitzvah in 1944. Fourteen years later they sure came in handy to help pay the $40 rent and buy gas for my '55 Olds.

The landlady left us an old studio couch that opened into a double bed and a floor lamp with a torn shade that sported a faded picture of a an old-time schooner in a storm. Under a loose floorboard in the kitchenette I pulled up a yellow parched newspaper from the year 1848. I have this treasured souvenir to this day.

At night it was noisy until well past 3 A.M. from French Quarter revelers walking past the courtyard on the street. The church bells from Saint Peter in Jackson Square rang each hour and the apartment was filled with the smell of hops from the Jax brewery nearby.

The only window faced the courtyard. After my first overnight in my little apartment I raised the shade in the morning. To our mutual surprise there was a flock of tourists wandering about the courtyard. They were part of a walking guided tour of the "Veux Carré." We waved to each other. I had become a tourist attraction in the heart of the French Quarter.

Another magic moment was the morning stroll through the French Quarter down to the Marketplace, close to the river, and to the Café Du Monde for chicory laced coffee and a warm beignet. Fortunately there weren't any Starbucks in 1958.

The delight of life as a young intern at Charity Hospital and as a bon vivant residing in the French Quarter ended too soon. Joy told me that she was pregnant. She related to me that her menstrual periods were regular "always like clockwork" and she was now three weeks late.

"Any nausea, any breast tenderness, any urinary frequency?" I inquired in a clinical manner. The response from Joy was, "Yes to all three questions."

Joy and I met privately at a nearby café. Joy had already pondered and knew her limited options if she were "with child." Like any woman faced with an unplanned pregnancy Joy had three choices:

1. Have a baby

2. Have a baby and adopt it out

3. Have an abortion

Joy said that she would have to drop out of nursing school as soon as the Sisters of Charity found out she was pregnant. She still had six months till graduation from the three-year program. Joy told me that if she had to leave school she would need to go back home to her folks. "My dad," she smiled and brushed away a tear, "would come looking for you with a shotgun and a preacher." I explained to her that I was allergic to both. I also informed her that I did not wish to get married but would help support the baby the best that I could. With that remark Joy promptly stated that she would have an abortion. I had silently hoped that Joy would decide on that choice. My immediate reaction to the word abortion was to think of my sister and the fact that an abortion was illegal and dangerous.

I suggested that first we should find out if she is definitely pregnant by doing a pregnancy test. Joy insisted that a pregnancy test result in her name, even if it were negative, would have her packing and out the door immediately. I explained that my plan would keep her anonymity. She could sneak a jar into the dormitory bathroom and void first thing in the morning. Then she would smuggle the urine specimen to the hospital in her purse so I could obtain her overnight specimen. Then I would order an A-Z pregnancy test on a fictitious patient. There were no computers then to automatically provide labels, printouts and requisitions. I would hand-carry the specimen to the laboratory. One of the intern's many duties was to obtain urine and blood samples and bring them to the lab along with the test request slip. We were also responsible to pick up the results and place the completed lab slip back into the patient's chart.

An A-Z test was all that we had at the time to help confirm a pregnancy. We did not order pregnancy tests very often because they were time consuming, expensive and required sacrificing a rabbit. There was no easy over-the-counter pregnancy test that could be purchased in a pharmacy and performed simply at home, and we had no sonography to confirm a pregnancy. The A-Z test was named after two Europeans (or Israelis?) named Asheim and Zondek. The test required an overnight concentrated urine specimen that was injected into the ear vein of a white virginal female rabbit.

Forty-eight hours later the cute bunny was anesthesized with chloroform and sacrificed. The rabbit's abdominal cavity was then opened and a trained laboratory technician would examine the rabbit's ovaries. If the woman were pregnant the rabbit's ovaries would be distinctly reddish in color from an inflammatory reaction due to hypersensitivity to the woman's hormone of pregnancy.

If the woman were pregnant her urine would contain elevated amounts of the gonadatropin hormone that is produced by her ovaries to sustain a growing pregnancy. If the woman were not pregnant then the rabbit's ovaries would remain a pinkish-gray color. The A-Z test was supposedly 98% accurate. I ordered this test infrequently and then only if clinically urgent. I decided that this time Joy's test was essential to us.

Of course the test was positive. At least the bunny was not sacrificed for naught. Joy once again reaffirmed her desire to both stay in nursing school and have an abortion.

At certain times throughout my life I've realized that life can be just like a scene from a movie. For some reason, this seems especially true of my time in New Orleans.

On an occasional Saturday, when I was off duty, I went to the Fairgrounds racetrack to enjoy the fresh air and to handicap the thoroughbreds. I was, out of necessity, a small time two-dollar bettor. By chance and by polite conversation I came to know a Truman Capote-like gentleman in a white linen suit. He knew his racehorses quite well; he studied the racing form and then he would place his selections "across the board." He soon learned that I was a starving young intern at Charity Hospital. As far as I could tell he was not a racetrack tout but he did make some selections for me.

He would take my racing program and circle the number of the horse that he suggested that I play. I would then place my wager on his picks that was usually two dollars "across the board." That is $2.00 to win, $2.00 to place and $2.00 to show.

There were some races that he did not circle any selection and indicated that this particular race was not worth placing a bet. I usually abided by his suggestion.

As far as I know I was placing my money on the same ponies as he was. I never heard his bet order at the pari-mutuel ticket window because he wagered at the twenty-dollar window and I stood in the two-dollar line. I won $240 that day. I was so elated with my newfound fortune that after the next to last race I invited my new racetrack companion to lunch in the clubhouse restaurant. He accepted an offer for a cocktail but declined lunch stating that he had social plans for an early dinner.

Over lunch we chatted and exchanged verbal resumes. I told him that my winnings today were more than three months salary as an intern.

He calculated in his head that interns earning $75 a month and averaging 96 hours of duty per week are averaging a bit less than twenty cents an hour. I laughed and made little of that inequity for I knew that internship was only a yearlong and the servitude was worth it.

I felt comfortable with this gentleman, a man in his mid-forties and a World War Two Naval officer. He may have been gay but he never made any overtures toward me.

I told him of Joy's and my plight and of our desire to terminate her unwanted pregnancy as soon as possible. He immediately jotted down his phone number and told me to call him in a few days. He said he would furnish me with a person's name that could help us. I shook his hand and thanked him. Incidentally, I had the occasion to meet him at the racetrack on two more occasions. Each time he wore a white linen suit and touted me more winners. What a guy!

The phone number given to me by my racetrack friend was that of an OB/GYN physician with an office near the Touro Infirmary; an old and well-established private hospital with a distinguished professional staff. Many of the instructors at Charity Hospital were part-time volunteer teachers. Their reward was the prestige that comes with being an associate professor on a medical school faculty.

I called the OB/GYN'S office and the receptionist informed me that the doctor was out of the country, on holiday in Europe, and would return in three weeks. I explained our predicament to her and she invited me to come by the office.

I obliged her request and presented her with my Charity Hospital Identification card with photograph. We discussed Joy's date of her last menstrual period and calculated that she was about 7 to 8 weeks gestation. Based on those dates Joy would be 10 to 11 weeks upon the doctor's return to New Orleans. We decided that we should not wait for his arrival.

Before the introduction to the electric suction machine technique somewhere around 1970, an abortion at 10 or 11 weeks could be quite hazardous and fraught with considerable blood loss. The technique employed in 1958 was simply a dilatation of the cervix and curettage of the uterine cavity (commonly referred to as a D&C). A pregnancy under 8 weeks was much easier and less hazardous to abort, we both agreed.

The receptionist/office manager offered me two options to terminate Joy's pregnancy: Mexico City or Havana, Cuba. The cost would be $1200 including round trip airfare and overnight in a hotel. I thanked her for her information as she handed me a written note with the aforementioned contacts. I left the office, went down the elevator to the lobby then turned around and went back up to the doctor's office.

The office manager was surprised to see me and inquired if I had forgotten something. I told her that I could raise $1200 from old War Bonds and, if need be, from friends in Miami. I went on to explain to her that I had a better plan.

I explained that I did not want Joy to travel to Mexico or Cuba by herself and I could not afford the airline ticket to accompany her. Besides that, Joy could not take the time off from nursing school. The nursing students do not get a vacation and it would be difficult for her to tell the nuns that she needed a few days off to fly to Mexico for an illegal abortion! If that is her only option then I think Joy would drop out of school and have a baby. "That is not want we want," I explained.

I told her that I had performed about ten D&Cs as an intern during my OB/GYN rotation; all of them successful and all of them were for incomplete abortions (miscarriages). Secure in the knowledge that I was completely competent with this simple procedure, I pleaded with her that I would appreciate it if she would allow me to do the abortion on Joy in their office while her boss is away. She took on a look of amazement and quickly responded, "Oh no, I would be fired if I let you do that. Besides you don't have a Louisiana medical license do you?" I admitted that I possessed only a Florida medical license. Then I reminded her that I did not need a license to perform an illegal abortion. "But most important," I quipped, "your boss won't know about it unless you tell him. Please help us out, you won't be sorry," I promised.

This woman was very kind and sensitive to our problem or maybe just hesitant to turn my desperate request away. Either way she agreed to allow me to perform an abortion on Joy in her office.

She told me that the office would be empty almost all week except for two prenatal checkups. They would be coming in to have their weight, blood pressure and urine checked and then the office nurse would listen to their fetal heart tones.

Joy was very pleased that she would not have to think about a trip alone out of the country. She had never traveled out of Florida except to come to New Orleans to attend nursing school. Joy confessed that she had visited a lay midwife who did abortions in her home in the suburb of Metairie and that she charged only $200 at eight weeks gestation. She also described the midwife's house as being cluttered and untidy. She mentioned that the "operating room" was a single size bed with a large plastic sheet. The instruments were on a bedside table lying exposed. Joy stated that she would have been scared to go there for an abortion. I told her that I would not have allowed her to go there at any rate.

The vacationing doctor's office was empty except for the office manager. She had set the room up with all the necessary instruments wrapped in a surgical sterile pack lying on a Mayo stand next to the metallic examination table. She had Joy change into a patient's gown and supplied me with a bright white scrub suit from the Touro Infirmary.

The office manager told Joy and me that she assists the doctor when he performs abortions on weekends or sometimes in the evening after office hours. "He does very few abortions, maybe five or six a month at most," she volunteered. She mentioned that he has a lucrative practice and does not do the abortions for great financial gain. Most of the abortions, she said, are referrals from close and trusted physicians and occasionally one from his practice. "I think that he performs abortions because he believes that it should be legal and he wants to help women like Joy." Then she looked serious and declared that, "My doctor could go to prison if he got caught. He is a hero to me." I assured her that she is probably a heroine to her doctor.

She placed Joy's legs on to the exam table's stirrups. I consciously pretended that Joy was another Charity Hospital patient in need of a D&C. I did a pelvic exam. Joy was not looking forward to this. She voiced complaints freely my every action, as one sometimes does with a confidant. I informed her that I needed to ascertain the size and position of her uterus and obtain accurate information. I was surprised to note that I was not nervous at all. The pelvic exam revealed her uterus to be about seven to eight weeks in size. That was consistent with her last menstrual period.

I opened the surgical pack. All the stainless steel instruments looked familiar but appeared to be newer and shinier than I was used to seeing. I inserted a lubricated speculum into Joy's vagina and slowly opened it until I could visualize her cervix. I could tell that she had never had a vaginal birth by the appearance of her unscathed cervix. There are telltale signs of an imperfect healing of small lacerations around the small cervical opening in women who have delivered a baby through their cervix. I then drew up 10ccs of 1% *lidocaine* into a glass syringe. (Today the syringes are plastic and are disposable.) Joy complained a bit as I injected a small amount of the anesthetic into the tissue of her cervix at the "12 o'clock" position to dull the area. I pinched this area of the upper or anterior lip of the cervix with a grasping instrument called a tenaculum. With this instrument I was able to elevate the cervix enough to visualize the soft tissue between the vaginal wall and the posterior lip of the cervix. Into this area I injected the remaining lidocaine at the eight and four o'clock positions. This injection is a paracervical block; to diminish discomfort during an abortion procedure.

This D&C would be different from a similar procedure performed for a miscarriage. The difference being that Joy's pregnancy was still intact and imbedded into the lining of her uterus. I was going to interrupt the intact gestation.

Several stainless steel tapered dilators were then gently and slowly inserted into the cervical opening. Each dilator increased in diameter by 2 millimeters. Gradually Joy's cervical opening surrendered easily to the dilators until the opening was 8mm in diameter, just enough room for the ensuing curette to be introduced into the uterus. The 3cm oval-shaped tip is designed for scrapping or curetting out the pregnancy tissue from the uterine lining.

Joy felt some moderate cramping and she squeezed the hand of my assistant. Joy was crying softly and I surmised that was partially from the cramping but mostly from fear and the sadness of surrendering her pregnancy.

The tissue expelled was consistent with the gestational age of eight weeks so I stopped curetting. The mind's eye can "feel" that the uterus is empty. The curette transmitted a "gritty feel" to my fingers. This sensation is a must for abortion providers because one cannot visualize the inside of the uterus.

Joy's bleeding was minimal so I removed the speculum and tenaculum and whispered to her that we were finished and all went well. My assistant, the office manager, congratulated me on performing my first abortion. In the years to follow after Roe vs. Wade I would accomplish another 40,000 or so, legally.

I drove Joy back to the student nurse's dormitory high-rise just in time for her 10PM curfew. She told me how relieved she was and thanked me for removing her "burden of worry." We kissed goodnight.

I called Joy's dormitory floor payphone the next day to see how she was doing. It was a Sunday so I knew she was not in class or on duty. Joy told me her cramping was mild, and her bleeding was scanty, less than a menstrual period. "I told you that I would do a good job", I boasted proudly.

The following day I called again to get a progress report. This time her roommate came to the phone instead of Joy. I asked her where Joy was. "Is she sleeping," I inquired. Oh no, she woke up this morning with some pain and fever. The Sisters sent her to the student infirmary at the hospital for observation and treatment," she informed me.

My pulse raced to the sudden rush of adrenalin. My mind whirled with all terrible thoughts; Joy is ill with a pelvic infection, she could die. We are both doomed. How could this have happened I wondered? I was certain that I had not broken sterile technique and that the instruments were not contaminated. I was equally sure that I had removed all of the pregnancy tissue. I had examined the products of conception after the abortion to check for placental tissue, the amniotic sac, and the small fetal parts for completeness.

It was certain that Joy would be expelled from nursing school only six months shy of graduation. That is if she lived. I would be discharged from my internship after the authorities learned of our "illegal misdeed". I was not allowed to visit the all female student nurse infirmary.

I was beside myself all day. Unable to concentrate on my hospital duties, I told my resident that I had dysentery and wanted to go to my dormitory room across the street for the remainder of the day. He reluctantly agreed to my request. I was both anxious and depressed. I was also angry that abortion was not a legal procedure.

The following afternoon I called the infirmary to check on Joy and I was informed that she had been discharged that morning. My thought was that she had taken a turn for the worse and had been transferred from the infirmary to a hospital bed for more intensive care. She must have a serious pelvic infection. Surely Joy would not be in the morgue!

Pelvic infection was a common complication from illegal abortions that were often performed under conditions that were less than aseptic. Again I was thinking about how careful I had been to assure sterile conditions for Joy's abortion. Perhaps the office manager had not properly sterilized the instruments. Not likely, but possible. I worried. I called the hospital information desk, disguising my voice like a true paranoid, to find out that Joy was not an inpatient.

I called Joy's dormitory floor and to my surprise it was she who answered the payphone. She had been trying to reach me at the hospital because she had heard that I was quite upset about her being ill. Joy laughed when I told her how worried I had been. She told me that she had a headache and a head cold with nasal congestion and a cough. The Sister diagnosed her symptoms as being consistent with "infected sinusitis" and shipped her off to the infirmary. That was Joy's admission diagnosis for her overnight stay.

Joy finished her schooling and became an R.N. I completed my internship and went on to be an OB/GYN resident. Our immediate goals were reached because we safely aborted an unwanted, unplanned pregnancy. We both left New Orleans and went our separate ways.

Residency

Chapter 11

Saint Vincent's and a Slice of Pizza

I drove my robin's egg-blue "88" Hydramatic Olds across the Gulf States from New Orleans, I realized that I was heading for new adventures of life. Having finished my year as an intern I was to begin a three-year training period as an OB/GYN resident.

As I motored through the "Redneck Riviera," I stopped for gas and greasy food along the way in places like Bay Saint Louis, Pass Christian, Biloxi, Mobile, and Pensacola. I was heading for Jacksonville, Florida. I had hoped to begin my residency training with the Tulane University service at Charity hospital in New Orleans. The Chief of the OB/GYN department was the temperamental and much feared tyrant, Doctor Conrad Collins. During my interview with him he read a report out loud to me stating that I had performed well as an intern and had delivered forty-seven babies during the two months of duty on the OB/GYN service. He also noted that I had chosen gynecologic pathology as one of my elective months. I was sure that that would impress him. Doctor Collins suffered from gout and subsequent renal failure from uric acid crystal damage to the kidneys. It was known that he was in constant pain and took his ill temper out on his residents. So I was not very dismayed when I received a cordial letter from him explaining that all the qualified interns could not fill the six openings for first year resident. He went on to state that the Tulane service provides preference for their medical school alumni, especially those who are residents of Louisiana. So I was heading for Jacksonville on the banks of the Saint John's River to begin my first year of residency at Saint Vincent's Hospital.

The transition from a huge state teaching facility like Charity Hospital to a Catholic private community hospital was not to my liking at first. Saint Vincent's facility and house staff was a far cry from Charity Hospital in every conceivable way. I arrived with a certain elitist attitude which I am sure did not go unnoticed.

In all fairness to the OB/GYN staff at Saint Vincent's Hospital, I learned a lot about the fine art and science of obstetrics from several well-trained physicians. Being a private hospital the care that was rendered, especially in the labor and delivery rooms, was more refined and personal then I had experienced at Charity Hospital.

At Saint Vincent's Hospital the chief of the OB/GYN service, Doctor Jackson Allgood, made sure that his house-staff-in-training got to deliver some of the private patients as our reward for the long hours we spent watching their patients in labor. This is how we were able to learn the art of following a patient in labor. Subsequently our presence enabled the private physicians to remain in their office or asleep in their bed at night until delivery seemed to be on the horizon.

These were pre-fetal monitoring days. We followed the progress of labor with one hand on the protuberant abdomen to feel the duration, quality and frequency of each contraction. We also listened frequently to the fetal heart tones with a stethoscope, noting and charting the beats per minute and performed routine pelvic exams to note the amount of cervical dilatation and the descent of the fetus into the birth canal.

So much of the present day fetal monitoring is expensive, impersonal and at times inappropriately technological. This is especially true if fetal monitoring is employed routinely. A low-risk and uncomplicated pregnancy should be followed in labor without the invasive technology of internal fetal monitoring. Every health practitioner should keep in mind that machines are programmed with a one-size-fits-all mentality, while patients in the real world are different from one another. I can't help but remember that doctors knew how to read the body much better when they had to rely on their own powers of observation rather than on machines and gadgets, some of which seem primarily targeted at commercial (instead of medical) interests.

The great rise in the C-Section rate in the past twenty odd years in the USA is not only due to physician fear of too many malpractice lawyers and a litigious society but also because of unnecessary routine fetal monitoring. When used inappropriately, fetal monitoring eliminates good clinical judgment. A perfect example of this is a true anecdotal experience I recalled from 1983 during my time at the Naval Hospital on the Marine Corps Base at Camp Pendleton, California.

A young medical officer was rotating through the obstetrical service as part of his Family Practice residency. I had the watch that night as OB staff physician. The young doctor rang me up as I lay sleeping in the hospital OB on-call room. He reported that a woman in labor was only five centimeters dilated but was having marked fetal heart beat deceleration (fetal bradycardia or lowered heart rate). I responded to his call immediately and met with him on the labor and delivery room deck. He approached me with the fetal monitor tracings and explained in a matter of fact tone that the fetal heart tones had decreased about twenty minutes ago. I glanced at the paper roll tracings through my still-sleepy eyes and noted the sudden dip in heart rate. "Did you turn her on her side?" I inquired.

The lieutenant replied that he had not done so. I asked him to show me the patient. It was obvious that he did not know which of the four labor rooms she was in. Without showing any signs of embarrassment, he asked the labor room charge nurse to show him which labor room the patient was in. He had not seen the patient even once. The nurse was following her labor and noted that the heart rate had slowed down so she promptly notified the resident who then called me. We were using routine fetal monitoring to satisfy the teaching protocol established by the consultants in OB/GYN to the U.S.Navy Surgeon General. This was pretty much the established modus operandi in most teaching hospitals in the eighties.

The resident, nurse and I entered the labor room. The patient was a large Samoan woman. Her husband, also a huge Samoan, was seated next to his wife's bed. He wore his Marine Corps "cammies" with the sleeves rolled up over his bulging biceps, as was the custom. His wife was lying as flat on her back as was possible. I asked her to roll over in bed and face the wall and assisted her in doing so. Within fifteen seconds her unborn child's heart rate turned to a normal 140 beats per minute; dramatically up from a low rate of eighty to ninety per minute. The dark- haired patient took a deep breath and told her husband that she felt better on her side and found breathing easier too. There was no magic performed. Every OB doctor knows that a full-term gravid uterus will compress the large vessel in her abdomen if she lies in a supine position. The vena cava, if compressed by the uterus, will disturb the return flow of blood to the lungs and to the heart. Turning her on her side released the compression and normalized the flow of blood and oxygenation to the fetus via the umbilical cord blood vessels.

This may be an extreme example of inappropriate reliance on technology but it clearly demonstrates that machines should be used as an extension of our minds, not as a replacement for experience, thinking and clinical judgment.

Unfortunately, it came to my attention that some of the physicians doing obstetrics at Saint Vincent's were poorly trained and not well disciplined in this specialty. It did not take long for the residents to know who these doctors were. For the most part these doctors were aware of their deficiencies and allowed us to assist them and to encourage them to ask for a consultation with another OB doctor when appropriate. Doctor Allgood suggested that we "look over their shoulders and keep them out of trouble as best that you can." They maintained their obstetrical privileges because they helped to fill the hospital beds and allowed the residents to learn by doing. Most of these doctors were in Family Practice, which, in the fifties, was still referred to as "general practitioners." On the other hand, most of the OB/GYN physicians were Board Certified and had been well trained and were skillful in both their clinical judgment and manual dexterity.

As OB/GYN residents we were responsible for the prenatal care and delivery of the women who lived in residence at the Catholic Home Society for unwed mothers-to-be. These women were our patients. The Catholic charity service provided not only free obstetrical care and gratis hospitalization but also room, board and maternity clothes. Their babies were all to be placed up for adoption with a qualified Catholic family. Most of the women, all young of course, were all white and from out of town. Most of them were from the Deep South or from the Eastern Seaboard. They had left home to avoid parental knowledge of their pregnancy or were sent away from home by their family to prevent embarrassment and possible condemnation. These unwed women, some girls in their teens, would deliver their baby and would not be allowed to see the baby, touch the baby or place it to their breast. But ignoring feelings doesn't simply brush them away. This attempt at preventing bonding (after 9 months of bonding in the womb) may seem dictatorial now, but it was the protocol then.

The women from the Catholic Home were obliged, as part of their prenatal care agreement, to have a general anesthesia for their delivery. That would ensure that the newborn baby would be whisked away to the nursery while the mother was still "asleep." The babies that were being placed for adoption were placed in a separate part of the nursery. Unlike the rest of the newborn nursery, which was open for viewing, in this area the window was covered with a shade. A casual postpartum stroll down the hall to the nursery by a single mother would be in vain for her to sneak a glimpse of her newborn baby. The adopting family was not allowed to see or meet the baby's biological mother. The same rule applied vice versa.

One of the patients assigned to my care was already seven months pregnant when I arrived at Saint Vincent's Hospital. I will call her Sonia Palocchio for our purposes. Sonia was a tall good-looking Italian-American blonde. She had large brown eyes that expressed shyness and reflected her apparent sadness. But Sonia was always outwardly cheerful during her prenatal visits. By offering her kind words I found it easy to get a smile on her young face. She was twenty-three years old in 1958.

Sonia had worked as a secretary for an insurance company in her hometown in Connecticut. When she discovered that she was pregnant and marriage was not in the cards she made contact with the local Catholic adoption agency. As was the custom in the pre-sexual revolution days, unwed woman departed from their home, family and friends to avoid the scorn of being pregnant and unwed thus leaving behind those that could have provided love and support for them.

The necessary contacts were made and Sonia was soon Florida bound. Where else could an unwed woman find a better place to migrate then the Sunshine State? In Jacksonville, the weather was mild, far from home and winter maternity clothes would not be needed. Sonia had told her parents that she had secured a new and better paying job as a broker for Prudential Life Insurance Company. "A piece of the Rock" was going to be hers she told her Italian-born mom and dad. Sonia never told them that she was pregnant.

It was no surprise that Sonia had had an uneventful pregnancy. Why shouldn't she? She was young, thin, healthy, a nonsmoker with normal blood pressure and she received good prenatal care. Sonia took her vitamins and iron supplement and attended prenatal classes as prescribed. One of the educational classes included a didactic lecture concerning the onset of labor and when to come to the hospital. The childbirth educators explained how to time the contractions (called "pains" in 1958) and how to keep tabs on the frequency and duration. Sonia's class was told to come to the hospital when the contractions were around five minutes apart. Once labor begins the process of digestion subsides. Sonia was told not to eat or drink once labor begins. Instructors also emphasized that they should leave for the hospital if the bag of water breaks. "You will feel warm and wet 'down there' if that should happen."

When Sonia arrived she was in active labor. Her roommate, who was six months pregnant, drove her to the hospital. It was about eleven thirty A.M. when the labor room nurse telephoned me in the gynecology clinic to tell me that my patient had arrived. After a brief glance at Sonia's chart and admission notes I entered the labor room.

"Good morning Sonia. How are you doing?"

"Just fine and dandy I think. It looks like you were nine days off on my due date," she replied with a grin. I smiled at her remark and placed my hand on her abdomen in order to feel her uterus contract. Labor was measured in terms of intensity and frequency with a hand not a fetal monitoring machine. Perhaps this method was not as accurate or as well documented as a machine but it did serve for a closer link between the patient and the doctor. Machines do not replace people.

The labor nurse's assessment was the same as mine. My pelvic examination revealed that the cervix was four to five centimeters dilated and thinned out or effaced about 75% of its thickness. The fetal head was well engaged into the maternal pelvis. Sonia's contractions were strong and lasting around 45 seconds with a frequency of two to three minutes apart. The fetal heart tones were auscultated with an over the head fetal stethoscope and were normal in frequency of about 140 beats per minute. All systems were normal and go!

I remember our conversation quite vividly. "When did your labor begin, Sonia?" I inquired.

"Oh, about seven or eight o'clock this morning. I think that the labor pains woke me around that time. I thought that I had to go to the bathroom because I felt cramping and pressure in my stomach," she placed her hand over the lower part of her abdomen. "Then I felt my stomach getting hard." I interrupted her jokingly and reminded her that the "big bump" that was getting hard was her uterus and her not her stomach.

"Speaking of stomachs," I went on, "When did you eat last?"

Sonia glanced at her roommate who was seated near her bedside. "Like I told the nurse, we had a slice of pecan pie and a glass of milk around nine o'clock last night. We usually have a snack about that time, just before bedtime."

I glanced at the wall clock just above the crucifix. It was noon. I felt another contraction and then listened to the fetal heart tone with the over-the-head stethoscope. I told Sonia that she and the baby were doing fine and that I would be going back to the clinic just downstairs.

It was my usual custom to tell a laboring patient that the fetal heart sounds like it is a girl. Sometimes they would ask me how I could tell that, and I would reply with exaggerated assuredness, "It is a girl because it sounds pink and pretty and it is a boy if the color tone is blue." I would then explain that one must be able to distinguish feminine tones from masculine ones. But this tongue-in-cheek dialogue could not take place in 1958 with Sonia because then it was customary for babies being adopted out not to be seen by their biological mothers. To know the baby's gender would only add to the grief and sadness as the years went by, or at least that was the popular wisdom at the time. It seemed logical at the time to all concerned parties, the patient, doctor, nurse and adoption agency that unwed mothers should deliver their babies under general anesthesia. Being completely asleep during their delivery would assure that they would not know if they had given birth to a boy or a girl. Later, they would be told of the baby's weight and general health for future medical information.

Labor and Delivery buzzed me in the clinic. The report given to me was that Miss Palocchio was having the urge to push. That of course could signal that she was fully dilated and getting ready to deliver. Gladly leaving the hot, humid and chaotic clinic, I went upstairs to check on Sonia.

Yes, the fetal head was entering the vagina. The cervix was fully dilated and the membranes were bulging in front of the baby's scalp. During the next contraction, a rather strong one, I easily ruptured the bag of water by pressing my two examining fingers against the protruding membranes. Then I reported to Sonia, "Well, young lady, it is time to go to the delivery room. Everything is going just fine. Your roommate must go to the visitor's waiting room and I will be going to change into a scrub suit. Try to resist the urge to push until I am in the delivery room with you. See you soon." It was 3:30 in the afternoon.

In today's climate and medical savvy along with childbirth education, the situation would be quite different. First of all Sonia's roommate would not have been asked to leave but would have been encouraged to be in the delivery room to participate in the birthing process and to encourage Sonia to bear down and push with each contraction. Furthermore, I would not have summoned the nurse anesthetist to the delivery room for a normal birth unless a complication was anticipated. Today it is uncommon for a patient to receive a general anesthetic for a delivery. This is also the case today when a newborn is being placed up for adoption.

Gordy was on duty. He was a tall, young, gay, capable and cheerful male nurse anesthetist. He introduced himself to Sonia, reviewed her chart and checked her vital signs. Gordy then provided Sonia with informed consent regarding a general anesthetic and made sure that her stomach was indeed empty, as she had previously stated, since 9:00 PM the evening before.

Sonia was placed on a gurney and wheeled into the delivery room. She dutifully panted like an overheated puppy during her contractions to make it impossible to bear down and push. You cannot effectively pant and push very well at the same time. (Try it and see for yourself).

Next, Sonia was gently assisted onto the delivery table. The nurse placed Sonia's legs in the stirrups. From the scrub sink area where I was washing my hands and forearms with an antiseptic soap and brush, I looked through the window into the delivery room and could see the nurse prepping Sonia's bottom with a similar solution. Gordy was preparing his equipment to enable him to put Sonia to sleep. The anesthetic would not be administered until I was gowned, gloved and had draped the patient's legs, abdomen and vaginal area. This was in order to minimize the amount of anesthetic time to protect the fetus.

"As soon as your next contraction is over, Mister Gordy is going to put you to sleep and I will see you later Sonia." She quietly nodded a yes and smiled at me. As soon as her next contraction ended Gordy gently placed a black rubber inhalation mask over her nose and mouth. Within two minutes Sonia was under anesthesia.

Gordy, seated by her head, was tilting up her chin with his fingers. He broke the silence in the room "She is ready anytime you are doctor." After the requisite vaginal exam to determine the position of the baby's head, I placed the forceps carefully around the sides of the baby's head. A small incision, called an episiotomy, was made with blunt scissors in the floor of the vaginal mucosa and perineal skin to provide more room for the fetal head. While applying gentle but firm traction in a downward manner, at the same time pulling the forceps toward my abdomen, the baby's head emerged slowly from under her pubic bone. The forceps were removed and the baby's head, which was face down, was rotated to the side and the nose and mouth were suctioned with a bulb syringe to remove mucous and amniotic fluid. By applying gentle downward traction on the head with the fingers of both hands, the upper shoulder popped out from under the bladder and pubic bone. Then slow traction in an upper direction produced the other shoulder from the floor of the vagina. The baby's back slid out with support and gentle urging from my hand. I then placed a newborn baby girl on my lap.

"Time of birth?" I inquired.

"4:12 PM," replied the delivery room nurse gazing at the overhead wall clock above the crucifix.

The umbilical cord was clamped at once to block the flow of anesthetic gas from Sonia's blood to the baby's circulatory system. A second clamp was placed on the umbilical cord and it was severed with scissors between the two clamps. As I walked toward the baby warmer unit, only a few feet away, my thoughts were spontaneously verbalized. "Listen to her healthy cry. Too bad no one can say, 'Congratulations, Sonia, you have a beautiful baby girl.'"

The nurse, a southern grandmotherly type, was busy foot printing the newborn and placing a bracelet made of lettered plastic beads for identification. All that fussing about made the baby cry. The nurse, without lifting her mask, said to the baby "Now, now, little one you are going to a good family with people who will love you so don't cry sweetheart."

Sonia's baby would not have Palocchio on her wrist in order to remain secretive as to her maternal biological origin. The bundled up baby was identified as "Baby Girl Jane."

By now the placenta had separated and delivered itself spontaneously with a small amount of encouragement by pressing gently on the firmly contacted uterus through Sonia's thin abdominal wall. I was beginning to repair the episiotomy. This was a three-centimeter incision from the floor of the vagina and through the skin and underlying muscle between the vagina and rectum. Sonia was to remain anesthetized until this repair was completed, a matter of ten minutes at most. The baby was whisked off to the nursery so that Sonia would be unable to see or hear her newborn.

I had placed the third suture into the small incision in the vaginal floor when suddenly Sonia's upper torso and head seemed to tighten up and raise itself upward off the delivery table. This was followed almost immediately by a muffled distant sound of a gasping, choking noise. Instantly I stood up off of the stainless steel stool. At that same moment Gordy quickly pulled the elastic rubber head straps off that secure the mask to the back of Sonia's head. The anesthesia mask was pushed off to the side of her face. Sonia's sleeping face was covered with vomitus. Gordy wiped her face with a hand towel and placed her head in a sideward position and began to suction her nose and throat with rubber tubing attached to a suction pump.

I turned a wheel at the side of the table that lowered the body in a head down position to allow better drainage of the vomitus. My heart raced as I heard the thick wet secretions being suctioned up. Vomiting while asleep on their back is not what you want a patient to be doing. The room permeated with the odor of vomitus. From the smell and the looks of it, it was too obvious that she had eaten recently. Gordy confirmed my fear. "God damned pizza," he proclaimed loudly as he continued to suction the vomitus out as best that he could.

When a person vomits while asleep, especially if they are drugged or anesthetized and lying on their back the vomitus can easily go down into the trachea and into the lungs. This is called aspiration and is a life-threatening emergency. Two bad things happen when someone aspirates vomitus: One, the air is obstructed by the vomit and ventilation is compromised and two, the vomitus is not only a foreign body but it is also very acidic from the gastric juices that were digesting the food. The high concentration of hydrochloric acid damages the fragile lung tissue.

Gordy placed a laryngoscope into Sonia's mouth while I helped position her head with the chin up. The suction tubing was passed skillfully into her trachea, guided by the light from the scope. Our worst fears were now painful reality. Sonia had indeed aspirated vomitus into her throat, trachea, bronchi and lungs.

Within a few minutes, which seemed like an eternity, a swarm of physicians were buzzing about the delivery room. The nurse had alerted them after she returned from the nursery. There was an anesthesiologist; an internist, a staff obstetrician and a few curious residents that had dutifully responded to the "Code Four" alert announced over the hospital P.A. system. Soon thereafter an E.N.T. specialist arrived from his nearby office. He seemed to take over the leadership of this makeshift team. I at once felt relieved as I watched the other doctors work frantically with perceived expertise to save Sonia's life. Her color looked frightfully dusky blue even with the oxygen flowing through artificial ventilation to her damaged lungs.

It was soon afterwards that Gordy and I had the time to chat and agree that we could detect the visible remnants and the aroma of partially digested tomato.

A Catholic priest assigned to the hospital arrived to give Sonia last rites or extreme unction or something like that. His sudden presence at her bedside in the recovery room gave me a sinking feeling in the pit of my stomach. I had this urge to tell him to leave at once, "Sonia will be OK," I said to myself as if I were speaking to the priest. Shortly afterward the anesthesiologist pronounced Sonia dead. The time was 5:37 P.M.

It was hard for me to imagine that it had been over an hour and a half since I had delivered Sonia's baby daughter. So much had happened so quickly and then all the efforts to save Sonia's life vanished so abruptly, like a cease-fire had been ordered. Life for Sonia Palocchio was over. She was dead at twenty-three years of age. A maternal mortality had occurred. I was in training to become an OB/GYN doctor because I had experienced profound joy in delivering babies and the young patients very rarely die, but perhaps for these reasons it is particularly tragic when they do.

Sonia's body was removed from the delivery room and taken to the hospital morgue pending an autopsy. There would be the filling out of a death certificate stating the cause of death as "aspiration asphyxia" with no mention of how nice a young woman she was while alive. Later there would be a postmortem conference to discuss Sonia's demise and the events that lead up to this unusual tragedy. The doctors in attendance would debate whether this death should be classified as preventable or unpreventable considering the circumstances involved, and how we might be able to prevent difficulties even when patients do give misinformation.

The Chairman of the OB/GYN department, Doctor Jackson Allgood, a soft spoken, southern gentleman with a ruddy complexion informed me that it would be my responsibility to notify the Home for Unwed Mothers and the patient's family and relate the terribly sad news to them. Doctor Allgood did his best to relieve me of my sorrow from this tragedy. He put his arm around me and quietly pronounced, "This was an unfortunate anesthetic complication and death. You did your obstetrical procedure as well as anyone could. Her full stomach was not your fault or even Gordy's. Now you must put this behind you but remember that general anesthesia has its dangers. Now go make some phone calls."

I tracked down Sonia's roommate who had already heard the bad news. She was on the ground floor in a small chapel off the main lobby of the hospital entrance. She was sitting on a small bench with her forehead resting on the top of the bench in front of her. She was crying quietly. I sat down besides her and placed my hand on her shoulder. "Lila, I know that you've heard the awful news about Sonia. She was a lovely woman and I am deeply sorry that she has died." Lila looked up and put her head on my shoulder. I had expected her to burst into tears and sob loudly.

I was prepared for such a reaction. To my surprise she managed a sad smile and brushed away a tear and murmured, "Sonia's baby is beautiful. I peeked into the nursery window through an opening in the drape. I saw the nurse weigh her and dry her wet hair. I knew it was a girl because the bracelet on her wrist had pink beads."

"Yes, she is beautiful and yes it is a girl," I agreed.

Lila blew her nose softly and inquired, "Did Sonia suffer before she died? Did she know that she had a baby? Did she ever see her daughter?"

"No, Lila. No, Sonia never saw her baby and she did not suffer before she died. She was put to sleep for the delivery. The baby was born without any difficulties and then Sonia died shortly after the birth," I replied with a heavy heart. Now Lila began to cry softly and she spoke while she sobbed. "It was all my fault. I know what happened up there. Sonia vomited and choked to death because we stopped to eat pizza on the way to the hospital."

Instantly the aroma of partially digested tomatoes returned to my mind. So that was it. How tragic, I thought to myself. Lila continued her dialogue of the events of that morning. She regained her composure now that she had confided her guilt feelings to me.

Lila told me that Sonia had woke her up at about 7:00 in the morning and told her that she thought she was in labor. Lila timed Sonia's contractions with her wristwatch the way she had learned in childbirth class. Sonia's contractions were about four to five minutes apart and were lasting around forty-five seconds in duration. Lila said that she went downstairs and notified the housemother. The housemother, a Mrs. Singleton, followed Lila back upstairs to see how Sonia was doing. After a short period of observation she agreed that Sonia was in labor. Lila asked Mrs. Singleton if she could drive Sonia to the hospital. She was one of the few women residing in the home for unwed mothers that had owned a car. When Lila decided to place her baby up for adoption she drove to Jacksonville from her home in Fort Walton Beach in the Florida panhandle near Pensacola. Mrs. Singleton agreed and allowed Lila to drive Sonia to the hospital. She instructed Lila not to go speeding through town like an ambulance driver. She emphasized that this was Sonia's first baby and there was plenty of time to get her to the hospital.

The drive to Saint Vincent's Hospital was quite familiar to both Sonia and Lila since they had both visited there frequently for their prenatal checkups. The trip would be about fifteen minutes depending on traffic and time of day. When they got off the bridge over the Saint John's River and onto the main street leading to the hospital they passed several fast food take out places and cafes. Sonia suggested to Lila that perhaps she was not in real labor but having those annoying "Braxton-Hicks" contractions that they had heard about in their childbirth classes. Lila said that she told Sonia that it would be best if they went straight away to Saint Vinny's and have her checked out to see if her labor was real or false. A pelvic exam will tell you what is going on, she assured Sonia. Sonia then began to beg Lila to just stop for a Coke and a snack. She explained that she was starving because they had missed breakfast and would probably miss lunch too while waiting around the hospital to find out that she was not after all in labor. Lila said that she shook her head no and reminded Sonia that they had been told not to eat or drink if you are in labor. She went on to admit that she too was famished and began to get an overpowering craving for some food. It was then that Sonia pointed to a pizza parlor and said that she was really up for a slice of pizza. Sonia pleaded that she had not had any pizza for a long time, especially for breakfast. Lila said they laughed as they pulled into the parking area. Lila remarked, "you Italians are always up for pizza." She also instructed Sonia that she could only have one slice and the rest would be for her to eat while waiting for Sonia at the hospital. Lila finished her recollections with a look of despair in her face, "we did wrong but Sonia is the one who paid for our foolishness." I tried to defuse some of the guilt that Lila was revealing. I told her that she should not shoulder the responsibility for Sonia's death. I reminded her that Sonia was three or four years older than her and besides that it was Sonia who had insisted that they stop for a snack. I could not restrain myself from asking her why Sonia had not told the nurse, the anesthetist or me that she had eaten only recently instead of repeating the lie that she'd had "nothing since yesterday." Lila explained that Sonia did not reveal that she had pizza and a Coke because she was afraid that they would not put her to sleep for the delivery. She also worried, Lila said, that they would be angry with her for not following instructions and then they would end up having her deliver awake like "going natural" or having a spinal. Sonia was also concerned about being awake and seeing the baby in the delivery room. She had told Lila that if she saw her baby she might have second thoughts about adopting it out. Lila told me that Sonia had wanted to keep the baby but she was convinced that her parents would disown her because they were strict, religious and old-fashioned Italians from the old country.

"Old fashioned Italians." This phrase kept rolling me from side to side as I tried to sleep back in my room in the resident's quarters across the street from the hospital. Those words were haunting and repetitive. They must have come back to me a dozen times that night, like a melody that seemed tattooed in my brain.

Sonia's demise was difficult for a young first year resident to deal with. I felt the combined heaviness of sadness and depression. Worse of all there was the uncertainty of how long this emotional down would last and how it would affect my work as a professional in training. I remember how I wanted my tired body and bereaved mind to escape into the unconsciousness of sleep. But even sleep did not allow escape from Sonia's death. The hot and sticky nights added to the restlessness as I saw Sonia' face in the back of my eyelids. After a week or so I was determined to get the facts into their proper prospective. A doctor must be able to deal with death because it is part of life. Sonia was as dead as any mortal could be…as much as a victim of a fatal head injury from a devastating motorcycle accident. Perhaps Sonia's death was a very important milestone in my medical education. A resident must learn from both positive and negative outcomes of medical care and its interventions. Sonia's death, as tragic as it was, was of value to me in the future when dealing with general anesthesia and the art of taking a history from a patient. I remained skeptical and was always adamant when I inquired about a patient's stomach contents. I would no longer inquire, "When did you eat last?" I learned from Sonia's death to query, "What did you *have* to eat before you came to the hospital?" I also learned from this event that general anesthesia without endotracheal intubation is a medical hazard.

All of these academic and cerebral gyrations were dwarfed in comparison to the horrid task of having to notify Sonia's family of her demise. I'm sure that I must have fallen off to sleep because the telephone aroused me at 5:00 A.M. It was the hospital switchboard informing me that they had reached Sonia's family in Connecticut. The hospital worked with the information they received from the home for unwedded mothers to be where Sonia had lived. Sonia's father was on hold. I introduced myself as a physician calling from Saint Vincent's Hospital in Jacksonville, Florida. He admitted that he was Sonia's father and that she lived in Jacksonville and was employed by Prudential Insurance Company. By his strong accent it was quite clear that I was speaking with an Italian-born immigrant. My heartbeat raced as I told him, "It grieves me to inform you that your daughter passed away last evening at the hospital."

The rest of the conversation I can remember quite clearly. First there was a pause at the other end of the phone line.

I had expected one. "Passed away? Our Sonia? Our Sonia passed away? Sonia has died?" His voice remained soft but had become agitated. "You mean to say that our Sonia is dead? My God what happened to her?" Before I could reply he put the phone aside and shouted to another person, presumably his wife, that he was talking to a Florida doctor about Sonia. I told him that Sonia had died as a result of a complication while delivering a baby. I also informed him that a priest administered last rites to her before she died. His response was one of doubt. "Doctor what are you saying to me? Sonia is not married and was not pregnant." He wanted to know if this call to him was a mistake or a joke of sorts. I assured him that it was neither. I told him that there is a baby girl in our hospital nursery that was born without any problems. I emphasized that Sonia was the mother of this baby and I had delivered her. As plainly and painlessly as I could I explained the cause of this tragic death. I summarized again that Sonia is dead and that the baby is very healthy. I could hear him crying and speaking Italian. A loud shriek came from a woman's voice at the other end. From the frenzied conversation I could envision poor Mister Palocchio attempting to gather strength and relate the awful event to his wife.

Within a few long moments a silence fell and I sensed it was time again for me to say something. I told Mr. Palocchio that I knew that this was a difficult time for him and his wife. I suggested that I call back in about thirty minutes or so. I explained that I would answer any questions they have at that time. They agreed and said that they will await my return phone call.

The interlude, I thought, would allow them time to comfort each other given the enormity of the sudden devastating news that had transpired during our short telephone conversation. I also felt a need to take a deep breath and place my emotional composure back on tract.

This sad vignette still lingers in my mind today, almost fifty years later. This is especially true when I hear the name Sonia or whenever someone mentions the city of Hartford. An OB/GYN resident's first encounter with a maternal mortality, because it is so unexpected, goes far beyond what may sound like just another "slice of life" anecdote. We study in books how unpredictable and life-threatening a normal delivery can suddenly become, but there is no way to prepare for the devastation of losing a patient. But the story is not without redemption. Out of something bad, something good would come.

Sonia had an older married sister living in Gastonia, North Carolina. Her parent's relayed the news of Sonia' childbirth and death to their daughter. Sonia's sister had been married six years and never conceived a pregnancy in all that time.

Sonia's remains were released to the family in Connecticut. Foregoing her sister's funeral, the older sister and her husband drove down from North Carolina to Jacksonville. There they easily completed the necessary hospital paper work and dealt with the bureaucracy and financial settlement with the Home for Unwed Mothers. Within two days they had obtained legal custody of Sonia's baby girl.

I met them at the hospital nursery. The older sister was an image of Sonia with short hair and a few extra pounds. It was an unexpected pleasure to have her embrace me with a hug as if to say that she was sorry for my sadness as well as for the death of her sister. The sadness was still there but it was overshadowed by the joy of a baby's soft cry.

The nurse handed the swaddled infant to the new mother. It was quite easy to recognize that this was a fine and deserving couple. The new mother looked at her baby daughter and whispered, "Hello my little Sonia. Buon giorno."

Chapter 12

The Sisters of Mercy

I had just finished delivering a baby in the late afternoon when the hospital operator paged me. I was wanted in the emergency room. While I changed clothes from a bloody scrub suit to my all white resident's uniform I spoke with the emergency room nurse on the phone. They wanted me to see a hospital employee who was having a vaginal hemorrhage.

The employee, as I soon learned, was a housekeeper-janitor by the name of Eula Mae Woods. I had seen her and spoke with her on a recent occasion when she came into the OB doctors lounge. She was tidying up; emptying dirty ashtrays and picking up littered used scrub suits. Most doctors smoked in 1958 as far as I can recall.

Eula Mae was in a corner cubicle in the emergency room with the curtains drawn around the examining table. We recognized each other and exchanged hellos. Eula Mae told me that she was four months pregnant and that this was the first sign of problems when she suddenly began to bleed and cramp and passed a few clots "The size of my fist" was her description. Her bleeding had come on with a sudden gush that covered her underwear and ran down her thighs. She went on to provide me with the history of the present problem. She had been cramping the past two days off and on "Like my monthly was wanting to come down." She was married, had three children and had suffered a miscarriage between baby number two and three.

On pelvic examination her uterus was about fourteen weeks in size. It was soft and tender. When I inserted a vaginal speculum large blood clots emerged and fell into the stainless steel pan below her. I noted that one of the clots contained some solid material that looked suspicious for being placental tissue. Her cervix was slightly dilated and a dark blood clot was protruding from its' opening. Eula Mae's vital signs were within normal limits except for a slight elevation of her pulse. This would be expected with her blood loss. I removed the speculum and asked her to sit up. I told Eula Mae that I was afraid that her miscarriage was in progress and that there was nothing we could do to stop it. She nodded that she understood and added that she had expected to "lose the baby" when she began to cramp. I explained to her that a miscarriage was Mother Nature's way of getting rid of "bad pregnancies" that are not growing normally. She responded with a smile and reassured me that Mother Nature knows best. I informed her that she would need a D&C to "clean out" the rest of the remaining tissue and clots.

I told the ER nurse to have the lab draw blood for a type and match for two units of whole blood plus a CBC (complete blood count). I also ordered an intravenous solution of 5% dextrose in lactated Ringers solution.

While I was searching for a suitable vein in Eula Mae's forearm, I asked the nurse to call the operating room and schedule a D&C as soon as a room becomes available. The ER nurse gave all the pertinent information about the case including the fact that the patient was an employee at Saint Vincent's Hospital.

Soon afterwards one of the Sister Superiors came into the ER to access the situation. The Sister Superior said hello to Eula Mae and told her that she was sorry that she was having a miscarriage. The nun then turned to me and informed me that arrangements were being made to have Eula Mae transferred to the Duval County Hospital by ambulance.

I complained that Eula Mae was an employee and she was scheduled for a D&C in the O.R. and did not need to be transported to the County Hospital. I of course knew right off what was happening but I wanted the Sister to spell it out in public. She did. She announced that Eula Mae did indeed need to go to Duval County because they had colored beds there and Saint Vincent's did not. She emphasized that point by adding that I knew that already. I responded that I did know that this was an all white hospital but that Eula Mae was an emergency because of the bleeding. I also told the Sister that I did not feel comfortable about her being transported across town from one hospital to another hospital. I reminded the nun that the trip to Duval would take at least thirty minutes. My response from the Sister was that she would make the decisions for both the doctor and the patient. She looked at Eula Mae and then spoke for her saying that "Eula Mae understands and she will be just fine especially with an IV running and having stable vital signs". Eula Mae, in turn, looked at me and smiled as she echoed the sentiments of the Sister. She assured me that it would be OK for her to be transferred by ambulance to the County Hospital.

I put in a call to the chief of the OB/GYN service, Doctor Jackson Allgood. He promptly returned my call while I was still in the ER. I gave him a brief rundown of the events that had transpired. He politely interrupted my monologue to inform me that the Sister Superior had already called him "about the colored employee's miscarriage". He went on to inform me that if Eula Mae's vital signs were stable she could be transported to Duval Medical Center.

I called the County Hospital and asked the operator to page Doctor Wesley Southerland. Wesley was an OB/GYN resident at Duval. He was a medical school classmate of mine. In fact from the first day of school Wesley and I were teamed up because of the alphabetical closeness of our names. We were assigned to the same cadaver for the entire freshman year in the Gross Anatomy lab.

Wesley, more of a true southerner than me, was less likely to be critical or amazed of such a medical transgression. Wesley agreed to take extra good care of Eula Mae and he thanked me for the personal referral. He promised to call me and give me a follow up on her case afterwards. We both agreed that Miami was certainly different than Jacksonville.

I remained in the ER until Eula Mae was placed in the ambulance. I was the resident on duty so I could not accompany her to the hospital. It is not likely that my presence would have made any medical difference anyway.

Before leaving the ER I turned to the Sister Superior who was conversing with the ER nurse and told her, "Sister do not expect canonization too soon." I left feeling better because of my caustic remark.

During the remaining four months at Saint Vincent's Hospital I felt the coldness of the nuns. I felt like an unwanted outsider. Actually that was what I was. Perhaps this feeling was due to paranoia or from the fact that all but one of the sisters ignored me by not nodding their habit clad head to wish me a good morning or a polite hello as they always had in the past.

What's more, Monica, a lovely young student nurse from far away Montana told me that she could no longer date me. Those were the orders from the Sister Superior. I told her that I understood but would miss seeing her. I asked Monica if I could walk her back to the student nurse's dormitory building. It was just down the street from the hospital and on the river's edge. She apologized and said that it would be best if she walked home alone. I said goodbye to her.

CHAPTER 13

Mount Sinai Hospital
(Back Home Again)

Adventures of an OB/GYN Resident
1958-1960

For some time, during and after WWII, the old and luxurious Nautilus Hotel in Miami Beach served as a Veterans' Hospital. Sprawled out over several acres of prime waterfront property on Biscayne Bay, it would later become Mount Sinai Hospital of Greater Miami. It is a private community hospital dedicated to serving the medical needs of the people regardless of their race, religion, or socio-economic status. We may not have been completely aware of it at the time, but the war effort had left a legacy of equality—all Americans had sacrificed for the effort, and now they were being rewarded.

My transition from St. Vincent's Hospital on the banks of the St. Johns River in Jacksonville to Mount Sinai Hospital in Miami Beach was for me like switching from Velveeta Cheese on Wonder Bread with mayonnaise to a diet of pastrami on rye with a side of kosher pickle.

I arrived the last year that the old Nautilus hotel would serve as a general hospital. Plans had already been completed for a brand new Mount Sinai Hospital. The local families who were well known for their philanthropy had raised the necessary huge sums of money. The new Mount Sinai Hospital would be across from the existing parking lot, just literally a stone's throw away from the old Mount Sinai Hospital. The architecture of the curvaceous 8-story edifice would take full advantage of its panoramic view of Biscayne Bay and of the Miami skyline several miles to the west.

The beautiful building conveyed more than newness and elegance for its own sake. It was perceived as a tangible indication of the hospital's dedication to insure nothing but the best and the state of the art in medical technology, research facilities and patient safety and comfort. The planners had included the old Mount Sinai Hospital to be utilized for the much-needed quarters for the house staff and student nurses.

Coming back home was a joy for me. My mother had been a widow for two years now. Moving back to Miami Beach to finish the last two years of my residency allowed us to be together at least once a week. I made an effort to dine with my mother at her home on Friday nights to celebrate the Sabbath. I would frequently bring along a house staff intern or resident from out of town or from another country.

Mount Sinai had many foreign exchange interns and residents. One of them was at Mount Sinai Hospital on a cardiology post-doctoral fellowship. He worked with Dr. Philip Samet, a pioneer in cardiac catheterization. Dr. Samet ran a well-endowed laboratory for research. The cardiac fellow, Doctor Gotz Scheele and I had become good friends. He was a fully trained medical doctor in the city of Kassel, in what was then in the Federal Republic of Germany. I asked my mother if I may invite Gotz over for our Friday night dinner, I informed my mother about Gotz having served as a teenager in the Hitler Youth Organization and at age 17 was conscripted into the Wermacht. Gotz had served as a medical corpsman on the Eastern front. When the Germans began their retreat in 1944, Gotz's division rushed west through Hungary and into Austria, not so much waging a defensive war but retreating from the Russian forces mostly in hopes of being made P.O.W. by advancing American armies.

My mother was initially horrified by suggesting that Gotz would be invited to our dinner table, "Your Nazi friend may have been one of those murderers that rounded up Jews to be shot in every shtetl in Poland!" I protested, "Mom, Gotz was a young German fighting for his Fatherland he was not involved with S.S. operations. Would you have expected him to be a pilot in the British Royal Air Force?"

For some reason the various groups that could not co-exist in Europe found a way to work and play peacefully together in America. This is true in the countries of Latin America as well as those of North America. Gotz worked side-by-side for 2 years with many cardiologists that were

Jewish and developed a deep respect for one another as teachers and practitioners. Doctors like Seymour and Rose London, Doctor Charles Werblow, just to mention a few, were dedicated research cardiologists and clinicians.

At dinner Gotz and I stuffed ourselves with Shabbat favorites like chopped chicken liver, baked chicken, potato kugel and home-baked pie for desert. My mother was polite enough not to mention the horrors of WW II or the holocaust at dinner.

The full magnitude of the holocaust was still not completely comprehended even in 1959; fourteen years after the war had ended. We had seen those horrid pictures of piles of human bodies reduced to almost skeletal corpses being pushed unceremoniously into mass graves by tractors inside the liberated concentration camps. The photo images of the charred remains in the crematorium ovens could not help but dehumanize the victims into a nameless mass of what was once a living, breathing human. Those images then still disturb me today. I remember vividly the thoughts and sadness I had then that linger on today. Not a day goes by that I do not think of all those innocents that were murdered because they were born Jewish. The magnitude and ferocity of the holocaust can only begin to be imagined when we read about and hear the oral histories describing the virulent, tenacious and dedicated fervor of the German people to commit genocide.

My mother did inquire about Gotz's capture by U.S. forces and his subsequent POW status after the war ended. Gotz was pleased to inform us that he was treated so well by his captors that he had hoped to stay a POW for as long as possible. He told us over a glass of wine that he became a waiter in the officer's club mess hall at a base in Germany and how the Americans supplied him with cigarettes, food, candy, jockey underwear and even cash tips for his duties as a waiter.

Gotz told us that his father, a physician serving in the Wermacht on the Eastern front, was captured by the Russians and sent to a Siberian gulag. He was one of the lucky ones because he made it home alive eight years after the war ended. My mother soon warmed to Gotz and his European charm after hearing his stories of the suffering of his family. The horrors endured by the German people of the Third Reich are not often remembered. In 1959 most of us thought that the holocaust atrocities were solely the deeds of the dreaded SS. We know today that the Wermacht and multitudes of ordinary Germans bloodied their hands willingly toward carrying out Hitler's Final Solution. At a different time and place I had asked Gotz if during the war he was ever aware of the mass killings in Eastern Europe by the SS. His reply was so matter of fact that I can still hear him say, "I did speak to a German soldier who had recently returned from the Eastern front. He told me that we were doing the unimaginable to the Jews in Poland. To me at the time that meant executing those guilty of sabotage. I never asked him what the unimaginable really implied." Even today the unimaginable is incomprehensible to me.

Gotz and I still corresponded until his death in 2002. He was a retired cardiologist in Kassel.

Having grown up in Miami Beach, I personally knew by name most of the physicians and many of the patients that were admitted to the obstetrical service at Mount Sinai hospital. Being a 28-year-old OB/GYN resident, many of my high school classmates were now having babies or fathering them. Hardly a week would go by that an old high school or college friend would be in the labor room.

I wouldn't always recognize their married name but I would soon remember them and greet them in a manner such as, "Oh my goodness if it isn't Gloria Goodman. So nice to see you again after all these years." A frequent response would be, "Well if it weren't Brucie Steir an OB doctor." Some would inquire as to whether or not I was going to do a pelvic exam on them. My reply to such a question became quite standardized because this social reunion in the labor room happened so often. I assured them that I would not perform a pelvic exam if they did not want me to and the labor room nurse could do the screening pelvic exam if they preferred. None as I can recall objected to my examining them. The discomforts of labor quickly erode modesty.

I attended to the labor and to the delivery of most of my friends either as an assistant or as the delivering physician in many cases. I had the honor of delivering so many of them especially when their private obstetrician was out of the hospital either sleeping at home or during the day in their office awaiting a phone call from the labor room. Most often the resident on duty would determine when to summon the patient's obstetrician to the hospital. After awhile I knew which doctor would arrive promptly and who would gladly miss the delivery for an extra few minutes of sleep. I also was quite aware of which deliveries would be better performed by me then by their private obstetrician. Those few, who I had decided were much less then competent, were usually called in an untimely fashion to assure that they would arrive after the fact. They would then poke their tardy head into the delivery room and say "Well it looks like everything went OK and besides, you are in good hands with our resident physician." The response was usually that they were pleased with being delivered by an old classmate.

My old college roommate, Ritchie Behren, became my roommate once again when I sent him to my quarters in the old hospital so he could rest with a little nap while his wife, Leta, was in early labor. Ritchie and I collaborated for me to do the delivery instead of Leta's private OB doctor. We had spoken of such a scheme long before the baby's due date. In return for "renting my room" Ritchie promised to name the baby Bruce if it were a boy. It was.

Jack Furman and I were good friends throughout high school and college. Jack went to law school while I was in medical school. We graduated on the same night and went out with our parents to celebrate. Several years later Jack got married and his wife was expecting while I was a resident at Mount Sinai Hospital. I had been best man at their wedding. When Jack and Iris arrived in the labor room I was notified immediately and got dressed and went over to meet them. The impending joy of the occasion was soon shattered when I was unable to detect the presence of any fetal heart tones. I listened and tried desperately to hear life instead of the deadly silence. I had learned to keep my composure in the face of such an event but Iris sensed that something was wrong. I asked her if she had any watery discharge. She denied such an event. I told Iris that I would do a pelvic exam to determine if she was in labor and to be certain that her membranes were not ruptured but still intact. I listened again for the sweet sound of fetal heart tones. There was horrid silence once again. There were not any fetal monitors available in 1959 to confirm the diagnosis of the absence of fetal heart tones. Checking for ruptured membranes with a piece of litmus paper on my gloved finger proved negative, which almost certainly ruled out an accidental prolapse of the umbilical cord as a cause of fetal demise. My pelvic exam revealed that Iris was not in active labor but only with mild barely palpable contractions. I told Iris that I would notify Howard Novell, her private OB doctor, and that he would decide as to her disposition. I went out of the labor room and straight away to my friend Jack who was in the nearby waiting room. This was going to be one tough meeting, one that I would have done anything to avoid.

I did not have to tell Jack that there was a problem. He sensed it on my face all at once. I told Jack that I could not hear the baby's heart beat and that I did not know why. I asked an experienced labor room nurse to listen for a fetal heart beat. She monitored the silence in vain as well. I called Iris's physician, Howard Novell. He had been one of my OB/GYN professors when I was a medical student.

Iris Furman was a healthy, vivacious woman and had had an uneventful pregnancy. There was no foreseeable reason that her pregnancy would in end in the eventual C/section for a stillborn baby girl. The induction of labor had been undertaken and it was unsuccessful. Although her pregnancy was at term, Iris's cervix was not "ripe" enough for inducing labor. (Ripeness refers to the dilation and various degrees of softening and thinning out of the cervix). An intrauterine fetal demise demands to be delivered as soon as possible for medical and psychological reasons. Thus a C/section was performed. I assisted Doctor Novell on this sad occasion. The baby was a completely normal, even beautiful, girl. The cause of her intra-uterine demise remains an elusive mystery. Jack and Iris went on soon afterwards to become the parents of two healthy daughters.

About a month before Iris came to the hospital without a fetal heartbeat, my fiancée, Joanne Miller had painted a Jack and Jill mural on the wall of the nursery-to-be at Jack and Iris's Miami home. The mural was quite professional and adorable so with a sense of pride I told my mother about her future daughter-in-law's artistic accomplishment. My mother was quick to point out that decorating or even furnishing a nursery before the baby was born was definitely bad luck. Apparently, God frowns on such arrogant behavior and some sort of evil eye may cast its spell.

Such inexplicable events are enough to make one either a believer or a born-again atheist.

Another of my University of Florida fraternity brothers, Jimmy Spector, married his college sweetheart. Eunice went into premature labor. All efforts to stop her labor failed. Her OB/GYN doctor arrived in the delivery room just in time to see how very small the baby was that I had just delivered. The tiny ex-fetus had all the stigmata of prematurely. His skin was shiny and almost transparent. His breathing was irregular and labored with noticeable rib retraction. We placed him in a warmer and called for the pediatrician.

Dr. J.B., Eunice's obstetrician, suggested that we place a towel over the newborn male so we would not build up the hopes of the parents that they had a viable newborn. He went on to say that a pediatrician would be obliged to conduct heroic measures to save the life of a doomed premature. At best, he predicted, the baby would have severe brain damage if it did survive and the parent's would receive a sizeable hospital bill for the prolonged intensive newborn care. He went on to emphasize that this was a sad but hopeless situation.

Ordinarily I would have agreed with him but I thought, "This is my friend's baby." I covered the baby with a blanket and whisked him off to the nursery. His birth weight was 2 pounds and some ounces. He was a tough, determined little guy. With the excellent and intensive newborn care he received, he eventually made it home against all odds. This was no small accomplishment in 1960. Over the years I heard that he was a completely healthy child and had become quite a good baseball player.

I met him at a wedding in Miami Beach in 1992. (The occasion was the marriage of Jack and Iris Furman's daughter.) The handsome thirty-two year old young man gave me a hug and thanked me for taking him to the nursery after he was born and not covering him with a towel.

Once again experience had demonstrated that the fine line of demarcation between health and illness and between life and death defies explanation. Theories and definitions abound, but the practice of medicine, like religion--for all our advancements and technological breakthroughs--remains full of mystery.

Chapter 14

A New Concept in Contraception

All of my duties as an OB/GYN resident at Mount Sinai Hospital were not limited to delivering the babies of old high school and college friends. Our residency training demanded long hours and frequent night calls and responsibility to provide care for our very active "charity" OB/GYN clinic clientele. In our outpatient clinic we provided prenatal care to indigent women who preferred Mount Sinai Hospital in Miami Beach to Jackson Memorial Hospital in Miami. That preference was in spite of the trip across Biscayne Bay over the causeway. The word around Liberty City or "colored town" as it was called before the term "inner city" came into being was that Mount Sinai's doctors were better and treated Negroes nicer because they were mostly Jews.

In addition to the mostly black patient population in our clinic service there was now an influx of Cuban refugees fleeing Fidel Castro and the communist way of life. Language problems would soon increase.

Searle Pharmaceuticals, after years of research and development, had a new medication that required a trial test before it could be evaluated for approval by the Federal Drug Administration. Mount Sinai was one of several trial test sites for their new medication called Enovid. It was to be a new concept in family planning.

Enovid was a newly devised method of contraception. It was a birth control pill. This new innovative modality was to be offered to women who desired contraception. Many women were fed up with diaphragms, condoms, spermicidal jellies, *coitus interruptus* and a lot of unplanned pregnancies. They were ready to try something new in family planning. Both female and male voluntary sterilization was not very popular in

1959 perhaps as a moral or religious issue or perhaps sterilization per se carried some of the ill feelings associated with forced sterilization perpetuated by the Nazis before and during World War II.

We were provided with detailed instruction sheets printed in English and in Spanish for the clients entering the study group. These instructions included contraindications, side effects and the fact that this was a trial study and they were not obligated to participate in it. In 1959 the peach colored Enovid contained 10 milligrams of a hormone in the estrogen family, perhaps more then 10 times the amount of hormone contained in today's oral contraceptive pills. If taken properly, i.e. as instructed, the effect would be to prevent ovulation. These 10-milligram tablets were not without their side effects. A large percentage of the candidates were experiencing nausea and vomiting and a good number complained of headache. So it was not a surprise that many of the participants dropped out in a short period of time because of these side effects.

After six months we analyzed our findings to date. There wasn't any database or computers to work with in 1959. We simply pulled the client's charts and recorded statistics. We were soon quite startled to observe that among the 85 pill users who had remained in the study they had experienced 14 pregnancies. All the women who entered the study were to begin taking the pills on the fifth day of their menstrual cycle (or five days after the beginning of their menstrual period). This made it fairly certain that none of them were pregnant to start with and to initiate the hormone at the onset of their cycle to suppress ovulation. These unplanned pregnancies meant that our study revealed a 16% pregnancy rate that was similar to the occurrence in couples that were using no method of birth control. Our report to Searle was equally disheartening to them. What went wrong? Other study centers, they claimed, had reported very few pregnancies.

To obey the study protocol we began to interview the women who became pregnant while taking the Enovid tablets. We noted that two of these women had miscarriages and one had returned to her native Havana to have a Cuban baby or an abortion. Abortion was illegal in the USA, but was still available, although not legal, in Cuba. Soon after Castro came to power abortion became less available in Cuba.

Ironically, the Cuban abortion providers left Cuba for Florida and set up illegal abortion clinics mostly in Miami and Tampa.

Of the eleven women with untoward pregnancies, nine were Cuban, one was Mexican and one was a Black Floridian. Aside from the latter, no pregnancies had occurred in the English-speaking women, the majority of whom were Black.

What soon came to light, with the help of translators, was that each and every one of these women who became pregnant had placed the Enovid tablet in their vagina. The bilingual instruction sheet clearly stated that they should "take one pill every night for 21 days. Begin on the fifth day after your period begins and etc." instructions continued. The translations in English were the same as those in Spanish except the word *"boca"* or mouth was not included in Spanish. Most of the Spanish-speaking women who did not get pregnant admitted that they were able to read the instructions in English on the flip side as well.

Searle Pharmaceuticals could not even report an honest appraisal of the incidence of nausea and vomiting because 23 of the participants had avoided nausea by placing the pill in their vagina. The concept of swallowing a pill to keep from getting pregnant was so revolutionary that the thought never occurred to them. Today this method is taken for granted.

The one good outcome of this flawed trial testing was that we urged the manufacturers to call the birth control pills hereafter "oral contraceptive pills."

Chapter 15

I Can't Be Pregnant

Night had fallen. The city was asleep. Deep into the night my phone awakened me in my room at Mount Sinai Hospital's house staff quarters. The hospital operator had just received a call from a woman in distress and the call had been transferred to the emergency room. The ER in turn transferred the call to me. I was the senior OB/GYN resident on duty. The ER nurse told me that she had a woman on the phone who was in pain and that there was a small foot coming through the opening of her vagina. "Well OK", I responded," Tell her to call an ambulance or, even better, have someone at home drive her to the hospital at once." The nurse interrupted me as I was about to give further emergency instructions. "She wants to speak with you. She wants to talk to a doctor."

"OK, for God's sake, put her on," I replied, trying to shake the sleep out of my head.

"Doctor," she said in a somewhat distressed voice, "Bad cramps in my belly woke me up and made me feel like I had to go to the bathroom. While on the toilet there was a gush of urine and then a foot came out of what I think is my vagina." I calmly told her that I already knew about that and strongly suggested that she is having a baby and it is coming in what we call a single footling breech. I went on to urge her to get to the hospital as soon as possible. "But--I --am-- not--pregnant," she chortled me by pronouncing each word separately for emphasis. "Well-- of course-- you-- are," I sarcastically responded, mimicking her tone and cadence. I tried to persuade her that the foot belonged to her baby and it was trapped and it needed to be delivered now. "Doctor, I am

44 years old, and I am not married and have never been pregnant and what's more my periods stopped almost a year ago," she retorted.

I was becoming irritated with this conversation. I asked her, "Ma'am, is that a small foot or an adult foot coming out of your vagina? Does this foot have a shoe on it?"

"No shoe on it. It is a small naked foot" she responded with a sob.

All I could say was, "Lady, I'm calling an ambulance now to get you over here pronto. Are you alone?" I asked. She was. I pleaded with her to just lie down and not to sit on this mysterious foot. I assured her that the ambulance would be there soon and that they would bring her to the delivery room and that I would be there to meet her. I instructed the ambulance driver not to try to deliver the breech baby and to go directly to labor and delivery.

About 30 minutes later the ambulance gurney rolled in. The two labor room nurses and I were awaiting their arrival and we had a laugh sharing the conversation that had taken place.

The woman appeared calm and had raised her head up from the gurney to greet us. She had propped her upper torso up with her elbows. She smiled and asked us to forgive her for bothering us at such an early hour (it was 3:30 AM). The woman looked her stated age. She had an Anglo-Irish face that revealed the lines of a smoker and/or a boozer. A quick assessment by the nurses and I placed her weight at about 220 pounds. Soon afterward she stated that she was 232 pounds and barely five feet and one inch tall.

As I pulled her sheet back and glanced between her legs I took note that indeed there was a shoeless foot of a baby protruding outward from her labia. The small foot was, as expected, a plum red-blue color from the constriction and it quivered about just enough to let us know that it was still alive.

I performed a pelvic exam on the woman. She smiled a very Irish smile and informed me that she had not had "one of those for ages." The pelvic was to ascertain if the umbilical cord had prolapsed down into the vagina alongside the leg when the membranes had ruptured back at her home. I lifted the protruding foot up with one hand and with the other I felt alongside the baby's calf and thigh. I did not feel any coil of umbilical cord. Its' absence is a good sign because the forces of labor pushing the cord against a cervix that is insufficiently dilated can cut off the flow of blood and the oxygen that it carries to the fetus. This baby had good fetal heart tones but time was of the essence.

I told the nurse in charge to call the anesthesiologist on duty to come over stat. We were going to do an emergency C/section. I called Dr. Harry Kraft, the chief of the OB/GYN service who also was on call this day. In obstetrical jargon I informed him that I had admitted an "elderly *primip*" presenting with a single footling breech." For good measure I added the fact that she was short and obese and that she was a smoker who had not had any prenatal care. The main justification for a C/section, as I pointed out, was that she had an irregular pattern of labor and was only 4 centimeters dilated. Doctor Kraft agreed that a C/section was clearly indicated and he offered to come in to assist me. I thanked and reassured him that there was a first-year resident on-call and that she would be available to scrub in with me. Doctor Kraft agreed and he went back to sleep.

When I was a resident the C/section rate in the United States was about five to ten percent of the total number of deliveries. It was required to obtain a consultation in writing if possible or by phone with another OB doctor to agree or not to agree that a C/section was indicated. The only exception was a woman with a history of a previous C/section. In that case the edict was quite clear: "Once a section, always a section."

Today the OB doctor would need a second opinion NOT to do a C/section on a woman having her first baby presenting with a footling breech. The C/section rate today runs around 20-25%. The reason that most breech babies are delivered by C/section is because it is perceived to be, and probably is, safer. Also the expertise of managing the labor with a breech baby and delivering it vaginally is all but a lost art.

In the days prior to a safe C/section, a single footling breech presenting through a partially dilated cervix was almost certainly a death sentence for both mother and fetus.

The section rate would be even higher today if it were not for the change in attitude that all previous C/sections needed to be repeated for safety sake. Today VBACs are performed, that is, vaginal birth after C/section. The dreaded fear of the uterine scar, from a previous C/section, rupturing during labor was shown over time and with monitored studies that uterine rupture was at best rare and easy to detect in the labor room and could be treated promptly in the operating room. As I write these memoirs today the obstetrical powers to be are now giving new second thought to this approach and questioning the safety of VBAC as new statistics on complications are being gathered.

I explained the reasons for a C/section to the patient. She promptly indicated to me that she would be "pleased to get that kid out of there." At last, I thought, she was finally convinced that she was going to have a baby. She signed the necessary consent papers to enable me to perform surgery on her. She asked me to call her sister in Chicago after the baby was born. I explained to her that she would be able to make the call herself, as she would be awake for the C/section. "We are going to be giving you a spinal block," I informed her. I also explained to her that if she were "put to sleep" the baby would be born sleepy from the drugs given to her.

I asked her if there was someone else that I could call before we wheeled her into the delivery room. I asked emphasizing the words "someone else". "Not really," she smiled. "You didn't get pregnant by yourself, did you?" I joked while the anesthesiologist, Doctor Axelrod, prepared the spinal tray. Her fast and witty response was not forgotten by any of us present on that early morning so long ago. She quipped, "I suppose that at Mount Sinai you people don't believe in the Immaculate Conception, do you?" And with that retort the matter was closed for discussion.

Her baby girl weighed in at a whopping nine pounds and ten ounces. Quite a lot of baby to have been overlooked! Doctor Feinerman was the pediatrician on call for the newborn nursery. He came in and examined the baby girl and declared that she was fit for "rooming in," fit for being with mother while she was awake. Later in the day when I was making OB rounds with the interns, the mother openly declared to me that she was very happy to have a baby girl and was overjoyed with her short and sudden pregnancy. She stretched her arms up from her bed and waved her fingers toward me as a signal for me to lean over her bed. She gave me a hug.

Later in the week in conversation with the mother prior to her discharge, she put together the puzzle of her pregnancy and the explanation for such an unusual case of denial. First she had ceased having menstrual periods about a year ago because of her age she assumed she had reached menopause.

Secondly, because of her obesity she did not notice any weight gain but admitted that she had developed what she thought was a "terrible pot belly."

Third, the fetal movements she felt over the past few months were perceived of as a nervous bowel disorder that she referred to as "gut rumbling." And finally her sister in Chicago attributed the reported breast tenderness to "change of life" and assured her sister that it would go away in good time.

Ever since that morning in 1960 I knew that *denial* was more than a river in Egypt.

Chapter 16

Muchos Bandidos

Another case of a woman in active labor without prenatal care was not so much a case of denial but of fear and alienation.

A twenty-two year old single Mexican woman who had immigrated to Florida with other migratory farm workers experienced the fear of a sudden confrontation with reality. She had been picking tobacco in North Carolina when she found out that she was with child. Her pregnancy state was confirmed by a nurse practitioner in a city clinic in Greensboro. That was her only prenatal visit. That solo visit six months hence was documented by a folded piece of medical record paper that she had placed in an envelope.

The young woman had been working the tomato fields near Homestead, south of Miami. When she became too big and too tired to pick tomatoes she went to live with a Mexican girl friend in Miami Beach. Her friend was a live-in domestic worker employed by a well to do family that allowed this young mother-to-be to share the maid's quarters.

When the young Mexican woman presented herself to the Mount Sinai hospital labor room she gave the nurse the information from her only prenatal visit some six months ago. It seemed that her estimated due date based on her exam in North Carolina and by the date of her last menstrual period would place her pregnancy about thirty-two weeks or about eight weeks early.

When I examined her gravid uterus it was obvious that its size was that of a full term pregnancy. I speculated that she was probably at full term and that her due date was calculated on erroneous data. Pelvic examination revealed the cervix to be six centimeters dilated. The fetal head was well engaged into the pelvis. The membranes were still intact and her vital signs were all within normal limits.

The labor nurse informed me in a musical tone, "I hear two fetal heart tones doctor." I grabbed her fetal stethoscope and placed the stainless steel band over my head that extended from my forehead to the back of the base of my skull. On her large protuberant uterus I firmly fixed the bell shaped listening device and heard what seemed to be two distinct heart tones. With the wall clock sweeping second hand I counted the fetal heart rates. One was 132 beats per minute and the adjacent rate was 124. The over-the-head fetal stethoscope was not as accurate as the electronic fetal monitor of today but it did provide bone conduction as well as auditory sounds for a reasonable degree of accuracy. "Yup, "I confided," I'm hearing two heart beats as well." I decided not to call for an x-ray of the pregnancy. I could hear two fetal heart tones and now with renewed vigor I could make out two fetal heads by external palpation. Why bother with an x-ray and all the hassle of getting them to come up to the labor room. I certainly did not feel it justified in sending the patient downstairs to radiology for fear of a precipitous delivery of a premature twin in the elevator or on the x-ray table. Why confirm what we already knew? Twins were coming soon. The fact that the first twin coming (Baby A) was presenting headfirst made me feel confident that the delivery of both babies would not be a problem. Usually Baby-A delivers spontaneously and then Baby-B is delivered feet first. This was in keeping with the obstetrical protocol for delivering twins in 1960. Today a C/section for twins would pretty much be routine. If baby-B would attempt to sneak out head first then I would push its head out of the pelvis and pull down both feet by inserting my gloved hand up through the dilated cervix. Needless to say this internal maneuver is performed under spinal anesthesia to relax the uterus and eliminate the patient's pain. Baby-B's delivery is safer if it is feet first followed by "the after-coming-head" because the head would usually not engage and pass through the cervix easily.

When the woman was ready to deliver we brought her to the delivery room and called for anesthesia and for a pediatrician to stand by. The delivery of twins should be considered as high risk because the very nature of the pregnancy is a built-in complication. The incidence of maternal morbidity from toxemia and postpartum bleeding increases with a multiple pregnancy. The infant mortality rate is increased as well primarily due to the frequency of premature delivery.

The increased weight of two fetuses and two amniotic sacs with fluid plus two placentas places extra stress on the cervix causing premature dilatation of the cervix and subsequently the premature onset of labor. Every precaution should be taken to enhance a good obstetrical outcome. That is the reason why women expecting twins are placed on bed rest in the eighth month. So many years of potential life are on the line here. The mother probably has about 60 more years of life and the two babies about 75 years each. That totals up to over 200 years of precious life.

Baby-A was expelled spontaneously by good old-fashioned pushing by the mother-to-be with choral assistance by the nurse and me. "Pujar, pujar", was the first non-vulgar word that I learned in Spanish. Baby-A looked like a four-pounder and she was carried off to the neonatal nursery. So far so good. Now it was time for the anesthesiologist to administer the appropriate medications to ensure relaxation of the uterus for Baby-B.

The uterus is, after all, a muscle and its relaxation is essential at this point in time to allow my hand to reach up through the dilated cervix and grasp the feet of Baby-B and pull by slow gentle traction downward and deliver as a breech presentation. The obstetrician must be very certain that he or she grasps the foot and not the hand before pulling that part of the fetus down into the vagina. A prolapsed arm does not allow a vaginal delivery. The arm must be reinserted back into the uterus. If this cannot be accomplished, then an emergency C/section must be performed. This maneuver, as I have described, is a blind procedure and the mind's eye must glide the baby out safely to join its newborn sibling in the nursery. Today I am sure that the medical and legal climate is such that this young woman would have undergone a C/Section straight away. That probably would be a safer journey for all parties concerned. Baby-B was delivered breech first followed by the after coming head without any difficulty.

Now that both baby girls were delivered safely and they were snuggled in the nearby baby warmers, it was time to attend to the expulsion of the placentas. I reached upward into the dilated cervix to assist the uterus in expelling the after birth. My fingers reached past the edge of the placenta and felt a bulging sac up above. I then palpated within the sac what felt like a fetal leg or arm. (We OB docs call those "small parts".)

"No, not another baby!" I exclaimed with astonishment. "Triplets!" I gasped. This was to be not just the first and only set of triplets that I would deliver, but the only set I would ever see delivered. This is no small statement. I delivered close to 6000 babies over a period of 28 years.)

Of course all of us in the delivery room were excited and somewhat nervous about the unsuspected little visitor, Baby-C. The mother was too groggy to truly appreciate what was happening in the delivery room. Either that or she was in a state of shock! No one in the delivery room could communicate with her in Spanish well enough for the rarity of this awesome event to be adequately communicated to her.

I did attempt some gringo Spanish from my end of the table. *"Tres ninas and muchas bandidas,"* I sang joyously to her groggy ears.

Now it was time to attend to the birth of Baby-C as soon as possible. The delivery was without incident. A baby boy was delivered in the same manner as was his sister Baby B: feet first. After the delivery the mother began to realize that she had had a multiple birth and started to moan incomprehensibly in Spanish, as if she were asleep and having a nightmare.

I do not recall the exact weights of the three newborns but, as expected, they were all in the 3-4 pound plus range and therefore considered premature. Babies with a birth weight that is below 5 pounds and 8 ounces are categorized as premature regardless of length of gestation. The pediatrician predicted that the triplets' prognosis was excellent and that all 3 should "survive and thrive." Undiagnosed triplets delivered from a woman without prenatal care was a startling event for the OB delivery room staff. The news spread rapidly throughout the hospital. Keep in mind that triplets and quadruplets are more common today. This gestation was not the result of fertility medications that are used so often today. These triplets were au natural.

Employees, house medical staff and administrative personnel found time to peek into the nursery window where the triplets were being proudly displayed. Because the mother was unmarried, privacy demanded that the bassinet identification was simply Baby-A, Baby-B and Baby-C. For the same reason, the newspapers were not notified by the hospital administration of the birth.

Two days after the delivery of the triplets we received more startling news. The mother, through a nurse translator, said that she wanted to place all three babies up for adoption. She made it quite clear that she was not prepared to raise one baby, let alone three. She stated sadly that she could not properly provide for the three little ones and that it would be best for her and for the babies to have a good family adopt them.

The hospital administration office regarding the rare availability of newborn triplets notified all of the known and reputable adoption agencies. Adoption would also be beneficial to the hospital, as the adopting family would be encouraged to participate in paying at least some of the hospital bill. The nursery cost for prolonged care of three babies would alone be substantial. Several local attorneys who arranged adoptions as a large part of their practice were also notified about the availability of the triplets. Time was not a big factor for finding a suitable family. Because of their prematurity, the babies would be in the hospital nursery for at least several weeks. As a result of their low birth weight and being delivered about eight weeks early, it would require weeks for their lungs to reach maturity and to regain their birth weight.

Over the next two weeks there were only two responses regarding possible adoption procedures. As the senior resident and the physician that delivered the babies, I stayed active and informed in the ongoing search for a suitable adopting family. I had promised the young Mexican woman that I would look into who was going to adopt her triplets. She remained adamant about relinquishing her babies. She remained in the hospital eight days. She needed extra time and care to treat postpartum hypertension and to correct her anemia. She was transfused with two units of blood. Actually she did quite well considering that she had no prenatal care and delivered triplets without a major incident.

While she was in the hospital she visited her three babies every day. She would slowly stroll down the hall from her room to the nursery window. The nurses would wheel the babies in their little beds up to the window so the mother could get a close-up look at her triplets. She had never shown or expressed any strong desire to visit and hold them. This meeting could have been in the nursery or in her room. If that had been her wish it would have been granted. Mount Sinai Hospital was, and probably still is, progressive, liberal and sensitive in their policies to protect people's rights. My experience back in the 1960's was that most hospitals had a policy to minimize contact between the mother and the baby that she wished to relinquish. The idea of course was to spare the mother the anguish of seeing and perhaps holding her baby before its departure and even more so to lessen the chances of the mother changing her mind as the maternal bonding sets in after a visit with her newborn. I can vividly remember even today the sadness and at times anger when women from the Home for Unwed Mothers in Jacksonville, Florida came to deliver at Saint Vincent's Hospital. They were not allowed to see their babies. First of all they were routinely "put to sleep"(anesthetized) so that they would not suffer the sadness of seeing and hearing their newborn baby in the delivery room. During their postpartum stay some of these young women would wander down the hall to the nursery and ask if they could just have a peek at their baby. The newborns that were being put up for adoption were not in the viewing area at the nursery window but instead were isolated in an enclosed area near the nurse's station in the newborn nursery. The request was always answered with a no because that was the strict order from the Sisters that ran the hospital. I wondered to myself then if that decree was just another way of punishing these young women for their perceived carnal sins. This attitude was not limited to Catholic hospitals but was the modus operandi for the vast majority of hospitals that delivered babies and placed some up for adoption.

An attorney that I knew from high school provided many of his clients with the legal work to obtain a baby by adoption. He told me that he always had a "waiting list" of prospective parents, the demand being much greater than the supply of newborns. He proposed that three different families would adopt the triplets and that he would arrange the necessary paper work and select suitable families for the babies. I told him the little information that I knew about the father of the triplets based on the mini-bio furnished by the mother by way of a translator. He was 26 years old, from El Salvador, about five feet eight inches tall with dark hair and brown eyes. He was in good health as noted by working the fields up to ten hours a day. My attorney friend thanked me for the professional referral and told me that he would begin the search for the adopting families.

I realized almost immediately that three different families meant three separate payments to the lawyer for services rendered. I was too embarrassed to mention that as a possible motive to him.

The attorney called me back two days later and insisted that none of his adoption seeking clients wanted the burden of three babies all at once. He went on to say that that one family was willing to adopt two babies. The family patriarch was a first generation Cuban-American lawyer. They were well to do and had two sons. One was their biological son and the other son had been adopted. The wife wanted a daughter but was unable to conceive again. The family told the attorney that they would be happy to adopt the two girls, Baby-A and Baby-B. They speculated that another family could easily adopt Baby-C, the infant boy.

The idea of breaking up "three of a kind" bothered me. It seemed insensitive and unnatural. When I told the nursery staff about the plan they felt sad like I did about this prospect. But then again we agreed that at least the Cuban-American family would be able to provide for the sisters and that seemed like a better choice then sending all three in various directions. We also agreed that none of us would want to adopt three little newborns. Having helped raise three children I can vouch for the enormous energy expended in doing so. The sheer logistics, chaos and financial outlay would be absolutely overwhelming for at least two decades. (A smaller scale effort akin to preparing for the D-Day invasion or climbing Mount Everest).

Mount Sinai Hospital had a very active Women's Auxiliary. These volunteer women, called pink ladies because of the color of their uniforms, provided volunteer services throughout the hospital. They ran the coffee shop and the gift shop; they assisted in the admission and discharge of patients and helped raise money for charitable causes related to the hospital. It was a common event for the pink ladies to donate a year of diaper service to an indigent patient being discharged with a newborn and very limited resources at home. In 1960 disposable diapers were not yet available. Around thirty percent of the obstetrical deliveries were from the Clinic Service, which were patients that were eligible for charity. This was before the state welfare system was in place. Most of the women who worked in the auxiliary were middle aged and from well-to-do families. Some were from families of wealthy hotel owners; real estate developers and some were connected to the local "syndicate" or underworld of illegal activities such as off track betting and drug dealing.

One common denominator shared by these affluent women was philanthropy. They were from the families that had helped raise the money to build the new hospital by donation and bond investments.

The news about the abandoned triplets soon made its way to the inner circles of the Pink Ladies. Some of the volunteer women had already gone to the nursery window to visit and peek-a-look at the three little celebrities. The women had heard through the grapevine that the likelihood of the babies being separated by adopting families was becoming a reality.

The impending adoption scenario reached the Mexican mother who was still residing with her live-in maid friend in Miami Beach. The news of the adoption plans caused her much grief and she became withdrawn and depressed. The woman of the house soon was aware of the new mother's sadness regarding the fate of her triplets. This woman was an officer and a very influential member of the Woman's Auxiliary. She soon thereafter related her concerns to her fellow Pink Ladies with the hope of some ideas to come forward to intervene on this sad existing situation. This triplet drama was the main focus of the meeting that was called within a few days. The question arose as to the possibility of the Mexican mother's desire to claim the babies as her own and cancel any adoption plans before it became legally too late. The women agreed in part, that if that was the case, that they could combine their influence and affluence to set up a trust fund to support the mother and the triplets.

The plan was ready to be set into motion if and when the Mexican mother wanted to claim and raise her babies. The support monies from the trust fund would be derived from the interest earned from the investments that would be made by the fund trustees.

The Woman's Auxiliary plan was discussed and put on hold until the mother could be approached with this generous and altruistic offer. The trust would buy a modest home for her in a Miami suburb with a significant Latino population. The trust would pay the monthly mortgage and provide for a regular stipend to enable the family to pay for the necessities of life. Free medical care would be available at Mount

Sinai Hospital clinics. It was common knowledge that raising three babies would preclude any employment for the Mother.

The young Mexican mother did not have to think about this offer too long. She was thrilled with the reality of being able to keep her three babies. Her depression and thoughts of suicide were rapidly replaced by overwhelming joy. The babies were now three weeks old and almost ready to go home.

The plan which was created by the Woman's Auxiliary was off and running without any foreseen glitches. I was present at the meeting in the hospital when one of the plan organizers, a Mrs. Leonard Wein, explained the trust plans to the mother via a translator. It was a happy and memorable occasion.

The two baby girls left the hospital after five weeks and baby boy C was discharged two weeks later. He was appropriately named Carlos.

Three years later I left the Miami area with my wife and two young sons. I was going to France to serve as an OB/GYN medical officer on a U.S. Air Force base. Before my departure I learned that the Mexican mother and her triplets were doing very well.

She had married a Cuban-American insurance broker and they had had a new baby daughter. It seemed that the trust fund and her husband were good providers.

CHAPTER 17

First-Born Baby

It is true that twin brothers can be born in two different years. It happened in France in 1965 at my small Air Force Base hospital.

A rather stout military wife I will call Rima Plum was pregnant with twins. Her multiple *gestations* were detected in the eighth month by X-ray of her gravid abdomen. I had ordered the X-ray (sonographic images were not available in 1965) because it seemed that there were two distinct fetal heart tones and the size of her womb as measured with a uterine caliper seemed too big for a single fetus pregnancy.

Rima's EDC (estimated date of confinement) was January 28. As with the majority of twin gestations Rima went into labor before her EDC. Her membranes ruptured on December 31st and soon afterward she went into active labor and progressed along in a normal fashion. Rima was taken into the delivery room at 11:32 PM. Yes, it was New Year's Eve. The first twin baby was presenting itself in a head first position. This is the preferred position for twin-A. Rima and her Air Force sergeant husband told me that they wanted their baby, if possible, to be the first baby of the New Year to be born in a USAF hospital or maybe even the "premier enfant" for nineteen hundred and sixty-five in all of France…but neither natal distinction was forthcoming. Rima's first baby, a boy, decided to be a 1964 income tax deduction and arrived at 11:54 PM.

Baby brother-B took his time to engage himself into the lower part of the birth passage. He needed coaxing with several good uterine contractions. By the time he was deliverable, with a minimal amount of assistance, a new year had begun. Baby brother Plum entered the New

Year at eight minutes past midnight. Both baby boys and their proud parents were healthy and happy that celebratory eve.

I mention this joyous anecdote because it reminded me of another first baby incident that preceded it by five years. The delivery of the Plum boys received minimal fanfare; only a small article in the Air Force Base newspaper heralded their birth. The Plums did not receive any gifts or awards. I did not even get a cigar from Sergeant Plum.

The first baby to be born at the new Mount Sinai Hospital in Miami Beach was destined to receive a myriad of gifts and newspaper recognition of this event. This was 1960, the year JFK was elected, and five years before the unpublicized birth of the Plum boys.

The old Mount Sinai Hospital had served the community originally as a waterfront luxury resort, then as a VA hospital during and after World War Two.

It was time for this gracious old building to retire. Replaced by a state-of-the-art hospital next to the old building, only a parking lot separated the old edifice from the new. The birth of the new hospital was a community-wide event of pride. Symbolically the first baby to be born at the new Mount Sinai Hospital would represent the birth of the gorgeous eight-story facility on the shores of Biscayne Bay.

The day of the big move was announced well in advance. Each hospital department worked out a scheduled plan to enable this opening to go smoothly and without interruption of good medical care. There was not to be any moving of medical equipment since all the medical furnishings were brand new and already in place in the new facility. Only personnel, medical records and patients needed to be transported across the parking lot. (Personnel are now called "Human Resources," a phrase that leads me to wonder whether another species is to be considered for employment!)

We had two patients in labor and several postpartum and postoperative women in the old hospital on moving day. They were wheel-chaired into a special van that looked like it had been a converted ambulance. The two women were in early labor were not ready to deliver anytime soon. They were transported without difficulty. The van was busy in use so we placed each of the mothers-to-be on a gurney with four wheels. Two people from human resources wheeled each of the gurneys across the parking lot out in the Florida sunshine and up to the sparkling new labor and delivery suite. I was one of the four-gurney pilots.

One of the women in labor was a private patient of Doctor Judd Breakstone; the other woman was from our OB clinic service. That meant that she was my patient, and that I might get to deliver the very first baby at the new hospital.

The local community shop owners, especially those from the fashionable Lincoln Road area, had donated merchandise for the family of the first-born. Various entrepreneurs and even politicians got on the publicity bandwagon and added a multitude of gifts for the parents of the first newborn at the new hospital. The public relations person from Mount Sinai hospital worked with the local newspapers to publicize the upcoming event and to enumerate the gifts awaiting this baby's birth.

There were flowers from florists, professional photography, weekends at several oceanfront hotels, a three-day cruise to Nassau in the Bahamas, and even one-year of free diaper service. (This was before the introduction of wasteful disposable diapers.) Numerous restaurants offered gratis meals and there were generous gift certificates for clothing for infants, children and for women as well. The pledged gifts were still coming in at the time of the big move across the hospital parking lot.

I had the honor of delivering the first baby just a few hours after we had moved the mother by gurney from the old hospital. Doctor Breakstone's patient did not deliver until after midnight on moving day. Nurse Ethel Bromwit, the head nurse of the labor and delivery unit, complied with the instructions to notify the administrative office after the birth of the first baby. She did so with delight.

The celebration and awarding of the many donated gifts was put on temporary hold by order of Mr. Samuel Gertner the hospital administrator. He inquired as to the particulars of the first-born baby and about its family members. He learned the following facts:

- The mother was from the clinic service.

- She had an uncomplicated pregnancy.

- This baby girl was her third child.

- The mother was single and on welfare.

- The mother was black.
- She lived across the Bay in "colored town," known as Miami's "Liberty City."

The woman that delivered the second baby at the new hospital was:
- A private patient and not on welfare.
- She had an uncomplicated pregnancy.
- This was her first baby.
- She was married.
- She was white.
- She lived in Miami Beach.

It became apparent that both of these women knew of the gifts awaiting the first baby at the new Mount Sinai Hospital. The woman who delivered the second baby knew that her baby boy was the second one to be born. The black single welfare mother knew that her baby had been the first to be born.

Mr. Gertner conferred with "other people" on the Board of Trustees. He informed Mrs. Bromwit, who in turn told me that the decision was to publicize the white married woman's birth as the first to be born in the new hospital.

This was for the sake of good public relations with the mostly affluent and all white community. He went on to explain in a rational way that the black single mother was receiving a gratis delivery and hospital stay as it were. Mr. Gertner explained that anyway that should be enough. This was the feeling of the "other people" whom he claimed to have conferred with.

Ethel Bromwit was enraged as she revealed Mr. Gertner's plan to me. My immediate thought was that the Board of Trustees would never be so dishonest and undemocratic. Mrs. Bromwit uttered some unkind but truthful words about the front office politics.

I went directly to Mr. Gertner's second floor office. I told his receptionist that it was quite important that I speak with Mr. Gertner as an urgent matter had arisen. I knew of Mr. Gertner as a good man and was quite sure that his motives were misdirected and would be changed by my reasoning and artful persuasion. I explained to him that I had delivered the first baby at the new hospital and that the woman knew that her baby was Numero Uno. Mr. Gertner argued in a sincere and professional manner that a single mother would want privacy at all costs and any publicity would surely be her worst nightmare come true. He went on to admit that a woman on welfare from across the Bay would never be well received by the media or by the community, and therefore would not provide good publicity for the hospital.

I, in turn, argued the opposite. Wasn't it clear that a black welfare mother being showered with much-needed gifts send a message to the entire Greater Miami area that the new Mount Sinai Hospital, just like the old one, was here to serve the public's medical needs regardless of socio-economic status or race. He agreed with my righteous "Lincolnesque little speech" and agreed that the new hospital would continue to care for the underprivileged. But he concluded that the new hospital was very costly and should reflect the majority of the community's population of working-class white people who are married. "Good" Americans, in other words.

I thought that his reasoning and conclusion were wrong. I told him that not awarding the gifts to the welfare mother would be an outrageous turnabout. The adverse publicity from the press, once they learn the truth, would offset any good public relations that he might have had in mind.

In return Mister Gertner gently admonished me by reminding me that I was a resident physician and therefore an employee of the hospital. Subsequently, it is my duty as a staff member to unquestioningly support the decision that had been made. His voice then became more conciliatory as he admitted to me that the decision to bypass the single black mother was not easy and not without controversy. The pros and cons, he said were weighed and openly discussed. The decision was appalling and painful for some of the board members but the majority ruled in this case. It was a victory for democracy. He admitted that he was one of the majority voters but said that he did what he thought was the most good versus the least good for Mount Sinai Hospital.

The next day a reporter and an accompanying photographer from the local Miami Beach Sun and Daily Tropics came to the hospital. They were there to do a feature story about the first baby born at the brand new local hospital. The public relations office paged me and asked me to accompany the newspaper people to the postpartum room of the woman who was to be the recipient of the gifts and publicity for her newborn. I was eager to see how this would play out.

I knew that she knew, and she knew that I knew that she had delivered the second baby and not the coveted first baby. Justice prevailed with a vengeance. The woman and her husband vigorously denied the celebratory event. They suggested that the real winner of the gifts was two rooms down the hall and that they should go to see her. I asked the husband to be sure, if questioned, that I was not involved with any of the change in events. I was afraid that I would be thrown off of the hospital staff if it were thought that I had told the reporter the truth.

I escorted the reporter and photographer two doors down the hall. The new mom was interviewed and photographed with her newborn baby girl. The smiling mother seemed quite pleased because she had heard some gossip from a nurse that there was some sort of conspiracy brewing to deny her the gifts and recognition. The reason given underfoot was that she was single and the hospital wanted to protect her privacy by not publicizing information so personal in nature. We all knew that was a shabby excuse. The happy mother told the reporter that she may not be married, but the baby has a father and he lives with her.

Two days later the article made the front page of the local newspaper. There was a photo of the beaming mother holding her newborn. The brief story also included a list of all the gifts pledged. There were a total of 42 sundry contributors for this event. The reporter editorialized about the new Mount Sinai Hospital, pointing out that the hospital was open to all, "rich and poor alike in the spirit of the old Mount Sinai Hospital." It went on to praise the hospital's policy and its philanthropic philosophy for the community's well being.

Mister Gertner never said a word to me about the incident. Rumor had it that he did take some heat from the Board of Directors. Somehow I thought at the time that everyone involved was probably pleased with how it turned out.

US Air Force

Chapter 18

How A Gynecologist Helped To Win the Cold War

1963-1968

When I first arrived at *Toul Rosieres* Air Base I was, as ordered, unaccompanied (that is, without my wife and two little sons. They would not be allowed to join me in France until I had obtained housing for my family.

Finding off-base housing in the villages surrounding the base was not too difficult unless you were looking for U.S. standards in housing.

But there was a "catch 22" imposed on me by the Wing Commander. Colonel Bob Boardman had deemed that five of our ten medical officers were Key Personnel and I was one of them. That meant that we were required to live on base. The lucky five were the two flight surgeons, two OB/GYNS and the General Surgeon. There wasn't any available base housing for me. Base Housing placed me on the waiting list for Officers Housing. I was number 18 on the waiting list and the turnover was apparently slow.

The other Key Personnel were of course the "fly boys", flight traffic control people, the jet engineers, and miscellaneous airmen that helped get those Phantom fighter jets off the ground and into the air...that was, after all, the mission of the Air Force.

After living alone in the BOQ for two months my name was the fifteenth on the Base Housing waiting list. I complained to Colonel Joe Claro, the hospital commander. I wanted my wife and two infant sons to be with me. I suggested to him that if I could not live off base and there isn't base housing available that I should be transferred to another base where I could be with my family. "After all it's not like we are at war," I reminded him.

Colonel Claro forwarded my complaint to Base Headquarters. That prompted some positive action. They immediately arranged for me to occupy two connecting rooms in the BOQ as soon as my family was on its way to France. Well those arrangements were fine with me. It would be like having two hotel rooms with a bathroom in-between. There would not be any kitchen but the Officer's Mess was just down the walk. The Officer's Club had fairly decent food at very reasonable prices and even served French onion soup, escargot and "Nouveau Beaujolais" for one dollar per glass. More importantly, they also had high chairs for my two little boys.

The deal was done. My dependents (as the military refers to family) flew to Paris and I met them at Orly airport. Instead of driving straight away back to the air base, a three-hour journey, I decided that my spouse and our 20 months and 5 months old sons would enjoy a guided tour of the historic landmarks of Paris.

"That's the Eiffel Tower--see boys how big it is?" I thought it would be a real treat to be able to tour the most beautiful city in the world with them. Mom was busy changing diapers and was suffering from jet lag and was not up for sightseeing. After a few more attempts at playing tour-guide past the Place de Concorde and *the Invalide* I was ordered to proceed to the base and to our new quarters.

I had set the two adjoining rooms up in advance. Our room had two single beds pushed together and a dresser. The bathroom separated our room from the boys' room. Their room had two porta-cribs, a dresser, and a playpen that I had recently purchased and assembled. The playpen was almost too big. It occupied almost half of the room but was deemed essential for two little boys. The arrangement was workable and at least we were together.

Meals were readily available next door at the Officer's Mess. We were able to dine in or take-out back to the BOQ. I usually showered and washed the dishes at the same time because the bathroom sink was quite small and there was no bathtub. The diapers were washed in the BOQ Laundromat. There were no disposable diapers available in 1963.

"Operation Europower" was to begin soon. It would involve all U.S., Canadian, British and French forces and was designed to be a show of power of the NATO forces. The exercise was to test the readiness and strength of the allies and to demonstrate their power to the Eastern bloc foes. This was at the height of the "Cold War."

Our airbase was a tactical reconnaissance wing. Our main aircraft was the old but useful B-66. Its main mission was to jam enemy radar with the latest technology. This was accomplished by electronic warfare equipment. They were used extensively several years later in Vietnam by many of these same flight crews. In 1964 the first Phantom jets arrived on our base. They too would be deployed from our air base as the war in Southeast Asia escalated.

This NATO winter exercise needed press publicity for the military establishment, especially the Pentagon people. The Department of Defense made sure that the press people would get the VIP treatment wherever they may be embedded. Even our small remote air base had a sizeable contingency of newspaper journalists and military personnel that arrived to cover the "war games."

My family was ordered without prior notice to vacate one of the two BOQ rooms that we occupied. I argued with the Base Housing Office to no avail. They claimed that the order from the Wing Commander was to have BOQ billets made available for the visiting "VIPs." The inconvenience, I was assured, would only be for a week, the duration of the exercise. I agreed that we would survive.

We placed both porta-cribs in our room with two single beds. There was, of course no room for the playpen. Our room was quite crowded.

As we entered the room the door was only able to open halfway, being blocked by one of our two beds. To enter the room interior we had to walk across both beds, but we survived the claustrophobia.

After the NATO exercise was over and the VIPs had departed we were ready to move into our two-room suite once again. To our great surprise, that was not to be. The BOQ manager had assigned that room to two new officer crewmembers.

"They have priority at the BOQ over dependents," I was informed. The manager, a middle-aged sergeant, started to add the Air Force cliché, "remember, Captain, the mission of the Air Force is to---". I interrupted and finished "yeah keep the planes in the air. I know that sergeant," I quipped, "but those fly boys in the sky will not perform well if they are worried about the health of their wives. My mission is to keep their spouse running well and finely tuned like an RF4C Phantom jet." My metaphoric speech did not impress him.

We were to stay in our crowded little room in the BOQ for two more months. Base housing finally came through with a vacancy. Even a small, very small, two-bedroom trailer was a delight to us. All the on-base 'houses' were trailers mounted on cement blocks. Even the Wing Commander resided just three trailers away. At least we had a kitchen and a small yard for the boys to play in.

Speaking of the Air Force's mission to "keep the planes in the air" reminds me of an incident that pitted moral ethics against the needs of the military. This required some deliberation before decision-making.

Captain David Appert, our wing's Senior Flight Surgeon, called me from base operations. He asked me if he could meet with me at the hospital to discuss a medical matter with me. David was a debonair and handsome single young physician from Chicago who both resembled and sounded like the late Peter Lawford.

I told Dave that I was getting ready to do a C-Section now and suggested that he come over in an hour or so when I would be free over a cup of coffee for a chat with him.

Dave told me that one of his pilots, a senior officer from his squadron, had picked up a case of gonorrhea while off duty in Madrid. Our wing flew south to Spain quite frequently for required flying time. This was especially true in the winter when northern France and most of northern Europe was socked in with heavy gray skies and poor flying weather.

Torrejon Air Force Base outside Madrid was a pilot's favorite rendezvous. Besides the friendly sunshine, the Officer's club was known for its parties and the BOQ was referred to as the "Torrejon Hilton." This nickname predated the infamous "Hanoi Hilton" of Senator John McCain fame.

"So David, you know how to treat gonorrhea, don't you? Surely you saw dozens of cases of clap at Cook County General in Chicago," I mused. David smiled and replied, "That is not the problem here. I have already given him a shot of penicillin and I also grounded him for a few days until his drip clears up. We don't like them to be sitting long hours flying with a urethral discharge because it can aggravate the prostate gland. This is a family problem now and that is where you come in."

David went on to explain that the pilot had intercourse with his wife after his Madrid trip but before he had noticed the discharge from his penis. "As soon as he noticed his drip he came into sick call to see me," David explained.

"The deal is we have to treat the Mrs. and not let her know the truth."

I responded with a sarcastic "what's this **we have to** business you mention. Why don't you treat her Dave?" Dave reminded me that Flight Surgeons do not see dependents. Dave reminded me that his job was to keep the planes in the air. I agreed to cooperate for the esprit de corps. We devised a cunning plan.

The next day Dave called the errant pilot's wife. I knew her and her pilot husband. She was a Georgia peach. Dave told her that her husband had a sore throat and that a recent throat culture was positive for beta-strep. He also informed her that it was contagious and suggested that she and her two dependent children go to the gynecology clinic to see Captain Steir.

Dave preferred to lie than to have the husband fabricate a story to his spouse. It was an honorable gesture. Dave of course had already explained the prefabrication to the pilot.

The deal was for the wife to come to see me for a throat culture. I set up an appointment for the same day that she called me as Dave had suggested. I had seen her in my clinic before for a routine gynecology exam so she was at ease with me. I gently swabbed the back of her throat with a sterile cotton swab. I repeated the same with her two Air Force brats. I told her I would notify her of the results. She thanked me and went on her way. I tossed the culture tubes in the wastebasket.

Two days later I called the pilot's wife at her base quarters. I informed her that her throat culture was indeed positive for beta-strep but both children's culture was negative. I advised her to come in to the clinic for a penicillin injection. I placed a bogus lab culture slip into her medical record marked "positive for beta-streptococcus."

Dave of course did what only a medical officer could do to a higher-ranking officer: he reprimanded the philandering pilot and told him to practice fidelity or use a condom. Mission accomplished.

Chapter 19

Where Were You When You Heard About JFK's Assassination?

Thanksgiving would be the first holiday that my family would observe at our military duty station in France. It was late November and the leaves had fallen revealing the man-made ugliness of our small rural air base in the beautiful French countryside.

Toul Rosieres Air Base was located in a sparsely populated farming area in the Lorraine Province halfway between the old cities of Toul and Metz. The German Wermacht had marched through this part of France no less than three times in the past one hundred years or so. The *"Bosch,"* as the French called the German invaders, captured and annexed Alsace-Lorraine during the Franco-Prussian War near the end of the nineteenth century. This area bordering the German Saar region to the north remained German until the end of World War I. In 1918, after the armistice, the Versailles Treaty returned these provinces to the French. This rejuvenated the sagging French pride and briefly rekindled the Napoleonic spirit of a century ago for a country that had lost so many of their young men in the trenches. They virtually capitulated all of it again in 1940 when the Nazis overran them. Much of the French Napoleonic pride morphed into a "collaboration with the conqueror" mentality. This reduced the success and patriotic bravery of the French resistance throughout World War II.

Twice in the twentieth century the combined allied forces, mostly British, American and Canadians was needed to oust the Germans from French soil.

The Roman conquers left behind arenas and viaducts. There is an intact viaduct that spans over the main road entering Metz. The

Germans left behind a sorrowful number of military cemeteries. Many sadly neglected cemeteries abound throughout the farmlands of Lorraine.

Not too far from our Air Base near a small village is a World War I military cemetery that honors the remains of fallen North African Moslem soldiers who died defending their French colonists. Their headstones are in the shape of a minaret. My thoughts visited the sad irony of an Algerian fighting on French soil and dying at the hands of Germans.

It was inevitable that my thoughts of this geographic irony would turn to the war in far away Vietnam. There we had young American boys being shipped home in hermetically sealed aluminum caskets from Saigon to Travis Air Force Base on mortuary flights. The reality of an eighteen-year-old Chicano from San Antonio being killed in a rice paddy by a Vietcong fighting for his motherland's freedom was incomprehensible then as it is now in our war against Islamic Iraq and Afghanistan.

Thirty minutes away from the Air Base near the village of Saint Michel there is a large U.S. military cemetery where the World War I fallen are honored. Approximately 5,000 or so are buried there.

The marble crosses with a scattering of Stars of David are in neat rows on gently rolling grassy hills. It is all green and well manicured. There is a stark but beautiful large monument that dominates the landscape and lends a somber note to the sad but idyllic scene. The American caretaker told me that the number of visitors diminishes each year.

An hour's drive away is the city of Verdun. Nearly one million combined French and German soldiers fought and died there in WWI.

The long siege and trench warfare resulted in the carnage comparable to that of WWII Stalingrad. The French said of the German army "They shall not pass" They did not. The corpses of the soldiers and even their horses lay on the ground and decomposed.

There is an ossuary at the site of the battlegrounds near Verdun. The ossuary is a large arena shaped structure with windows all about. Inside the ossuary are the skeletal remains of French and German soldiers. As I walked around it peering through the glass enclosures it was difficult to not condemn these soldier's leaders for allowing such carnage to take place and to spend their youthful lives. For the glory of their country they killed each other and now their remains lie next to each other helter-skelter for eternity. The ossuary is not a monument that invites an emotional feeling of patriotism or that evokes a tear to the eye but instead an overwhelming disgust and sorrow. It was not built to be a monument dedicated to the fallen heroes but a convenient place to house corpses rotting on the battlefield. The ground all about was too filled with shrapnel, shells, barbed wire and mines to dig graves. Even today there is so much metal in the soil around the battlefields that trees and crops cannot grow.

Our air base was on leased ground from the French. It had been agreed upon between the U.S. Department of Defense (DOD) and the French as part of the Armed Forces Agreement that when our "mission" was completed and we were to abandon the base that all of the fixtures on the base would become the property of the host country; i.e. France. Because of this arrangement the DOD in the Pentagon decided to spend as little as possible on repairs of the infrastructure and furthermore not to build any substantial on-base housing.

As a result U.S. military base facilities all over France were indeed shabby and second world as compared to the U.S. military bases in Germany, Japan and at home.

Base housing at Toul Rosieres was dismal at best and hard to come by. No new housing was built to accommodate the influx of Air Force personnel and their families. The need for increased manpower was due to the never ending needs in fighting the "Cold War."

Most of the families lived off base in ancient farmhouses in nearby villages. There they could live among the local French and learn how to survive in quaint but rough and shoddy old hovels. The good news was that their military housing allowance was more than their rent.

Some of the Americans learned the art of French country cooking which were mostly delicious stews and soups cooked with leftovers from the previous day's meals. Very few improved greatly in their mastery of the French language. *"Au revoir"* still sounded like "Irv Renoir" to the French ear. Many an airman from the states could be heard uttering a "mercy buttercup" to show their thanks to a local citizen. In the 1960s the French were rather intolerant of their language being abused by

Americans and even by French speaking Canadians. I had six lessons in French at the on-base Berlitz language school. Thinking that I was cool I ventured into a café in nearby Nancy and had an Alsatian beer and a plate of delicious *pomme frites*. Still thirsty I pointed my index finger at the empty beer glass as I caught the eye of the aproned waiter. I said politely, *"Encore de bierre, s'il vous plait."* He in turn nodded his head and replied *"Oui monsieur."* Soon afterwards he appeared before me with a plate containing a slab of butter. He placed it before me and smiled slyly then uttered *"voila monsieur."* I could not readily find the translation for "wise guy" in my Berlitz handbook. I did note later that the French word for butter is *le beurre*.

The base surgeon was Homer Petrou. He and his wife Barbara were from North Carolina and lived in a trailer on base with their two children. The Petrous invited my wife and me to dinner. Also invited were Gus and Libby Conley. He was the base pediatrician. They were also, like the Petrous, Tar heels.

Homer reminded me of a young Henry Fonda, except with a more sullen personality. He seemed shy and was a slow talker with a wry sense of humor that had good ol' country boy flair to it. His wife Barbara was very pretty and seemed to be a devoted wife and mother. Gus, the pediatrician was a blonde with a crew cut. He was, like me, short and muscular. He had big twinkling steel blue eyes and a devilish Paul Newman smile. His wife, Libby, was a schoolteacher and had striking Irish looks. Not being considered key personnel they did not have to live on base. They were the lucky ones who lived in a nearby French village. The Medical Officer of the day could handle any pediatric emergency quite competently until Gus could arrive in about fifteen minutes or so. I could call Gus on the phone if I were going to do an emergency C-section so he could be present to care for the newborn.

This particular evening I was on duty. The other OB/GYN and his family were away for the weekend. Whenever we were off duty we would sign out and go somewhere. Any place would be better than staying on the dismal air base. Besides most of Europe was at our doorstep. The geographic location of our base plus the horrid quarters we lived in made frequent traveling a delightful must. If you look at a map of Europe you can see the city of Nancy, thirty kilometers from our base. Wow and ooh-la-la only three hours to Paris, two hours to the Swiss and

Luxembourg frontier, and one and a half hours to the German border. If you had the right connections at base operations you could probably fly "space available" in a C-42 (a.k.a. the Gooney Bird a twin engine prop job) to England for the weekend and stay at the plush Officer's Club in London called the Columbia House right off Hyde Park and the Marble Arch.

There weren't any cell phones or pagers available at this time so I took call by telephone from Homer's trailer. I had a patient in early labor and wanted to be sure that the labor room nurses knew of my whereabouts.

The six of us sat down to a nicely prepared table. We drank toasts to each other's good health, to the Air Force, and to the French--- *"A votre sante!"*

Towards the completion of dinner I received a call from the hospital. The airman on duty that called me was Al Blanco, a nineteen-year-old tough Italian kid from Utica, New York. Airman Blanco was calling to let me know that the woman in labor wanted to go home because her contractions were getting weaker and further apart.

My memory reviewed the patient's chart. This was to be her third baby and she lived in Pont-a-Mousson a town about thirty kilometers from the air base. I told Airman Blanco that I wanted her to remain in the hospital at least overnight because of the distance from her home to the hospital and the possibility of "black ice" on the country roads this time of year. Being newly arrived in France I did not yet know about the deadly thick fog that permeates the late autumn nights in the province of Lorraine.

Airman Al Blanco then startled me by asking, "Have you heard about the president being shot?"

"President Kennedy?" I inquired, hoping that it was another president.

"Yes, someone shot him in his car in Dallas today."

The time in Dallas was six hours earlier than for us having dinner in France. I hung up stunned after asking Blanco to call me back when he had more news about the president.

I returned to the dinner table feeling a wave of depression and bewilderment at the possibility that JFK might be dead. It was quite apparent to my wife, Joanne, that I looked upset. I had decided not to share this dreadful news with the others just yet. It was so upsetting to me that I was hoping it was just a prank or a rumor. I assured my wife that I was all right and began having dessert with the others. Ten minutes had not past when the dreadful phone rang once again. It was Airman Blanco calling. He laid it out loud and clear without any noticeable emotional tone to his voice. "Someone has shot and killed President Kennedy," he announced. I asked him if he was sure the president was dead. "Yeah he was shot in the head and was pronounced dead at a Dallas hospital."

I returned to the table and announced the dreadful news to the others. They were shocked. Homer thought I was going to tell a joke and that was the opening line. I repeated the information from Blanco a second time because they only starred at me in disbelief like I was only kidding. I told them that this was not a joke. Someone asked who shot the president. I told them that I did not know. In my own mind I can remember that my suspicion turned to the LBJ and Ladybird clan and their powerful Texas connections almost immediately. I did not share that private thought at that time.

Our pediatrician, Gus, broke the silence. Gus flashed a sheepish smile, gained his composure and said, "Oh that's not such bad news. After all, Kennedy is a Catholic and a Democrat." My wife spoke up almost immediately. With anger in her voice she reminded Gus that President Kennedy was also a son, a husband and a father. How could Gus possibly heal sick children when he held this attitude toward human life, even the life of his own president. Gus smiled sardonically feeling alone and embarrassed. Then I remember standing up and feeling sorry for Gus having made such a hatefully cruel comment hoping to lighten up the mood at the dinner table. I also reminded him that President Kennedy was also our Commander-in-Chief.

With that said we quickly bid them a goodnight and excused ourselves. We walked down the hill past the hospital towards our base quarters. It was cold and dark and we were silent except that I could hear Joanne gently crying.

Chapter 20

Where Are Those Baby Girls Today?

Once a week, or whenever she got around to it, the hospital commander's secretary would plop down a batch of birth certificates on my gray metallic desk for me to sign. She would leave them in my office in the hospital's outpatient clinic area. Invariably she attached the same note: "Please sign these birth certificates ASAP and return them to me so I can deliver them to the mayor in the village. I remain your humble servant, Emily." Emily was an American civilian working as a clerk for the Department of Defense (DOD). She was the secretary for Colonel Joe Claro. Colonel Claro, a senior medical officer and constant pipe smoker, was our hospital commander at the 608th Tactical Hospital on the *Toul Rosieres* Air Base in Northeastern France near the city of Toul.

Less than a kilometer away from the front gate of the base is the village of *Rosieres-en-Hay*. There is one main street, a narrow winding road that goes through the typical ancient, drab French farm village about two or three blocks long. Like most villages in this part of France, the one-story houses and barns enjoin each other. The backyards of the small old houses reach out to their farmland. There was a bar and small general store that seemed to be always closed. The Frenchman who owned the store also sold and delivered propane gas in heavy round metal containers. Without his services, the base trailer dwellers would have had no heat or fire for the stoves. He had worked out a deal with the base and had a propane monopoly…in other words, we were at his mercy for survival through the winter. The first time I needed a propane tank refilled, I placed a clearly visible sign in our trailer window as instructed by my Air Force neighbor. The sign read simply

"GAS." It was written in large letters with a red crayola on a piece of white cardboard.

The day went by. Nothing. We did not get our empty container picked up nor replaced. The trailers on either side of ours had their propane gas replaced that very day. The propane-delivery monsieur only delivers once every two weeks during the winter and about every three weeks throughout the rest of the year. The weather was cold and we would be out of propane within a few days without replacement. Even with the trailer heater on full blast and a portable electric heater, the interior remained cold during the night. On very cold nights, we dressed our three-year old and one-year old boys in thermal underwear and one-piece nylon snowsuits as if we were preparing them for an all night hike on the blistery tundra. In the morning the poorly insulated interior showed us their icy windowpanes. This sight of ice motivated me to drive out to *Rosieres-en-Haye* with the empty propane container and the ignored sign I had posted. The propane man did not respond when I knocked on his house doors. I had met the village mayor before when I delivered several birth certificates to his farmhouse. That was the week that Emily, the hospital secretary, was away on holiday.

The mayor, a man of about sixty years old with a ruddy complexion and bloodshot blue eyes, greeted me and invited me into his house. We went immediately into the adjoining kitchen. Only the kitchen had adequate heating in French village farmhouses when I was stationed there in the early 1960's. I was offered a bowl of *soup* but declined and instead accepted a cup of tea. The farmers, I was told, always have soup on their wood-burning stoves. They thrived on their *potage du jour* (soup of the day*)*.

I showed the Gitane-smoking mayor the one word sign that I had placed in my window. Then I explained *"Pas le gaz pour moi."* I thought that meant "No gas for me." Having recently been put down and embarrassed by a French *garcon* for using very bad French, I was hoping that I did not say something rude or inappropriate. Perhaps I thought the mayor would think that I did not want his soup because I did not want to get gas. The mayor looked at the sign and broke into a laugh. He smiled and said to me *"Gaz not Gas"* as he pointed to my sign with one letter that I had misspelled. I am not certain if the propane guy was being arrogant or he was illiterate for any non-French word. I changed the "S" to a "Z" and asked as best that I could for the mayor to help me to get propane gaz for my frozen trailer. He assured me many *oui-oui's*. And I departed offering him several *Merci-beau-coup's* and an opened pack of Salem filtered cigarettes that he was pleased to receive.

Two days later our "*gaz*" was delivered. The exact number of francs were required and given to the dour French propane man. No needless words were exchanged in either language. To this day I remember that someone long ago told me that a Frenchman is an Italian in a bad mood.

The birth certificates for the American babies born at the base hospital were in French and in English (not unlike the label on a bag of Canadian cookies). The delivering physician had to sign the certificate before it was delivered to the village mayor. The mayor would not only place his signature on the certificate but also sealed it with a mayoral stamp in dark red ink. The mayor would get five francs, the equivalent of one dollar, from the DOD for each certificate signed. Our hospital averaged about twenty deliveries per month.

I sometimes wonder what became of LaChaum Moseley. I noticed this unusual name when I signed the certificate. It had a nice sound to it, that is, if I was pronouncing it correctly. From the birth certificate, I remember that the mother was from Pigeon Creek, probably in Mississippi or Alabama. I had just finished postpartum rounds and remembered that LaChaum's mom was still in the hospital. At lunchtime I wandered over to her bedside and told her that I liked the name LaChaum.

"Am I pronouncing it correctly?" I asked her.

"Yes, that's right, Doctor."

"It has that nice French sound *La Chambre. La Chambre*, you know, *La Chambre*, the room in French."

"Oh, yes, of course, it does have a nice French sound," I assured her.

Then there was the birth certificate that I refused to sign. Looking back now I realize that I had been too opinionated and serious about the whole incident. It had become a base hospital topic of conversation and philosophical debate among the Air Force doctors and nurses. Most of them sided with my refusal to sign the birth certificate of Pebbles Farley.

I had asked her mother, an older Air Force dependant wife about forty-four years of age, if she did not mean Pebbles to be her daughter's nickname. "Oh no, Doc," she insisted, "Sergeant Farley and I just love Pebbles from the Flintstones. We even named our Labrador Wilma after one of the Flintstone characters."

I suggested to Mrs. Farley that her baby daughter could very well become a surgeon and the hospital's paging system would blare out, "Dr. Pebbles Farley, you are wanted in the O.R." She was quick to point out and put me down by reminding me that doctors are paged by their last name. I retorted, "How about if she became a judge and the bailiff had to shout, "All rise for the honorable Judge Pebbles Farley." Or if she should marry a US Senator from Missouri, where she is from, and the press would print Senator Symington and his wife, Pebbles. She laughed, lit up a Lucky Strike and told me I was being silly for a doctor. I couldn't fathom what she could be thinking that made this decision appear to be reasonable to her.

I spoke with my hospital commander, Joe Claro, and told him that I felt that I did not want to sign the birth certificate with such an absurd name. The colonel reminded that it was the child's name and it was her parents' decision, not mine, I should sign it.

"Make me feel good and sign it for me, Colonel," I asked him.

"Nothing doing" he retorted, puffing on his pipe and frowning at me.

Several days later the other Ob-Gyn doctor came back to the base from leave. I had placed the Farley's certificate with other certificates on his desk waiting for the signature of Dr. Gordon Hanusek, M.C., U.S.A.F. Gordon signed it without reading the baby's given name.

I often wonder if the Mayor in the village understood the name Pebbles and what he might have thought about a baby being named "the room."

Chapter 21

Abortion and the French Connection

Thirty kilometers from the picturesque city of Nancy, the provincial capitol of Lorraine, was a small *Toul Rosieres* Air Base. From there the French wife of an American Air Force sergeant went to the city to have an abortion.

I am not sure if I should call this misadventure an illegal abortion or not. France, of course, is a Catholic country but quite secular in matters of morality and politics. At least that was my impression back in 1965.

A well-known Parisian OB/GYN told me, "We keep abortion out of politics." He went on to explain that it is not for politicians to decide what a woman can do with her unwanted pregnancy. This he said was a personal matter and was a decision that would ultimately be decided by the woman and her physician and not the State. If the woman or the physician wishes to abide by the Catholic dogma against abortion then they will not terminate the pregnancy."

In essence what he was saying was "pro-choice" before that term became a label for the people who believe in reproductive rights and freedom to choose. Pro-choice became the rallying cry in the abortion debate that persists even today, over 35 years after Roe vs. Wade.

I met this French OB/GYN physician in Paris at a three-day gynecology conference/workshop on laparoscopy technology and technique. The meeting was sponsored by the then prestigious American Hospital of Paris. The USAF allowed me to take time off for continuing medical education. The military is very good about encouraging their physicians to attend worthwhile meetings to enable them to keep up with the latest advances in medicine.

They "cut orders" for me to travel and paid me a per diem for room, board and travel expenses. The only requirement the USAF asked in return was that I wear the military uniform to all meetings.

During a conference lunch break the suave French *acouchier(*obstetrician*)* and I chatted over a coffee and a Napoleon cognac. The topic of John F. Kennedy's recent assassination came up. He expressed his sorrow and told me how much the French loved Jackie and John. I was in France when the tragedy occurred so I knew from personal experience what sadness and mourning the French people experienced on a grand scale. Mass was held throughout France including on our Air Base in a huge air hanger to accommodate the locals as well as the military personnel.

We also spoke about LBJ and wondered what his policy would be in Vietnam. The French physician's thoughts and hopes were the same as those expressed by a French Air Force colonel. This pilot was the French liaison officer to my base; He had served in Vietnam and had seen combat, including at *Dien Bien Phu*. We conversed over a cognac at the Officer's Club bar. He strongly urged, "You Americans should not get too involved in Vietnam." He suggested that the best course of action toward their civil war would be non-interference. "Only the rich Vietnamese landowners want you Americans to help them hold on to their wealth. Get out of there before it is too late. Do not be foolish like we French were." He also mentioned, to my surprise, that "Ho Chi Min was not a Marxist communist. He simply did not want to see a divided Vietnam." The colonel, an educated man, compared Min to Abraham Lincoln who also fought to keep his country together.

The French OB/GYN thought that if we elected Barry Goldwater, instead of re-electing LBJ, there would possibly be a nuclear strike against Vietnam, China and North Korea that could escalate into an international apocalypse. I assured him otherwise and dramatically changed the subject.

I asked him for a contact in Nancy for a physician who would perform an abortion in his office. He did not seem surprised or offended but could only offer me a name of a physician that performed abortions in Paris.

I had already referred several women; dependent wives of military men, to a Frankfurt, Germany OB/GYN for first trimester abortions performed in his office. My German friend, who had been a post-doctoral cardiology fellow at Mount Sinai Hospital in Miami Beach, provided the Frankfurt contact for me.

The Frankfurt abortion provider turned out to be a good contact. There had been no complications and his cash fees were by all standards quite reasonable. His fee included a post-abortion visit. I believe that most of the women came to see me at the base hospital for their follow-up examination. Their medical records indicated a routine gynecology visit with no mention of a recent abortion.

The reason I asked the Parisian OB/GYN physician for a contact in Nancy was because of the sergeant's French wife who had her abortion in Nancy unbeknownst to me. This young bride came into our emergency room with a raging pelvic infection. Being a native of Nancy, she preferred to have her pregnancy terminated on her "home turf." Very few Frenchmen in this province traveled to Germany although it was a little over an hour to the frontier. They felt uncomfortable visiting *Allemagne* because they did not speak German and there were still ill feelings against those *Bosche* who had occupied their land three times in less than 100 years.

A local physician performed her abortion in Nancy eight days prior to her visit to our E.R. My colleague, Gordon, the other OB/GYN medical officer was on duty when she arrived. He admitted her and promptly started her on intravenous antibiotics and a much needed blood transfusion.

We saw her together on rounds the next morning. Her admission temperature was 103.6F and now it had dropped to 102F. Her pelvic and abdominal examination was extremely tender to gentle touch and she guarded against our palpation. She was critically ill with a pelvic abscess located behind her uterus. Her laboratory results were consistent with a serious acute infection, i.e. a very high white blood cell count. After two days on I.V. antibiotics the French wife was not any better. Her blood pressure showed signs of dropping on the third day. We feared that she was beginning to go into septic shock, a life-threatening emergency. This syndrome occurs when certain toxins are released by bacteria as they enter the blood stream.

I telephoned a Colonel Paul Stavig at the Wiesbaden Air Force Base Hospital in Germany. He was the Chief Consultant in Europe for the

Air Force Surgeon General. I expressed the anxiety that we had for this young woman's life. In the practice of OB/GYN almost every woman is very young. We mutually agreed that she was in dire need of a transfer to a larger military hospital for optimum care. The colonel said that the best equipped and staffed hospital, and one with an intensive care unit, would be the *Landstuhl* Army Hospital in Germany. He told me that he knew the hospital commander there and would arrange for her transfer. That same day we air-evacuated her in a cargo plan along with a nurse a corpsman and her Air Force husband for the one-hour flight to the army hospital. Gordon and I were in touch with the army OB/GYN physicians on a daily basis by military phone. They had a team of military doctors at work devoting a lot of energy, skill and resources along with technology and medications that our small hospital did not possess.

After several critical days, when her life was hanging in the balance, she began to respond to a new "miracle antibiotic" which I now believe was a *cephalosporin or clindamycin*. Several days hence, when her fever had subsided, the army doctors performed an exploratory laparotomy on her. They removed one badly infected fallopian tube and ovary, a so-called T.O.A., or a tubo-ovarian abscess. They also surgically closed a three-centimeter perforation in the dome of the uterus.

This wound occurred at the time of the abortion almost two weeks prior. The French physician inadvertently allowed an instrument to pass through the safe confines of the pregnant uterus and into the abdominal cavity. Usually a uterine perforation is diagnosed and treated almost immediately. At other times it can be undetected, as it was in this case.

Gordon and I were very pleased that we had transferred our patient at the right time. She recovered normally and was well upon discharge. Over lunch in the hospital dining room we discussed the issues of illegal abortion.

Chapter 22

The Guilt of Our Fathers

The events that led up to World War II began on November 11, 1918, the day that World War I ended with the signing of the Treaty of Versailles. The day would become known as Armistice Day. Several centuries from now both world wars will be called the Twentieth Century Wars since they are only 21 years apart and historically connected. Those horrendous events were ever present in the minds of those who had lived through it in Europe.

My visit to the city of Verdun in northeast France 19 years after the fall of the Nazis provoked anger in me directed against the Germans.

Verdun was the sight of a prolonged and momentous battle in World War I. The French held their ground there despite the horrendous conditions that made trench warfare infamous. The carnage and historic significance is comparable to Hitler's ill-fated attack on Stalingrad.

After the French capitulated in 1940, the Nazis occupied Verdun with great pride. Verdun was where many Germans had lost their lives fighting for the Kaiser and the Fatherland in 1915-16. That was only 25 years before their sons would return and conquer France.

In 1964 I visited Verdun and attended Rosh Hashanah services at the small synagogue. The majority of the congregation was Algerian or Moroccan Jews who immigrated to France after the French were forced out of their African colonies and Arab rule prevailed. There were a few local French natives who had survived the Holocaust. Through conversation I learned that some had survived the horrors of the extermination camps, others had fled to England while a few said they were with the French resistance.

It seemed to me after three years in Europe that every Frenchman had joined the resistance and fought the Nazis and every German was against Hitler and his henchmen.

The locals told me, through our Jewish military liaison officer, that during the Nazi occupation the synagogue was converted to a stable for horses belonging to the *Wehrmacht*. The old wooden pews were removed and stalls were set up in their place. All of the Jews were rounded up and were deported to a staging area near Dracy and then sent by train to extermination camps in the East. Few of them survived.

During the postwar occupation of Germany by the Allies, many U.S. GI's married *frauleins*. Many German women were pleased to be with American military men. The GI had prestige and dollars and was a willing "sugar daddy." There was also a surplus of German women to choose from. The combat losses of the vanquished *Wehrmacht* were somewhere approaching nearly 6 million men including thousands of POWs still languishing in Soviet gulags.

Once married, the GI and his German bride would return to the U.S.A. either as a civilian or as a military family.

On our air base in France there were many airmen who were married to foreign women. The most numerous non-American wives were British, German, French and Japanese. I can recall meeting wives from Italy, the Philippines, Holland, Belgium, wherever the GI was stationed …he came, he saw, he conquered. Or as some Marines like to boast, "We conquered, we saw, we came." Our air base had two OB/GYN physicians assigned to the hospital, Gordon Hanusek and myself. We rotated night call and weekends as well as the prenatal visits of our OB clients. We wanted to be certain that they would have seen both of us at least three visits each whenever possible. This enabled the pregnant client to become familiar with both OB doctors since we never knew who would be on call to eventually deliver her baby. With few exceptions, this protocol was satisfactory to the clients.

Gordon and I were about the same age. We were both married and with children. Our personalities were somewhat similar as well. I would say that we were not authoritarians and possessed a liberal attitude for obstetricians in the 60's. We encouraged childbirth classes, breast-feeding, rooming-in if desired and husbands in the labor and delivery rooms. Most military hospitals did not welcome fathers in the delivery room at this time.

One airman expressed his delight to learn that he could be with his wife when she delivered their baby. I had assured him that was our policy unless there was a C/section. He told me that he was not allowed in the delivery room for their first baby at an air base in Texas. The husband's role in the delivery process was important to them. The airman was an M.P. He had bravely risked his military career by handcuffing himself to his wife as she was being transported to the delivery room. He proceeded to assist his wife with the breathing and pushing learned in their childbirth classes. The delivery room nurses and doctor thought his act of defiance was justified and courageous and humorous. His act of resistance against bureaucratic arrogance helped to open the door for fathers in the delivery room in U.S. military hospitals.

One day the German wife of an airman, after a routine prenatal visit with me, she asked if I would deliver her baby when she went into labor. I explained the on-call rotational system that Gordon and I had incorporated. She in turn assured me that she understood the rationale and advantage of such a policy but would feel much more comfortable if I attended to her delivery. I explained to her that if her delivery took place during the daytime work hours that I would be available any time but Doctor Hanusek and I alternate night and weekend calls. Then I inquired from her if there was a problem or a misunderstanding between her and Doctor Hanusek. She responded with a definite, "Oh, *nein, nein*, he is a good doctor and seems to be a nice person." She ignited my curiosity so I asked her what was the problem. She pronounced my name with the German sound: *shtier*, but spelled Stier. That was how my grandfather said his name to the official on Ellis Island in 1899. He was told that in America we use a softer sound and suggested that he change it to Steir or Steer.

"Doctor Shtier, I feel uncomfortable with Doctor Hanusek because I am a German and he is a Jew. I was a child during the war but I never felt any hate for Jews. I had heard that the Nazis killed the Jews because they were our enemy. So Doctor Hanusek probably hates Germans. I know that he would not harm me because Jews, especially American Jews are not that type of people. My husband would also feel better if you delivered our baby." She appeared somewhat embarrassed but relieved to have confronted me with her dilemma.

My initial reaction was to laugh and tell her that I was Jewish and Gordon was a Christian but I hesitated to do so because I thought it would be very embarrassing for her if I were to reveal the facts. She seemed like a nice woman. I decided to go along with the misunderstanding since I could not think of a way to get around it. So I played along with this harmless deception by telling her that I would deliver her baby if I were not away off the base on leave.

She was quite delighted and relieved of her self-imposed stress. She even gave me a hug along with her *danka*. At that moment I knew that I could not reveal the truth and embarrass or maybe even anger her needlessly.

As it turned out I was on duty the evening that she went into labor. I delivered her baby boy after an uneventful labor. It was her first *kinder*. A few hours after the delivery I went to make rounds on the postpartum patients and I checked on the new German mother who was sleepy and doing well.

Her husband was at the nursery window admiring his new son. The young airman asked me if he should have his son circumcised. "What do you recommend?" he asked. I inquired whether he was circumcised. He replied that he was. I said, casually, "Then yes, have a matching pair, like father like son." He smiled and asked me if I had any children. I told him that I had two little sons, and anticipating his next question, I volunteered that my sons were circumcised, as was I.

I decided that this joyful moment would be the best time to reveal my true ethnicity. I asked him to escort me back to his wife's bedside. There I told them that I had circumcised my own sons on the eighth day of life according to the Jewish tradition. To make the truth complete I went on to reveal that Doctor Hanusek also has two sons who have been circumcised but were raised Catholic like their father.

The German wife was visibly embarrassed but not angry. I eased her discomfort by grasping her hands and telling her that I felt that time heals all wounds. "You and I were not responsible for the nightmare of World War II. You were in diapers when the war ended," I reminded her. She laughed and thanked me for delivering her baby boy.

Later the thought came back to me that time does not always heal all wounds as I had stated. There was that ironic possibility that lingered in my mind that her father might have been one of those willing executioners committing mass murders against the Jews in Eastern Europe not so long ago.

PRIVATE PRACTICE

Chapter 23

To Cut or Not To Cut?

Seattle
1968-1980

I've never read the bible. I have never read the "word of God." I am a Born-Again Atheist and a very secular Jew. The only prayer that I say at times of need is: "God please protect me from your followers."

I have read some of the wisdom of the Talmud and I memorized my birthday portion of the Torah for my Bar Mitzvah in 1944. That was during the time, unknown to me, that my European relatives were being systematically murdered in the extermination camps by Hitler's henchmen.

I do not know what the holy scriptures say about circumcision. A rabbi once told me "God commanded Abraham to circumcise his son Isaac." This was the "Covenant with God" and Abraham complied with the holy order (Genesis 17:10 states that the Lord decreed "this is my covenant.... every man child among you shall be circumcised"). I am not certain of whether this was before or after God commanded Abraham to sacrifice his son Isaac. As we know now God was only testing Abraham's faith. He sent down an angel to grab his knife-wielding hand poised to slit Isaac's young throat. Perhaps God was only kidding about the circumcision order as well.

I had often wondered why the Covenant subscribes circumcision to be performed on the eighth day of life,. Most baby boys born in the United States are not Jewish. These gentile baby boys are circumcised on the first or second day of life and certainly before mother is discharged from the hospital. Some hyperactive obstetricians perform the task shortly after the baby boy is born when they are still in the delivery room. They justify this by claiming, "circumcision causes pain and pain leads to crying which in turn helps clear the baby's lungs." But not everyone is in agreement that traumatizing a newborn gratuitously is a good idea.

The nursery people prefer that they wait a day so that the baby can be kept warm, receive an injection of vitamin K and be generally evaluated and examined by their pediatrician.

I believe that the ancients, in all their wisdom, pounced on day eight for medical reasons that were unappreciated by them at that time. They based their dogma on eons of observation. The newborn's blood does not clot as well at birth as it does a week or so later. Newborns are short on vitamin K that plays a role in the blood clotting process. By the eighth day of life the liver has produced adequate levels of vitamin K from intestinal absorption. Also by observation they noted that some newborns began to turn a yellow color several days after birth. Some of them got well and some died after a week or two. If the newborn did not turn yellow after a week then that meant that they probably would not become jaundiced. The jaundiced babies of course were the second or more newborns of an Rh-negative mother impregnated by an Rh-positive father causing incompatibility and subsequent damage to the red blood cells.

Mothers who are Rh-negative and have an Rh-positive man no longer need worry about the " Rh" incompatibility and a baby sensitized with antibodies that can harm the fetus in-utero.

Since 1968 we have a pharmaceutical product named *Rhogam* that alleviates this problem.

Neonatal sepsis among our forbearers was probably as frequent as maternal mortality. Infected babies surely suffered a high neonatal mortality. Aseptic severing of the umbilical cord was a significant contribution to decreased newborn infection.

These modern days we provide semi-sterile vaginal deliveries and have escaped the scourge of neonatal and maternal sepsis. We obstetricians and midwives have learned of the importance of a clean delivery room and sterile instruments as needed.

It has only been less than 150 years since an Austrian doctor named Ignatz Semmelweis begged the doctors attending births at the Viennese hospitals to please wash their hands after leaving the morgue or wards on their way to the delivery room. It was a known fact that women giving birth at home had a lower mortality rate from infection than those delivering at the city hospitals, and yet Semmelweis was considered crazy at the time for thinking that this fact might be related to microbes spread when hands were not washed. For his audacity to posit such an outlandish theory he was the recipient of hidden and overt anti-Semitic rage.

Today infection is rare thanks to sterile operative technique being used. And newborns receive an injection of vitamin K to enhance the blood clotting mechanism so post-circumcision bleeding almost never occurs.

It must have become clear by scientific deduction of the ancient Hebrews that most newborns that are healthy after a week of life will probably survive to childhood. These lucky baby boys would be deemed low risk for circumcision on the eighth day of life by a process of elimination.

The newborn male of today can be circumcised shortly after birth if so desired by the parents. The Jewish baby boy can now be circumcised during his short hospital stay or he can remain uncircumcised, a growing trend among secular Jews, especially in iconoclastic communities like Berkeley, California. Observant Jews may have a traditional ritual circumcision at home on the eighth day of life. This is a social-religious celebration called a *brit*. *(brit* or *brith* is Hebrew, *bris* is Yiddish) This is a fun time for everyone except the baby boy and his mother. Most Jewish mothers are not too pleased with this social gathering because they understandably dislike someone causing their baby boy to cry and shed a little blood, and they feel that they still look fat and tired so soon after the delivery.

The person that performs this ritual at home is called a *mohel* (pronounced moil). He is a quasi-religious guy trained by another mohel or he could be an ordained rabbi and a trained mohel as well.

So what happened to God's command that Abraham should circumcise his son? Well just think about these little Jewish baby boys having this surgical procedure performed by an untrained father. Abraham must have had great faith indeed to perform this newfangled surgery on his own beloved son. God only knows!!

One need not be a Talmudic scholar to realize that a trained and experienced person-- now called a mohel, should perform this ritual procedure. Abraham's descendants undoubtedly said to the town mohel, "Look you circumcise my son and I'll make you a nice suit." I suppose most commerce began that way.

I have written about my theory of how the task of ritual circumcision became the mohel's job and relieved the father from the covenant equation because I obeyed God's command and I circumcised my sons.

Both of my sons, Philip and Robert, were born at Mount Sinai Hospital in Miami Beach sixteen months apart. I assisted on the first delivery and delivered our second son. Their mother and I had agreed that if I can do routine deliveries and circumcisions as an OB/GYN physician then I should be able to deliver my own babies and obey the command of God at the same time!

The grandparents of course felt otherwise because they did not know about the biblical history and Abraham's duty to obey his God. They only knew that a *mohel* performed a *brit* on a Jewish baby boy. They finally agreed to disagree with our radical approach to this traditional event.

I explained rationally that as a fully trained OB/GYN doctor I had delivered both boys without incident and had a "standby obstetrician" in the delivery room area in case of an unforeseen medical complication.

We agreed that if they buy the wine, sponge cake and a deli platter that I would hire a real live *mohel* to say the blessings in Hebrew while I said the same in English and performed the ritual brit. I circumcised both of our sons in a routine manner and without complications.

Five years later I found myself with my family in far away moistly green and beautiful Seattle. During that five-year hiatus we lived on an Air Force Base in a rural area of Lorraine in Northeastern France for three years and at Travis Air Force Base in California for two years. I requested and received an honorable discharge. My enthusiasm for military life waned as the bloody and needless war in Vietnam went on. I had witnessed too many mortuary flights returning from Vietnam loaded with caskets headed for Travis Air Force Base.

I entered civilian life as a junior partner in a well-established OB/GYN practice. We were expecting our third child shortly after we arrived in Seattle. All the packing and moving in the sixth month of my wife's pregnancy may have added to the obstetrical emergency that ensued in the seventh month.

My wife suddenly developed bright red vaginal bleeding. It occurred in bed while we were asleep. The warm ooze awakened her. She pulled back the covers to show me the bloody sheet. It resembled a Japanese flag.

I knew straight away that sudden painless bleeding in the seventh month would most likely be from a low-lying placenta. The normal and usual site of implantation of the placenta is in the upper portion of the pear-shaped uterus. When it is implanted in the lower segment, above or near the cervix, it is called a placenta previa. During the third trimester of pregnancy the lower part of the uterus begins to thin out and lengthen, allowing an imbedded placenta to partially detach itself from the wall of the uterus, thus causing sudden painless bleeding.

Now it was imperative for my wife to stay in bed until the pregnancy became closer to term, like say, thirty-six weeks into the gestation. That was still four or five weeks away. The bleeding will usually subside; at least for a while, and every day the fetus gets closer to term and further from the morbidity of prematurity. There were two events to avoid with placenta previa: vaginal intercourse and too rigorous a pelvic exam by an overly enthusiastic physician.

I listened for the fetal heartbeat with my ear to her gravid abdomen. It was easy to find and sounded good, completely normal. There was no sign of labor or further bleeding.

My practice partner and my wife's doctor, Sheldon Biback, was away on vacation so her new obstetrician was lying next to her in bed. I thought a second opinion was in order so I called a newfound friend named Thorpe Kelly. I knew Thorpe to be a light-hearted, jolly good Irish-American and arguably one of the busiest and most skilled OB/GYNs in Seattle.

Thorpe agreed with the probable diagnosis of placenta previa. Since her bleeding had ceased after the initial gush and she was in bed, staying there was the treatment of choice. To move her to a hospital would likely increase the chances of further bleeding and could induce labor. We did not want to deliver a baby in the seventh month.

I called Joanne's parents who lived at the New Jersey seashore. Her mother dropped everything and flew out to Seattle. She took over the task of minding two wild little boys, ages five and six and a half. We also had a live-in nanny.

My wife remained on strict bed rest throughout the next six weeks. She had a bedside commode and a hospital-type bed stand on wheels. She was fighting day by day from going stir-crazy. One of the few times that she was home alone was when her mother went out grocery shopping, the boys were in school and I was in my office less than a mile away.

The postman rang twice. This caused our Dalmatian, Dmitri, to bark incessantly. Long after the postman departed, Dmitri continued his annoying barking. JoAnne could no longer tolerate the barking and got out of bed and went down the stairs to the front door where she proceeded to smack the stupid dog with a rolled up newspaper.

She hemorrhaged on her way back upstairs. She called me at the office. When I arrived home straight away she had stopped bleeding and was in no apparent distress. I called her obstetrician Thorpe Kelly. We agreed that now that she was only three weeks from term it would be advisable to take her to the hospital for evaluation, observation and possible delivery. Shortly thereafter her mother returned and the boys came home from school. I drove Joanne to Northwest hospital for admission.

This was the suburban hospital that Thorpe Kelly and I performed most of our inpatient OB/GYN. Thorpe came over to say hello and ordered the necessary lab work and routine orders for a third trimester bleed. He ordered a "soft tissue placenta-gram" to attempt to visualize the location of the placenta in relation to the uterus and the baby. Today sonograms are used to identify the location of the placenta. Sonograms, like antenatal gender identification, were not available in 1968.

The placenta-gram revealed, as we had suspected, a low-lying placenta that was ominously implanted too close to the opening of the cervix. The head of the fetus was adjacent to the edge of the placenta as if it were a pillow.

Thorpe Kelly went back to his office in the Ballard section of Seattle, about five miles away. JoAnne was typed and cross-matched for two units of whole blood to be held in reserve in case of a serious hemorrhage. The labor room nurse started an I.V. in JoAnne's arm to have an open vein in the advent of an emergency.

Four hours after arriving at the hospital JoAnne began to cramp and to feel her uterus become intermittently firm like a flexed muscle. She was in labor. Soon afterwards she began to pass small blood clots from her vagina. This is a warning sign, like a smoking volcano, that more bleeding is soon to come. The edge of the placenta, rich in blood vessels, is slowly shearing and tearing away from the uterine wall. Blood accumulates in the lower segment of the uterus where it will clot and then pass through the cervical opening and out of the vagina.

I called Thorpe Kelly at his office in Ballard. Thorpe's office manager informed me that he was just finishing a delivery at Ballard hospital next door to his office. I told her to contact Doctor Kelly and tell him that my wife, his patient, was in labor and passing blood clots.

There are three delivery rooms at Northwest hospital. One of these rooms is set up to be available for caesarian sections. I instructed the nurse-in-charge and the on call in-house anesthesiologist that Doctor Kelly was on his way to the hospital and that they should transport my wife to the C/section room and prepare for a "double set-up." The purpose of a "double set-up" is to perform a pelvic exam on the patient in a delivery/operating room and have the room set-up for an immediate C/section if needed or to proceed on with labor hoping for a safe vaginal delivery. The pelvic exam is to evaluate the relation of the fetal head to the placenta and to palpate the cervix to discover any significant dilatation.

We transported JoAnne on a gurney cart to the operating room across the hall. It was unusually quiet in the labor and delivery suite on this summer afternoon. Usually there are one or two patients in labor or in the delivery room. The doctor's lounge within the labor suite was also void of any obstetricians.

JoAnne passed more blood clots as she was moved from the gurney to the narrow operating table. I ordered a unit of whole blood that had been set aside hours before. The nurse used a hand held Doppler that magnified the fetal heart sounds. Significant internal and external fetal monitoring was in its infancy and unavailable in 1968. The fetal heart rate showed some signs of distress. We began to administer oxygen to JoAnne via a nasal catheter. She appeared to be calm and her vital signs were normal. The administration of oxygen was to saturate her blood and thereby deliver more oxygenated blood to the fetus via the placenta and umbilical cord. I continued to look out the O.R. door hoping to see Thorpe Kelly.

Doctor Gerald Flowers, an expatriate from England, was the anesthesiologist on call. He administered a spinal anesthetic without difficulty. I was at the sink outside the O.R. scrubbing up and looking through the window with one eye on JoAnne and the other eye peering down the corridor looking for Thorpe.

I felt assured and comfortable about performing a C/section on my wife. This was a procedure that I performed very frequently during the past ten years.

In the O.R. JoAnne smiled and whispered, "Hey Brucie let's get our kid out of there." She could not point to her abdomen because both arms were affixed to boards for I.V.s, monitoring and restraint. I told her that was exactly what I was going to do. I reminded her that I delivered our two boys and now it was time for the third baby.

After prepping and draping the lower abdomen I checked the level of anesthesia by pinching the skin with surgical tweezers over the area to be incised. The level of numbness was appropriate for the procedure to begin.

"Any sign of Doctor Kelly?" I inquired.

"Not yet," came the reply of the circulating nurse. She then added, "Are you up for doing this section now Doctor Steir?"

"Yes, of course I am. I have been doing this sort of thing for a living the past ten years. It isn't as if I was going to open her chest. This is my area of expertise," I boasted.

With a scalpel I made a seven-inch transverse incision through the skin just above the shaved pubic hairline. This is commonly referred to as a "Bikini cut." The incision was then carried down through the sparse layer of fatty tissue just below the skin. Small bleeders were clamped and tied with thin chromic suture. My assistant was a very capable O.R. nurse who had scrubbed in with me many times before. She cut the ends of the ligatures down to the knots. The underlying abdominal muscles were easily separated in the midline with my index fingers gliding them laterally in order to expose the shiny white fascia below.

This thick sheath of connective tissue was opened with blunt scissors also in a transverse manner.

Thorpe Kelly now appeared at the scrub sink. We made eye content. I was pleased to see him and acknowledged his presence with a nod of my head.

I lifted the peritoneum--a thin shiny, almost translucent layer of tissue that separates the outside world from the interior of our abdominal cavity. This is opened easily with the rounded tips of scissors.

Thorpe came into the O.R. and the circulating nurse gowned and gloved him. "Sorry I'm late. I got here as fast as I could. The answering service told me that you had called just as I was delivering a baby at Ballard. How's it going?" he inquired.

I assured him that everything was under control and that we had a good spinal and we were ready to open the uterus. I asked Thorpe, "Why don't you take over and I will assist you. O.K.?"

Thorpe, a burly jovial man with a Brooklyn sense of humor agreed and jokingly quipped, "I would be honored to take over and hope that this patient has good medical insurance for the primary surgeon."

Thorpe, a Columbia University trained OB/GYN, began to systematically open the uterus. He first dissected the outer thin layer off of the lower segment of the uterus that is also the roof of the urinary bladder. He pushed it downward and I placed a wide retractor over it to place it out of harm's way.

The muscle of the lower uterus was opened with a transverse incision exposing the amniotic sac. The clear, yellow tinged fluid was allowed to escape with a welcomed gush from a small puncture with a scalpel.

"Thorpe, I want to lift our baby out if it is OK with you."

"Be my guest," he replied as a matter of fact. My opened right hand reached down into the opened uterine cavity and felt its way below the baby's head. I could feel the ear and the curly wet hair as I lifted the head through the uterine incision. Thorpe used a blue bulb syringe to suction the mucous from the baby's nostrils and mouth. I lifted the lower shoulder out with gentle upward traction of the head. The shoulder and arm popped out of the uterine incision.

Then, as almost routine, the upper shoulder and arm slid out from below the uterine incision. The baby was lifted upward with one hand behind the nape of the neck and the other hand on the lower back.

Our newborn daughter was placed on the drapes above the surgical area. She gave forth a lusty, healthy cry. The umbilical cord was doubly clamped and cut.

A sleepy voice came out from behind the draped off area. "What do we have?"

"Well JoAnne, we will not have to deal with another *bris*," I shouted.

"Is it really a girl?" she cried.

The anesthesiologist administered medications to relax her abdominal wall in order to ease its closure and serve as a sedative for the mother. I picked our baby up and moved toward JoAnne's face.

"What is the name we decided on?" I asked.

She looked and replied, "Oh it is a baby girl. Her name is Laurel Anne."

I had chosen the name from the neighborhood where we lived in Seattle called Laurelhurst.

Laurel Anne cried and I handed her to the nurse. Our pediatrician, Lester Mackoff, was waiting for Laurel Anne in the newborn nursery.

Chapter 24

Abortion Is a Sin unless.... I need one

For almost everyone else it was just another gray and rainy day in Seattle. For my OB/GYN practice partner and me it was a special day. Roe v. Wade had just become the law of the land. In 1973 abortions in the state of Washington could be performed only in a hospital setting and only with in-patient status. That meant a hospital admission and included the occasional scorn, sarcasm and humiliation of hospital staff directed at a woman who chose not to have a baby. Having to be admitted into a hospital to obtain an abortion also greatly (and unnecessarily) increased the cost of the procedure. The state law was almost punitive for women. But alas and at last it was legal!

On that day in January 1973 when abortion became legal I had scheduled, in advance, four consecutive abortion procedures in the same operating room at Northwest Hospital in Seattle. That was where we delivered all our OB patients and performed almost all of our gynecologic operative procedures. My partner and I had supplied the hospital with the necessary instruments and vacuum suction machine.

While I was at the scrub sink preparing for case number two I was verbally assaulted. The chief of the OB/GYN service strolled by on his way to another operating room. He did not even stop but just slowed down as he stabbed me in the back with this comment, "Well, tell me, Bruce, how many babies are you going to kill today?"

He was down the hall before I could answer him. It was just as well because I do not usually spout out *bon mots* like Oscar Wilde. I was not expecting such a salutation from a man who I thought was my friend. It took a moment or two for me to digest what I had just heard. It then dawned on me that he had recently left his wife and children, ironically, to marry a young born-again Christian. Her influence on him was not only on his attitude about abortion but also on the décor in his office. The anti-abortion doctor's waiting room was recently adorned with several large paintings that appeared to be reproductions of various scenes from the life of Jesus and his followers. It drove his practice partner of many years to move out and dissolve their very successful professional relationship. He told me that he too was a good Christian and a family man but he could no longer tolerate his partner's judgmental intolerance veiled as Christian zeal.

The anti-abortion doctor had his office in the same medical building that my office was in. We were on different floors and obviously we tried to avoid each other.

About a year after that nasty scrub-sink encounter I received a phone call from him. He said hello, skipped the polite formalities of meaningless conversation, and reminded me that he was anti-abortion and he knew that I was doing abortions on a regular daily basis. He said that he would very much appreciate my doing an abortion on his teenage family member. He concluded his request by offering me a compliment of sorts. He told me that he was sorry to have to call on me for such an unpleasant favor but he wanted his relative to be in "good hands" with an experienced abortion provider. This time, at least, he did not call me a "baby killer."

I was shocked at the hypocrisy of it, but as a doctor I was glad to be of assistance in helping with this crisis.

A few days later his eleventh grade blood relative came to my office for her appointment to have an abortion. At this point in time the state of Washington was allowing abortions to be performed in an outpatient facility. If the law had not been changed and his young relative had needed to go to a hospital for an abortion then she would have gone out of town or had an illegal abortion or perhaps would have the baby and leave school. As it were, she was shy and uneasy, as one would expect, this being her first OB/GYN examination. Her pregnancy was only eight weeks gestation. I performed her abortion under local anesthesia without incident.

During her visit we did not discuss anything about her family's abortion philosophy or their religious activism.

I provided her with oral contraceptive pills at her request and my suggestion. After she left my office I called her family relative downstairs and told him that all had gone well and that she was fine. He thanked me.

His rude insult was the first of many that would come my way in the years to follow as an OB/GYN abortion provider. Most abortion providers, I'm sure, at some point have had a similar experience. I am also sure that my fellow abortion providers do not think of themselves as "baby killers," just as manufacturers of contraception do not think so. We are women helpers. That is what an OB/GYN physician is supposed to be.

Abortion should not be a morality issue. Abortion should not be a political football. Abortion is about a woman's reproductive health. It is that simple. Abortion is a surgical or medical procedure that involves a woman and her abortion provider physician or nurse specialist. Politicians, theocrats and vindictive misogynists have no place in this private and difficult decision-making by a woman who wishes to exercise her right to choose how she will live her life. We are not at the mercy of our reproductive processes as the animals are; we can choose how we will live. As the old T-shirt slogan goes: "Not the church/ Not the state/ Women must decide their fate."

One day perhaps we will have the courage to welcome each and every child into this world with open arms as it deserves to be welcomed. That will require a complete reordering of priorities and infrastructure, including interpersonal infrastructure. The top two reasons women have abortions, marital status and economics, are not personal at all but institutional and as such can be solved. Until then, abortion is necessary.

I do not need a poll to tell me that only 22% of Americans are anti-abortion. But the legality of abortion should not be decided by a popularity contest. That is unless those voting are sitting judges on the United States Supreme Court.

Chapter 25
A Larger Venue Is Needed

The first night out on a backpacking trip in the Mount Rainier National Park in Washington State, Doctor T and our children all sat around a bonfire to tell stories, keep warm and roast somores for snacking. After the children turned into their tents, Dr. T and I drank some wine that we had hauled along in our aluminum framed backpacks.

It had occurred to me for several years that Dr. T was a very busy OB/GYN physician. He had been in Seattle for a good number of years. Dr. T and his partner delivered more babies than any other obstetrician at the Northwest Hospital in Seattle. Dr. T alone performed approximately ten hysterectomies a month. That was in addition to other surgeries such as exploratory laparotomies, C-sections and sterilization procedures. Dr. T was raised in New York City and trained at Columbia Presbyterian Hospital in Manhattan. His low complication rate reflected his excellent training in operative skills. In addition, Dr. T possessed Clintonesque looks and personality; he had a rakish good-old-boy demeanor about him. Dr. T was a real Irish *mensch*.

I too was in a well-established OB/ GYN practice. My older partner had been in Seattle for about the same length of time, maybe even longer than Dr. T. My partner and I were scheduling about two hysterectomies a month between the two of us.

At the campsite fire I asked my friend, Dr. T, how his practice generated so many hysterectomies as compared to my practice. Before he could answer I conceded to the fact that my practice had a younger clientele than his, partly because my practice was near the University of Washington campus. Dr. T. candidly responded, " I have a salmon fishing boat with monthly payments, and an expensive home with high mortgage payments, two offices, two children and a wife that likes to shop." He smiled an Irish smile and placed his large hand on my shoulder and added, "Besides, anything that bleeds every month has got to be bad." That is an old gynecologists' joke that I had heard before but this time it did not seem too funny.

Dr. T was never to my knowledge, confronted by the Surgical Tissue Review Committee for performing unnecessary surgery. Had Dr. T been troubled with complications that would have raised the red flag and brought his misadventures to the attention of the Review Committee. For example, when a surgeon performs an appendectomy, he/she must dictate or write a pre-operative diagnosis of appendicitis. This pronouncement should then be followed by a post-operative diagnosis of appendicitis. If the surgeon removes too many normal appendixes with a pre-op and a post-op diagnosis of appendicitis, the Committee would discipline him or her. This could be a mere a slap on the wrist warning or at worst a suspension of surgical privileges for a specified period of time.

In gynecology, when a uterus is removed (a hysterectomy) with a pre-operative diagnosis of "dysfunctional uterine bleeding," the pathology tissue report can be a "normal uterus." Abnormal uterine bleeding such as inter-menstrual spotting or prolonged heavy periods (menorrhagia) will not always be due to abnormalities that can be seen grossly or microscopically in the removed uterus. Abnormal uterine bleeding is frequently due to a hormonal imbalance between the functions of the pituitary gland, the ovaries, and the uterus. So gynecologists can treat dysfunctional uterine bleeding with hormone therapy once they rule out endometriosis, pelvic tumors (including cancer) and ovarian cysts. If hormone therapy fails to solve the problem then usually a D & C is performed. If the D & C shows normal tissue and the woman continues to have abnormal bleeding, then some gynecologists will suggest a hysterectomy. This common operative procedure can be performed by removing the uterus by way of the vagina, especially in women who have had a previous vaginal delivery, or by the abdominal route as needed.

It's now been documented that too many unnecessary hysterectomies were being done in this country in the not-too-recent past.

The doctor's lounge for the labor and delivery room suite at Northwest Hospital was a frequent hangout for the OB/GYN doctors. It was there that they could chat socially, make phone calls, have a cup of coffee, take a nap, dictate a surgical procedure such as a C-section or follow a patient's progress in labor.

The week following the backpacking trip to Mt. Rainier National Park, I found myself dwelling on the flippant, self-serving and comical reason that Dr. T had suggested as the source of his numerous hysterectomies. I mischievously placed a poster on the bulletin board in the doctor's lounge. It was handwritten with a black marking pen. The sign read, "There will be a meeting of all the women who have had hysterectomies by Dr. T. The get-together will be at the Kingdome stadium in Seattle." Hours after I posted the sign and had left the hospital, I had the sinking feeling that it may not be taken as a joke but could be misconstrued as a vindictive message and not one of good humor.

I returned to the doctor's lounge to remove the sign the following morning when I visited the hospital to make rounds. I discovered that it had already been removed.

Two days later there appeared a new message printed on a notepad sheet and attached to my silly note and posted on the bulletin board. The new sign read:

"CHANGE OF VENUE:
KINGDOME TOO SMALL
MEETING WILL COMMENCE
WHEN ADEQUATE SIZE FACILITY BECOMES AVAILABLE"

Once again Dr. T's cavalier attitude regarding unnecessary surgery was overlooked, as were the pain, inconvenience, and expense suffered by scores of women. He was insensitive but had a sense of humor. Maybe he was doing a service that he thought was good gynecology. Unnecessary surgery is, after all, a relative term not unlike affluence or hypocrisy.

Chapter 26

Easter Egg Hunt In Seattle

It was raining on Easter Sunday. That is not much of a surprise when you are living in Seattle. I was enjoying an early dinner at nephew Fred's restaurant in downtown Seattle in Pioneer Square near the brand new Kingdome stadium. That was in 1974. Since then the Kingdome was imploded and a new stadium was built.

Fred's restaurant was the Salad Gallery. Like the Kingdome it has also vanished into mismanagement oblivion. The eatery was called the Salad Gallery because it specialized in large healthy and affordable salads of every type imaginable. They also displayed the art of a one-person show that decorated the walls.

My answering service beeped me on my pager. They informed me that Ms Q was having an urgent gynecology problem and needed to speak with me.

I knew Ms Q, having delivered her baby some two or three years back. She was a pleasant woman but not too swift in the IQ department. Since her baby's birth she had become somewhat neurotic following a divorce.

Q. told me that she was sorry to bother me on a Sunday, especially Easter Sunday and hoped that she did not wake me. I assured her that I had not been asleep (it was 7 P.M.) and she was not to worry about bothering me.

She related by phone that her two and a half year old daughter had put an Easter egg into her vagina. "Are you certain that it was an egg?" I begged quizzically. "Yes it was an egg" she insisted. "One of those colored ones for the Easter holiday."

Needless to say the disproportion in size ratio between her little daughter's vagina and an Easter egg had me confused and wondering what was going on. I asked the worried mother how her daughter was reacting to this bizarre penetration.

Q. stated that her daughter was crying and touching her vaginal area but did not appear to be crying from pain. She also told me that she could see the entrapped Easter egg when she used her thumb and index finger to spread open the small lips of her daughter's vagina. "Now," I said calmly, "an Easter egg might go into *your* vagina because you are a grown woman and you have also given birth to a baby. But your little girl's vagina is much too small to accommodate an egg."

Little girls often insert small objects into their vagina. An eraser from a pencil, a Roosevelt dime and a paper clip come to mind from my own clinical experience. I removed those foreign bodies with the aid of a nasal speculum gently inserted near the opening of the vagina and a surgical tweezers for the removal of the misplaced object. But never an egg!

I queried Ms.Q as to why she thought this misplaced object was an egg. She insisted that it was so because she had placed five Easter eggs on a small plate for her daughter to enjoy. Then she told me that she noticed that there were only four eggs on the plate and her child was sitting on the couch crying and touching her "private parts". Then Ms Q finally made the egg misadventure clear to me. She asked her daughter where the foil wrapper was. The little girl opened her hand to reveal the colored foil wrapper.

"O.K.", I claimed, "so she put an Easter egg chocolate candy in her vagina instead of her mouth" Ms Q agreed that was indeed the case. She asked "What should I do now Doctor Steir?"

I gave that some thought for three seconds. You can take her to the E.R. or you can place her in a tub with warm water. "Mind you", I warned, "not too hot so you won't scald her." Then I began to think out loud. "The chocolate should melt if it hasn't already because the vagina is 98.6 degrees."

Ms.Q. said she would try the hot bath treatment and if it did not expel the Easter egg then she would go to the E.R. and call me. I reminded her once again that she must not make the water too hot and should test the temperature with her elbows before submerging her child. I also strongly advised her to refer to the object as an Easter chocolate candy and not as an egg. She agreed to do so.

I told her that I would call her back in an hour to find out how it went. I urged her not to put any object, like her finger or tweezers into the vagina.

On my call back to Ms. Q she assured me that the warm bath water had turned a murky brown and smelled like a Hershey bar. Her daughter had stopped crying and had just helped herself to another Easter egg candy. This time she had placed it in her mouth.

US Navy

CHAPTER 27

The Sailor From Twenty-Nine Palms

1980-1985

In 1980, after twelve years of skyrocketing malpractice insurance premiums while I was in private practice in Seattle, I decided to get out of the rain. I joined the United States Navy. I actually had seen a recruitment poster outside the gate of the Sandpoint Naval Station. This military facility was one block down the lake from my waterfront home. The poster was seductive. It promised pay, travel, adventure and advancement. I called the recruitment officer and expressed my desire to enlist. I also informed him that I had served in the Air Force from 1963 till 1968. He informed me that the Navy was in very short supply of OB/GYN physicians. He went on to state that if I had received an honorable discharge and if I could "fog a mirror" then I was as good as in the Navy.

As a Board Certified member of the American Board of Obstetricians and Gynecologists I was eligible to re-enter the Armed Forces with one rank higher than at my discharge twelve years prior. I was honorably discharged from the Air Force as a Major. One rank higher would be a Lieutenant Colonel. In Navy ranks that is equivalent to a Commander.

When I was asked if I had a duty station location preference on an enlistment form I did not hesitate in requesting my geographic desire. The form asked for preference number one, two and three.

All three of mine were Navy hospitals in California. My desire to be stationed in California was not based on good weather but on the fact that my three children had moved from Seattle to the Bay Area with their mother after our divorce in 1973.

When I finally received my orders to report for active duty I was pleased because the Navy came through with their promise to station me in California. My orders read for me to report to Camp Pendleton Marine Corps Base near San Diego. I knew that the Navy had a large hospital on this sprawling training base. The Marine Corps does not have its own medical corps. They use Naval facilities for their medical and dental care.

After my drive down the "left coast" from Seattle to Oceanside, the hospital commander and the seven OB/GYN Navy physicians that I would be working with greeted me cordially. At least that is what I had assumed until I was handed a new set of orders. I was ordered to report to the Navy Branch Hospital at the Marine Corps Base at Twenty-Nine Palms, California. This "satellite facility" of Camp Pendleton is located on the high elevation of the Mojave Desert about one hour from Palm Springs.

Twenty-Nine Palms is a combat exercise base. It is where our Marines learn their combat skills and test their new weapons. Ground and air war games are carried out here in the security of the isolation of the desert. This is where the infantry grunts learn warfare skills alongside tank maneuvers and where the Marines employ new anti-tank devices and tank drivers learn to destroy these weapons. Except for the Joshua trees, the bleak vast desert expanse and purple-hued mountains might make you think you were on the moon. That notion is dispelled when fighter jets roar in over the base and release rockets that slam into discarded tanks for target practice. I was in awe at their accuracy as viewed from a command outpost many miles out in the desert. These fighter jets are usually aircraft carrier based perhaps one or two hundred miles away. They arrive in combat formation within fifteen to twenty minutes, hit their targets and then disappear.

Temperatures at Twenty-Nine Palms can range from 45°F to 105°F in the same day. This is where I was to serve as the solo OB/GYN physician and Senior Medical Officer for almost three years. Ours was a small but busy hospital. We delivered around 25 babies a month and supported an outpatient clinic that served a base full of male and female Marines plus the dependents of the active duty and retired Marines.

The Navy had billeted two OB/GYN medical officers for Twenty-Nine Palms. As it were there was another Navy OB/GYN on board when I arrived. I soon learned, much to my dismay, that she had recently received her orders for a humanitarian separation from the Navy. So with her departure I was "it." I would be on call for obstetrics, as we say today, 24/7—a heavy load for any one physician to bear. Camp Pendleton, my mother superior hospital, turned down my request to transfer one of their seven OB/GYNs to fill the recently vacated billet.

The OB/GYN department at Camp Pendleton was a good old boys club. They were "fat" in doctor billets and intended to keep it that way. They must have figured out that being on call in the hospital every seventh night was better than every sixth night. The Chief of the department, Captain Jim Hebert, was a prince of a man having served on active duty past his twenty years for retirement purposes. Jim sensed that there was an inequity of their staff manpower as compared to mine on the lonely desert outpost two hours away. He made a generous compensation for me.

The Captain so decreed that every month I would be granted a 96-hour, or four days' relief from duty by way of sending one of their doctors to Twenty-Nine Palms. This "96", as it was to be called, would not be counted against my 30 days of annual leave allowed by the Navy. This "96" would begin on Thursday afternoon and end on Monday afternoon. During this free time I could stay home and stare at the vast desert landscape or go off to wherever I pleased. I did not stay at home. Not even once.

As for the visiting OB/GYN from Camp Pendleton they were welcome to stay in my three bedroom, air conditioned on-base house with all its amenities or they could rent a room at the Bachelors Officers Quarters (BOQ) just down the street from the hospital. All but one of the physicians agreed to stay in my on base quarters. The lone dissenter was Ali, an Iranian born U.S. Navy medical officer who thanked me for offering up my home but stated that he would rather stay in the BOQ then lower himself to the task of feeding Lover, my elderly orange-stripped cat.

The civilian pharmacist at the base hospital, at my request, told me which doctors were performing abortions in the area. I knew from experience that I would need such information sooner or later to refer patients. Abortions were legal in all the states since Roe v. Wade passed in 1973. The procedure was off limits in all military hospitals at home and abroad…and still is today.

The pharmacist told me of an OB/GYN in Palm Desert, a suburb of Palm Springs that performed abortions in his office. When I called him he invited me to come down and to meet him and visit his office facilities. After my short visit the doctor was kind enough to offer a discount to all military women and dependent wives or daughters needing or wanting an abortion. He realized that the salary of an enlisted Marine was barely above the poverty line and that fact would justify lowering his usual fee. Before I left his office he inquired as to when I thought the military would begin to allow abortions performed at their facilities. "When is the military going to get in step with the law of the land? Roe v. Wade was seven years ago." I responded with a simple and factual answer. I told him that it would never happen as long as we have Reagan and his ilk in power. Middle-aged men do not get pregnant. If they did then the anniversary of Roe v. Wade would be a national holiday.

The first woman to see me in my gynecology clinic who wanted to have an abortion was a lance corporal's wife. She was in her early twenties and was the overweight mother of two young children. Her Marine Corps husband was away on temporary duty (tdy) on a "float" aboard a ship on a Pacific Fleet Exercise. Those floats usually lasted three to six months in duration.

Her husband had been gone about eight weeks and by pelvic exam she was about ten weeks pregnant. The gestational age coincided with her menstrual history.

I learned the hard way early in my OB/GYN career never to assume two things: that every pregnancy was a wanted one, and that every woman was a straight heterosexual. With these assumptions in mind it was comfortable for me to say to a patient with a newly discovered pregnancy, "Are congratulations in order?" Bear in mind that a woman has only three options when she discovers that she is "with child":

1) Have a baby and keep it.

2) Have a baby and adopt it out.

3) Have an abortion.

The Marine's wife was referred to Doctor Durante's office for her abortion procedure. This was her choice. Her husband was not involved with any decision-making or information. Clearly the physical and emotional burden of yet another child was hers to bear and raise and not so much as for her Marine husband.

It was at her visit that Doctor Durante's question became meaningful and buzzed around in my mind. When would the military provide an abortion at a military hospital or pay for one at a civilian facility? After giving her preoperative instructions for her abortion procedure and the written directions to the clinic, she inquired how much money she would need to pay for the abortion. I told her that Doctor Durante's fee for less then twelve weeks gestation was $300. That is not a staggering amount of money for a surgical procedure but is a definite dent in the budget of a lance corporal's family. She also asked me if Doctor Durante or I would have to notify her husband. I told her that it was not a requirement to do so. That would be for her to decide. I reminded her that even if the military allowed me to perform her abortion that they would be obligated to notify her Marine husband aboard a ship or wherever he was located.

The next referral for an abortion was for a Marine captain whom I had delivered only four months prior. She and her Marine Corps officer husband had failed to use proper contraception. A well-meaning relative assured them that breast-feeding moms cannot get pregnant because they do not ovulate as long as they are lactating. The truth is that breast-feeding moms usually do not ovulate in the first six months postpartum. The key word here is *usually*. Both husband and wife were present in my office when I confirmed the new pregnancy. They both agreed that another baby was not wanted at this time.

After providing them with the necessary information needed regarding the abortion procedure, I launched into a derisive commentary on the sad state of affairs that has been caused by the military's refusal to provide coverage for an abortion procedure for active duty personnel. I asked them if they were told when they joined the Marine Corps that the military would provide them with medical and dental care. They responded in agreement that the recruiter did promise that benefit. The husband interjected that the recruiter's spiel was that if the medical service was not available at their duty station then they were allowed to go on *"Champus"* for that service and the military would pay the provider through an insurance company like Blue Cross. Champus is a program that allows military active duty and their dependents and retired military people to receive civilian medical care when the nearest military facility does not have the capabilities needed. This arrangement is even more prominent today with so many military base closures over the past decade.

I reminded them that Champus would not cover the abortion and that they would have to pay for the procedure. The husband replied that he never thought about *Champus* paying for an abortion procedure. "We knew that would not be covered," she said.

It made little sense to me that having an abortion was not a recognized part of their medical care just as having a baby is. I explained that I could, with their permission, admit her to the hospital today and perform a tubal ligation for sterilization. That would be covered by the military. In fact, I told them, here at Twenty-Nine Palms I perform about three voluntary sterilization procedures a week. That is part of their medical care and their reproductive care. The sterilization procedure prevents future unwanted pregnancies and an abortion terminates an existing one, so what really is the difference? An existing pregnancy that is not wanted is an accident or a mistake. It doesn't really matter which it is. People make mistakes and as long as they do there will be erasers on pencils and delete keys on keyboards.

My diatribe continued. The Marine couple was beginning to show interest in my annoyance with the federal attitude on abortion in military hospitals. I told them that the U.S. political people in power are telling the military doctors who are capable and willing to perform an abortion that they do not care if abortion is the law of the land according to the Supreme Court. "You won't be doing any abortions in our military facilities. What's more, if the woman wants an abortion she can go off base and have one, but we aren't paying for it. Now I believe that is chutzpah," I concluded.

The Marine officer, a gorgeous woman and a Mormon, asked me what is a "cute's bar." I explained it as best as I could. Chutzpah, I explained, is a Yiddish or Hebrew word used to express extreme gall, audacity or insolence by being very nervy. As an example I related the well-known story about a man who murders his parents. He is apprehended and stands before the judge and pleads, "Your honor, you wouldn't send an orphan to prison would you?" Now that is chutzpah.

I then suggested to the couple that they write to their home state Senators or Congress people and complain that the Marine Corps is not providing them with the medical care that was promised to them when they enlisted. Because they are both officers, I thought that should have an impact. A squeaking wheel gets oiled, I thought.

I went on with this verbal scenario for the next few years whenever I needed to refer a client to a civilian abortion provider. That was between the years of 1980 and 1985 during which time I served as a medical officer in the Navy. Even after the Clinton administration in the White House for eight years it is still forbidden to perform abortions in a military hospital. President Bill Clinton's efforts to change that ban in overseas military hospitals, like in Germany or Okinawa, failed.

During the Gulf War I worked in a woman's clinic in Oakland, California. On two occasions I saw military women who were being seen for post-abortion checkups. Their stories were quite similar. One was a sailor who had become pregnant while serving on an aircraft carrier in the Persian Gulf. The other was a soldier, age eighteen, who found herself in that predicament while serving on a base in Kuwait. They both were told that they could go on leave back to the U.S.A. if they so desired an abortion. They would not have any priority on a military flight because their need to go home was not considered an emergency or a medical necessity. They could hop a military flight as a standby but because of their lower enlisted status their chances of being on a manifest list was dim. They could not afford a commercial flight home. They related to me that their senior corps women advised them to go on leave to Israel.

They flew to Cairo and then on to Tel-Aviv via Air Egypt, a one-hour flight, for a roundtrip airfare of roughly $175 at the time. When they arrived at Ben-Gurion Airport they had instructions to look for a military shuttle bus that would take them to an Israeli Defense Force base near Haifa. Their official leave papers did not explain their mission. They were housed overnight at the base hospital and fed in the base mess hall. The young sailor was surprised that everyone spoke near-perfect English. The large number of women in uniform on the base also amazed the soldier.

They were admitted to the hospital in the morning and met the Army doctor who was to perform the abortion. They had a sonogram to confirm their pregnancy. Their dog tags confirmed their blood type. Their abortions were performed under light intravenous sedation. It was of interest to me, as an abortion provider, to learn that their abortion was performed under direct visualization with a sonogram machine. This is a discipline that is not always adhered to in the U.S.A., but certainly is the best way to assure that the abortion is completed properly and safely.

They were encouraged to stay overnight in the hospital. One did but the other woman decided she was feeling well enough to hop a bus to Jerusalem to visit some of the holy sights before flying back to Kuwait via Cairo. Neither woman had to make any financial payments. They were told that "military allies" are entitled to medical care at no expense.

While I am remembering the policies and attitude of the military regarding abortion, allow me to digress to an interesting experience I had in Alaska.

The U.S. Navy has a base on the small island of Adak. This is near the westernmost end of the Aleutian chain that fans out from the main landmass of Alaska and stops short of Siberia. During World War II the Japanese landed on several of these islands but were eventually repelled. I was told that Adak had underground nuclear missiles at the time. The base has a small Navy hospital. The pediatrician, surgeon and OB/GYN physicians are rotated to Adak from Navy bases in the "lower forty-eight," mostly from large Navy hospitals in California. The rotation is for six weeks and is unaccompanied by family. For most people six weeks on Adak is enough.

Recently, having become single, I was pleased to have a six-week reprieve from my desert hideaway. I would never have a free trip to the Aleutian Islands again, so why not go? Besides I was reading about the fighting that took place there in World War II and was fascinated that the Japanese had attempted to invade Adak. The Navy recruiters always push that "pay, travel and adventure" slogan. So off I went to Adak.

Most of the military assigned to Adak are Marines. Marines do a lot of saluting. They seem to seek out officers just to render them a snappy salute. That is what I recall as my fondest memory of Adak. In order to return the salute I had to place my left hand on top of my military hat and salute with the right hand. The wind that blows across the Aleutians was always present and never less then thirty knots. Even the snow blew sideways. The tough part was when I was carrying a package out of the Post Exchange and trying to return a salute without losing my hat. I soon learned to return their salutes with an exaggerated nod and a sincere smile.

There was a serene and mystic beauty in the distant landscape from Adak to the islands on each side of the chain. The snow-capped mountains seem to rise right out of the horizon. Their sight was breathtaking, especially as the sun was rising or setting in the distance.

A sign on the small island lured me to the "Adak National Forest." The surgeon and I drove the short distance in a Navy van. The interior of the van contained a large slab of concrete between the front and rear seats, I was told, to decrease the possibility of the van overturning and becoming a victim of the relentless Aleutian winds. We should have known that the sign was strictly GI humor. The so-called National Forest consisted of a single silver birch tree surrounded by a six-foot chain link fence. Trees do not grow naturally on Adak because of the cold wind. The other sign of note also turned out not to be a joke. It was an official looking black and gold road sign warning that stated simply, "Caution--Otter Crossing."

Once a week, weather permitting, a Navy PBY seaplane flew to Tanaga and Kanaga, nearby islands just west of Adak. These islands are, as I was told, considered Indian reservations for Aleut natives. The PBY picks up those Aleuts who have appointments at the Adak Naval Hospital. Apparently the Bureau of Indian Affairs (BIA) had an arrangement with the Navy to provide medical care for them. I saw two Aleut women patients during my six-week tour on Adak. One was for monthly prenatal checkups when she was in her fifth and six months. When she would be 36 weeks (eighth month) she would have a weekly pelvic exam, then she would be admitted to the hospital when her cervix felt "ripe" or imminent for the onset of labor. She was obese and hypertensive and admitted to being an alcoholic but denied consuming alcohol during this pregnancy.

The other Aleut woman who came to Adak I only saw once. That visit became the focus of local news on the base, not unlike small-town gossip. This Aleut woman spoke very little English. In fact she rarely spoke at all. She told me that she had missed two periods and could tell that she was pregnant. My pelvic exam revealed her to be seven or eight weeks pregnant. After I confirmed her suspicion she told me that she wanted to have an abortion. She offered no reason and I did not feel the need to ask her for one.

I left her in the clinic and walked down the hall to the office of the Hospital Commander. As a non-physician he was a member of the Medical Service Corps. Commander Green was a career officer and a pleasant, mild-mannered man who had invited me to his home shortly after my arrival on Adak. I remember that we dined on Alaskan moose. Or was it elk?

I told him about the Aleut woman in my office and asked the commander where to refer her for an abortion. He remembered that there had been a similar situation on Adak about a year earlier. He told me that the woman was a young unmarried sailor who wanted to abort an early pregnancy. The Navy flew her to Elmendorf Air Force Base near Anchorage. Her flight was on a routine weekly Navy "milk run." She then went to a nearby civilian Anchorage clinic to have her abortion. She then waited around for the remainder of the week for the military flight back to Adak.

Commander Green suggested that the Aleut woman could do the same scenario as the sailor did. He reminded me that the Navy does not pay for the abortion but there is, of course, no charge for the flight on the Navy plane. I provided this information to the Aleut woman and her husband who had flown in with her. Her Aleut husband introduced himself and then informed me that he worked for the BIA on his island. He asked me if I knew that the Navy would allow his wife to have her abortion at the Adak base hospital. I replied that all I knew was that the military does not provide abortions. He told me that because of the long flight to Anchorage and the cost of abortions there was an agreement between the Navy and the BIA that the abortion could be performed at the Adak Navy Hospital if the physician is willing and capable of doing so.

Her husband looked me in the eye, stepped back one pace and put his hands in his corduroy pants pockets and asked me, "Doctor can you do the abortion here on Adak for my wife?" When he mentioned the BIA-Navy agreement regarding abortion procedures on Adak my thought was that it would be possible. I told the Aleut husband that I would check on that agreement with Commander Green, the Hospital Commander.

Vern Green confirmed the fact that the Navy had indeed entered into an agreement to allow BIA dependents to have abortions on Adak. He also admitted to personally being pro-choice but added that that as far as he knew the agreement had never been consummated. To him I then chortled that we were going to perform Adak's first known legal abortion tomorrow. I informed him that I was going to admit the Aleut woman to the hospital and schedule her abortion for the next morning. As I was leaving his office, Vern snapped back in a friendly tone telling me not to be surprised if the Surgeon General of the Navy in Washington orders you not to do an abortion in this hospital. I asked him how the Surgeon General would know of this. He told me that he would inform their office that we would be activating the Navy-BIA agreement. He suggested that it would be best for the Surgeon General to be informed beforehand then to learn of this from angry anti-choice personnel after the fact.

No problems arose from Washington. It was after all their agreement and not mine. The only obstacles that developed were local but surmountable ones. The nurse anesthetist, a gay male officer, refused to participate in the abortion procedure on "moral grounds." I told him that the C.O. or I could order him to perform his duties and besides, we both outranked him. I knew from previous experience that I could safely perform the procedure with local anesthesia plus a little intravenous sedation. That would make the procedure easy, especially for an Aleut woman used to the hardships of life. I told the nurse that he was excused from the case. The laboratory technician corpsman refused to perform the routine preoperative blood and urine tests. He asked the surgeon, a fellow church-going Catholic, to tell me of his unwillingness to be an accomplice to the crime of murder. The surgeon passed the indignation on, appropriately, to Vern Green, the C.O. I told Vern that I was quite annoyed with this morality attitude and even suggested that this was ground for the young corpsman to be charged with insubordination and dereliction of duty. We ended the impasse with a compromise. I would draw the blood and obtain the urine specimen and the reluctant corpsman would do the blood count and urinalysis. I stood over him as he performed the simple lab tests. My presence was annoying to him but it gave me a sense of vengeful empowerment.

The Aleut woman and I got along well in the operating room. I injected her cervix with a local anesthetic for the abortion procedure. A Navy nurse who was enthusiastically pro-choice assisted me. For the instruments I opened a D&C surgical pack. It contained all that we needed. For a suction machine we utilized a portable Gomco machine that is used in surgical cases where suction is needed. The abortion went off quickly and without incident. I had limited experience with Native American women in the labor and delivery room. But this I did know: they do not complain about perceived discomforts and rarely about pain. The Aleut woman was, as expected, the same as her sisters in the "lower forty-eight."

The surgeon who rotated to Adak was from the Navy Hospital in San Diego. We arrived at the same time and had become good friends. He was a practicing Roman Catholic. He and I jogged and biked together and played ping-pong every day. He was fiercely competitive and beat me almost every game. After the abortion drama we never played ping-pong or dined together in the officer's mess. He remained cordial but aloof and was no longer very friendly toward me. I assisted him on an appendectomy and a *cholecystectomy* in the O.R. before returning to my base in California. Our conversations remained limited and nothing was mentioned about the Aleut woman and her legal abortion on Adak.

ABORTION PROVIDER

Chapter 28

The Anti-Abortion Woman and the Hired Baby Killer

Back in the early 90's I attended what would turn out to be a memorable *Superbowl* party at my ex-wife's house across the Golden Gate Bridge in Sausalito. Instead of the usual banter about football or the half-time show, the conversation somehow took a joyless turn into the topic of abortion. My daughter-in-law's best friend was soon admonishing several pro-choice women for their views regarding a woman's right to choose to have an abortion. She declared that abortion was murder and that abortion providers were nothing more than "hired baby killers." I took that comment quite personally but as an invited guest and eavesdropper I did not challenge her. Who wants to engage in moral, religious or political issues at a Superbowl party?

To me there is no point in defending the individual freedoms at the heart of the pro-choice issue. It would be like trying to defend the abolition of slavery. To me a valid point of opposition does not exist.

She went on to state adamantly that she was proud to be a pro-life activist and an Operation Rescue supporter. She even boasted that she had partaken in abortion clinic picketing in San Francisco. I continued to refrain from getting involved with this all-women debate. Besides, I was there to enjoy football. My daughter, however, was quite irate and did not spare her any of the pro-choice rhetoric. Laurel, having been raised in Berkeley was adept at defending her political leanings with some added spice learned, no doubt, from her mother who was the party hostess that afternoon.

About three months later, in the early spring, I entered one of the operating procedure rooms at the Pregnancy Consultation Center in

San Francisco. This was one of several clinics that I worked at as a contract physician abortion provider. This was a Saturday morning clinic and I had become accustomed to the usual flock of protesters on the sidewalk and in front of the clinic building.

The orange-vested pro-choice escorts were always there in equal force to keep the anti-abortion zealots at bay and the clients out of harm's way. Their presence assured me that I was safe and could enter the clinic from my parking place without an adrenaline rush. I should be void of fear and anger to enable myself to provide an abortion procedure to the usual 20 to 30-odd women waiting their turn to have their unwanted pregnancy terminated so they could get on with their lives. Each one had a reason and a story to tell as to why they wanted to or needed to not be pregnant. My job was not to ask them about their stories but to provide a safe, dignified and affordable abortion. For many of these young women this procedure was much more than a matter of convenience. It was a life saving intervention.

Over the many years as an obstetrician I delivered several thousand babies. Nearly each and every delivery, with few rare exceptions, was a delightful experience but I must confess that I hardly ever received hugs or heartfelt thanks. In contrast, during my twelve years as a full-time abortion provider, the women frequently expressed profound gratification. This was not surprising considering that they arrived at the clinic with a burdensome problem and left without one.

Financial and family pressures rank at the top of the list of reasons women have abortions. As one earthy woman said to me after I completed her abortion, "If you can't feed 'em don't breed 'em." Later that year I read that appropriate remark on a bumper sticker at a strip mall in Chico.

Just three months later I was in the clinic preparing for an abortion procedure when I picked up a medical folder from the chart holder affixed to the door and I realized that the name seemed familiar to me. Sitting on the operating table dressed only in the familiar paper gown was my daughter-in-law's friend from the *Superbowl* party. We recognized each other immediately. She was somewhat taken aback and appeared startled at the amazing coincidence and irony of it all. She clutched her paper gown closer to her bosom as if to show her embarrassment. I decided not to remind her of any of her passionately stated convictions.

This was not the first time I was confronted with a turn of events like this in the abortion clinic. This was such gross hypocrisy as well as a perfect illustration of the phrase "judge not lest ye be judged."

Her presence here was stressful enough for her. I did not have to add to it with words of cynicism. She, however, could scarcely hide her emotions and timidly confessed that she was still nevertheless staunchly anti abortion. She went on to say in an aggressive tone, trying to keep from crying, that she was after all a single, working woman and could not afford to lose her job or even afford maternity clothes, prenatal care or let alone to raise a baby.

There were many thoughts and words that came to mind at that moment, especially the option of adoption. Adoption, after all, is so very often advocated by the "pro-life" people. But instead I said to her in a reassuring manner, "I understand." Then she was sedated and I did her abortion and left it at that.

Just before she left the clinic to go home she left a note for me with the recovery room nurse. Her message to me was: "Thank you for being non-judgmental with me."

Chapter 29

Have Speculum, Will Travel

Flying to Redding in Northern California almost every Friday was usually an unpleasant chore. The flight on United Express was an early A.M. departure that was almost always either delayed or cancelled because of bad weather, mechanical problems or whatever reason United decided on for their benefit or for our safety considerations.

So often the flight would be delayed for hours with the passengers waiting impatiently in the boarding area. I soon learned that if a flight was being delayed hour after hour that it would invariably end up being cancelled. I would keep in touch with the clinic in Redding by telephone and give them the flight update as soon as I knew of it. Too often I needed to rent a car and drive the 225 miles to Redding, a boring three and a half hour drive on Interstate 5 straight through the endless Sacramento Valley. That was even worse than the airport troubles.

We never cancelled the clinic because of bad weather or cancelled flights because there were too many patients scheduled and they were already waiting in the clinic. Having to reschedule 20 to 30 women to return another time would have been a disaster.

The Redding clinic was one of four outpatient facilities run by the Feminist Women's Health Center. I was most fortunate to be their Medical Director for over ten years. They are hard working; dedicated women who strive to make abortion and other reproductive services available and affordable to women in Northern California.

The Redding clinic offered abortion services only once a week. Many of these women came to Redding after a four or five hour drive over mountain roads and as far away as the Oregon border and the far reaches of the Northeast corner of California, around the Alturas area.

Most of these women were welfare recipients and were on Medi-Cal. Many had to borrow money for gas and hitch a ride with a friend. Most winter Fridays there were clients who would arrive late because of snow in the Trinity Alps northwest of Redding. I can recall a sixteen year old that was so desperate to be seen and to have her abortion remain a secret that she hitchhiked by herself from Eureka, a five-hour drive away. We paid for the gas to have a clinic escort drive her home.

I either flew or drove to Redding every Friday for twelve years. For almost two of those years, 1993-1994, two Federal Marshals greeted me at the airport. They would accompany me to the men's room to stand guard and watch me don a flak jacket. The clinic had provided me with a bulletproof vest. (During my time in Vietnam as a flight surgeon 25 years prior I had never worn a flak jacket and never felt the need to wear one.)

The two marshals and I would then walk to their unmarked car parked at the curbside of the relatively small airport terminal. The drive to the clinic was 15 minutes or so. The usual protesters were present outside the clinic but they were tame and did not demonstrate with bullhorns or block the entrance to the parking area. Their docile demeanor was probably due to the visible presence of law enforcement officers and the recent incarceration of their anti-choice leader.

This federal protection given to me was ordered by the U.S. Attorney General's office. This followed the indictment of "U.S.A. plaintiff vs. Ronald M. Walters, defendant." The violation was a felony: "Mail Threatening Communications." A Grand Jury charged that Walters, a local anti-abortion activist, "Did on or about July 19, 1993 knowingly cause to be delivered by the postal service a letter to Dr. Bruce Steir, Feminist Women's Health Center, 1901 Victor Avenue, Redding California 96002. Said letter contained a threat to injure the person of the addressee in violation of Title 18, U.S. code, section 876."

A copy of his letter was attached as exhibit A. It read:

"Dear Dr. Bruce, Goodbye. Testify that he has cursed both God and the King. Then take him out and stone him to death."

This threat and silly, non-syntactical bible reference was enough for the federal attorneys to indict Ron Walters. Subsequently he was sentenced to six months in prison. This was followed by probation and an injunction prohibiting him from close proximity to the clinic.

I had walked past the menacing gestures and verbal threats of Ron Walters every Friday for years. He was seemingly the leader of the pack of picketers who turned out in force to greet the clients as they entered the clinic grounds. The harassment that these women and girls had to endure was shameful and disgusting. These were clients who had traveled for as far away as five hours by car to obtain abortions. These were mostly indigent, rural women or teenagers who had made the difficult decision to terminate their unwanted and unplanned pregnancy. The last thing the clients needed was to endure the taunting of these self-righteous, hypocritical, misogynistic, right wing fundamentalists.

The harassment did on occasion cause a client to turn around and return to her car and drive away before she could enter the clinic. Most of them, however, came back a week or two later with determination not to let these picketers get the best of them. One client's boyfriend became so irate at the picketers tormenting and unkind words that he grabbed the nearest one and decked him with a solid punch to the face. The police were of course summoned and the angry assailant was arrested for assault and battery. The clinic escorts and I scraped up $1500 to meet his bail.

There is one good thing to say about these misogynistic activists: they were determined. On hot days (105°F) and in freezing weather (25°F) they were there rain or shine every Friday. Our clinic escorts, all local volunteers, were also there braving the weather and tolerating the anti-choice mob.

Ron Walters was "the crazy guy with the bullhorn." He would yell quotes from the bible along with gratuitous obscenities at the clients, clinic workers, and of course at me, the "evil baby killer."

The Federal Marshals stayed in the clinic all day. They sat in the kitchen at the table next to a window from where they could keep watch over the picketers. But mostly they read magazines and drank coffee to pass the time as best they could.

At the beginning of their doctor protection service I could sense that they were not very fond of being in an abortion clinic. The marshals rotated the Friday-in-Redding duty so that over the course of two years I met several marshals. One thing that they all had in common was their professionalism as federal employees. None of them voiced any anti-abortion sentiments. The only time that I overheard a negative opinion was when I informed them one Friday that this would be a long workday. I explained that there were 38 clients scheduled today. That usually meant that we would perform around 25 or so procedures. The remainder would be "no shows" or clients that were too early or too far along in the pregnancy to fit into our protocol. Only once did I overhear a marshal say to the other with some annoyance, "Thirty-eight woman scheduled! You would think that these country girls would have enough smarts to know how to keep from getting pregnant. They should learn to keep their legs together!"

After a few months of clinic duty it was all too clear that the marshals had become decidedly pro-choice. They may have been anti-abortion or pro-life at the onset of their visits to the clinic but after awhile they could see with their own eyes how important a service we provided for these "country girls."

They showed their change of attitude by asking questions of me and the other health workers who wandered by the kitchen table.

They inquired as to "how old is that girl? She looks like she is fifteen or sixteen." Kitty, the clinic manager, replied, "No she is thirteen, just a baby. Now she can get on with her life and finish school and hopefully not get pregnant for a long time."

They also seemed to be more interested in the activities of the picketers. They realized that each time they stepped outside the front door the picketers would put down the bullhorn and lower the volume of their insulting rhetoric. Some even lowered their protest signs to half-staff.

The marshals, all married men of course, assumed an air of a protective father, especially for the teenagers who entered the clinic.

At the end of the workday the marshals would drive me back to the airport and await my departure from Redding to San Francisco. Then they would drive back home to Sacramento.

After I was arrested and charged with homicide, one of the marshals called me at home and offered to be a character witness for me if I went to trial. He told me that he knew quite well that I would not leave a patient in distress and that I would not rush out of the clinic to catch the last plane out until the last patient had recovered satisfactorily. The marshal stated that he was aware of the many times that I would miss the last flight out and have to rent a car and drive the three and half hours home. I thanked him for his voluntary offer to testify on my behalf.

After a while we all got to know the picketers by sight and more or less knew what behavior to expect from them. Some Fridays two or three would show up, and at other times as many as 20 protesters would show up to annoy all of us. We had clinic escorts. They were local volunteers who were there to help us make abortion accessible. They would, as the name implies, escort the clients from their parked car on our private lot to the clinic entrance. This allowed the clients to feel less vulnerable and more protected. The barrage of heckling was mostly ignored as much as humanly possible. Some clients were intimidated and some showed their disgust by displaying anger.

Over the period of the 12 years that I worked at the Redding facility, there were a handful of clients who responded to the protesters by making a U-turn in their car and departing with tears. As far as I know, every one of these clients returned in one or two weeks to have their abortion. On their second trip to the clinic they knew what to expect and were prepared to handle the hassle in a positive way. Delaying their abortion of course prolongs the stress and psychological drama that goes into the difficult decision-making that takes place when a woman or girl decides to have an abortion. The delay also increases the risk factor for the procedure. The complication rate, although very low, does increase with time elapsed. An eight-week pregnancy is aborted almost always without incident, whereas a twelve-week gestation requires more time, different instruments and an increase in cramping and bleeding. Without realizing the harm they were causing, the only tangible result of the protests during those long Fridays (aside from causing bad feelings and knotted stomachs) was to endanger the lives of the women who felt forced into delaying the procedure.

One client and her male companion were so angered by these picketers that they walked several feet out of their way to grab one of their anti-choice signs and trample it on the ground. The clinic escort quickly intervened to prevent a head-on confrontation. There were several altercations between protesters and clients and the clinic escorts. The Redding police were called several times by either side and came to the clinic to investigate the various charges. They usually came out reluctantly and asked questions. Most of the complaints came from our clinic manager who was protesting the picketers' violation of a Shasta County injunction that prohibited protests from taking place in close proximity to the clinic boundaries.

One well-known middle-aged woman, a regular clinic picketer, came into the Redding clinic one Friday with her daughter in tow. Kitty, the clinic manager, recognized the picketer immediately and wasted no time in asking, "What in hell are you doing in here?" The mother explained in a brash tone that she did not wish to come into the clinic but her daughter needed to have an abortion and refused to go to the clinic without her mother. Her pregnant daughter, she went on to say, was only seventeen and a senior in high school. The dour picketer mother then attempted to justify her presence by stating that her daughter knows how anti-abortion she is but told her that it was OK for her to go to the clinic because the daughter was going to have the abortion and not her mother!

That was the strangest use of logic any of us had ever heard. The picketer mother was shown the door in no uncertain terms. She was advised by the clinic manager to take her daughter elsewhere. "She should have come without you knowing that you are so anti-abortion. Now you can see how you like driving with your daughter for three hours to Sacramento or to the Bay Area and then three hours back home in the same day. Hopefully you and your daughter will be greeted by yelling picketers wherever you go!"

She left with her daughter in a huff. After my experiences with so-called anti-abortion types who were dead-set against abortion until the moment one was actually needed, I was ready to perform her abortion and allow the mother into the procedure room to hold her daughter's hand. But I was out-voted by the clinic staff. Not that my vote would have counted anyway.

Chapter 30

A Botched Operation for Christmas:

(Politics, Not Science, Determine the Outcome)

Was it a "botched abortion" or a "surgical complication"? That is a matter of prejudicial semantics depending on who is discussing the ill-fated event.

Eleven days after Sharon's tragic death following a second trimester abortion, my wife Yen, came very close to dying too. Her near demise was one day before Christmas.

Throughout our courtship and after our marriage it had become apparent that our energy levels were disparate. Simply, I enjoyed getting out and doing things. Yen's preference was to stay home and do things. Nonetheless, I made several attempts to introduce her to the outdoor thrills of mountain biking, skiing and hiking.

Yen tried all three and found them not to her liking. She, having grown up among the privileged class in Vietnam, usually avoided the sun and strenuous activities. Besides the cultural differences, there was also her almost nonexistent stamina. Her pulse rate at rest while visiting Lake Tahoe's 7,000-foot elevation was one hundred beats per minute. After an easy ten-mile bicycle ride on a flat riverside trail, her pulse rate became imperceptible and she hungered for air. I assumed that she was just out of shape.

Like so many physicians that I have known, we pay attention to our patients and their complaints, kvetching, and sundry symptoms and ignore those of the people that we love. Yen's persistent and nonproductive dry cough that she suffered with for over two years was written off by me, her physician husband, as a psychological ploy to stay home and thus avoid a Sunday in the park with Bruce.

My old college roommate and fraternity brother, Richie Behren and his wife Leta invited Yen and me for a winter visit to their townhouse in Vail, Colorado. I skied with Richie almost every day. Yen stayed indoors and coughed. She coughed all night and disturbed everyone trying to sleep. I felt that I had been the cause of her cough neurosis and was sure that her illness was psychosomatic. I easily dismissed the various medical conditions that could be attributed to the etiology of her cough and lassitude.

When we returned home to San Francisco from Vail I finally decided that it was time to have Yen see her primary care physician at Kaiser Permanente. After a few appointments and chest x-rays and some abnormal laboratory findings it was determined that my wife was ill. Her chest x-rays revealed evidence of enlarged nodular masses around the lungs and the soft tissue near the heart. The radiologist determined that these suspicious lesions in her chest were nonspecific. That means that they did not know what they were. The differential diagnosis that was being entertained was troublesome. They would have to establish whether this was tuberculosis, Hodgkin's disease, *lymphoma* or *sarcoidosis*. The latter being a not-so-rare disorder that resembles *tuberculosis* on x-ray but is not an infectious disease. *Sarcoidosis* is a disease of uncertain etiology and can affect multiple systems of the body such as lung, liver, skin and even the eye. It is thought that there is a relationship between *sarcoidosis* and an overactive immune system.

It was now essential to obtain a tissue biopsy of the enlarged lymph nodes that were in the chest cavity or *mediastinum*. A biopsy would obtain tissue that could then be microscopically examined for a definitive diagnosis. The radiologists attempted several painful and unsuccessful maneuvers with long spinal needles directed at the enlarged pulmonary nodes. These insertions were performed under sonogram guidance but to no avail.

The pulmonary specialists and the thoracic surgeon planned a more invasive procedure. Obtaining adequate tissue from a biopsy was imperative for establishing a diagnosis.

Yen was scheduled for a *mediastinal* biopsy. The thoracic surgeon scheduled the procedure for the 24th of December, the day before Christmas. The surgeon assured us that that she would be well enough to go home the same day or at most there would be an overnight stay.

If you place your index finger in the midline at the front of the base of the neck, that is, between the clavicles, that area is called, anatomically, the *sterno-clavicular* junction. Or to simplify it in lay terms it is where the breastbone meets the two collarbones. This is where the thoracic surgeon showed Yen he would make a very small incision. Through that incision he would pass a scope called a *mediastinascope*. This instrument has a fiber optic light at one end and a magnified lens at the other end for the surgeon to view the interior of the thoracic cavity. Gynecologists perform a similar procedure with a *laparoscope* to visualize the pelvic organs. There is an aperture on the *mediastinascope* to allow a snare-like instrument to pass through the hollow of the scope. The biopsy forceps then pinches a piece of the enlarged lymph node. The tissue is then retrieved by withdrawing the forceps up through the scope. This is all done under the direct visualization of the operator.

When performing this type of surgery it is imperative that the operator possesses tremendous skill in eye-hand coordination. I know of this necessity because I had to develop this skill as a gynecologist when I first learned how to perform laparoscopy in the operating room. I suppose that is why one refers to the "practice of medicine."

The procedure was explained to Yen and me. She was admitted to the hospital on the morning of Christmas Eve day. Her mother and I sat in the nearby family waiting room. This was to be about a one-hour procedure under general anesthesia.

After two hours I became restless and annoyed that the doctor had forgotten to come to the waiting room to see us. I walked down the hall to the closed operating room doors. I pressed the square metal push pad that pneumatically swings the doors open. An orderly dressed in a green scrub suit appeared. I told him of my concern. He left and returned shortly afterward to tell me the doctor was finishing up and would be out to see me very soon

After three hours had passed by I repeated the same activity with more annoyance than worry. This time an O.R. nurse greeted me and said, "The doctor is finishing up and will be out to see you soon." As a physician who performed gynecological surgery I was aware that something was amiss in the O.R. I wanted to go back into the operating suite and look through the window of the room where my wife was lying. My street clothes and common sense kept me at bay.

As every physician knows, a family member is more likely to have a medical complication than an unrelated patient, or so it seems. This thought did cross my mind but I dismissed it as I remembered how many doctor's wives and daughters I had delivered without any complications.

When at last the thoracic surgeon appeared at the waiting room door his demeanor was not unlike that of a defeated warrior. He appeared stoop shouldered in his scrub suit and doctor's white coat. He looked pale and stern faced. The surgeon wasted no time in delivering the reason for the long delay in the operating room. Before he could utter a word my autonomic nervous system took over and prepared me for the worst, news that my wife might be dead.

That horrible moment ended when he informed us, "Yen is O.K." He went on to tell me, "We had a torrential hemorrhage during the procedure. We nicked the pulmonary artery with the biopsy forceps during the procedure."

The "we had" is a phrase that is uttered by most physicians. "We had a complication" or "We ran into some trouble." This is an unconscious ploy to share the blame of disaster with the innocent patient so as to involve them with the negligent act. This is partially true is it not? How could there have been a complication if the patient was not in the operating room? I've noticed that this play on words comes from the mouths of generals as well. "We suffered grave losses at Normandy."

The unapologetic surgeon went on to describe that on his last attempt to retrieve lymph node tissue his biopsy forceps was between the heart and the great vessels that emerge from the aortic arch. The surrounding lung, he admitted, hindered his visualization. As he tried to manipulate the scope to see the target for biopsy the forceps inadvertently lacerated Yen's pulmonary artery. Although I had been a gynecologist for many decades and worked almost exclusively below the navel, I still knew that the pulmonary artery was a very formidable vessel that brought oxygen-saturated blood to the body with every beat of the heart.

The adrenalin rush hit me. My mother-in-law quickly noted my grave concern as her facial expression changed to anguish. The surgeon at once assured us that Yen's hemorrhage was brought under control by performing an emergency *mediastinotomy*. Fortunately there was another pair of experienced surgical hands in the operating room area who was available to immediately assist in this life-threatening emergency. The opening of her chest was done by incising the skin overlying the sternum and then using an electric surgical buzz saw that splits open the entire length of the sternum in a longitudinal manner. Retractors then hold the chest open to allow visualization of the lacerated artery. Prior to opening the chest the surgeon attempted to stop the hemorrhage by placing gauze packs inserted through the scope. That would be wishful thinking at best because packing will not stop arterial bleeding of that magnitude. After the two surgeons ligated the bleeding artery they closed the chest wall. The ten-inch long incision in the severed sternum was approximated with wire. You can see the wire on a chest x-ray today.

After the upended thoracic surgeon departed to return to the I.C.U., I explained to my Vietnamese mother-in-law all of the horrific details of what had transpired in the O.R.

I calmed her down with a hug and then she decided that our consolation was that Yen is alive. Yen required seven units of blood replacement in order to stabilize her vital signs.

My visit to the I.C.U. was emotionally draining. My feelings fluctuated between anger and sorrow. My mind played unwelcome games with me. Was my wife's near death tragedy in some way a retribution for Sharon's demise only eleven days ago?

Sharon and Yen shared some commonality. They both went to see a physician for an outpatient surgical procedure. They anticipated going home soon after the procedure was completed. Of course the sad difference is in the ultimate tragedy that befell Sharon. Yen is alive. Not gone. Sharon is dead. Gone forever.

As a physician and husband I felt somewhat responsible for my wife's surgical complication. Given my medical knowledge, I had pursued the search for a diagnosis of her persistent prolonged cough. If I had been a non-medical person perhaps the mediastinal biopsy would not have taken place. It is just conjecture on my part. The near fatal biopsy was performed to rule out diseases that could be fatal. How ironic it would have been for her to die finding out that her biopsy showed a disease that is not fatal if treated properly.

When I stood by my wife's bedside and realized how close she came to dying, I cried. I had a good cry that made me feel better. The last time that I cried was in the early eighties when I learned that over 200 U.S. Marines were blown up by Hezbollah terrorists while they were asleep in their quarters in Lebanon. At that time I was a Medical Officer stationed at the Marine Corps Base at Camp Pendleton in San Diego County.

Yen was in the I.C.U. She had tubes and drains seemingly everywhere that an orifice was available. There was blood dripping into her vein along with a morphine derivative into another vein. There was a nasal catheter delivering much-needed oxygen. There was continuous monitoring of her vital signs and chest electrodes were monitoring her cardiac status. A Foley catheter drained her bladder and a suction machine drained seepage from her chest cavity. The whole works were going at once; all this sophisticated equipment, expensive, sterile, and frightening high technology. I leaned over the side rails at her bedside and called her name. I asked her how she was doing and told her that I loved her. She replied with a raspy weak voice that she was itching all over. I looked at the I.V. drip and noted that there was morphine being dispensed periodically in small doses. I told Yen that her itching was probably from the morphine. Most people on morphine usually tolerate the side effects of nausea and itch quite well because of the built in opiate-induced euphoria that they experience.

Yen's chest was bandaged and had drains attached to suction bottles. I was not yet prepared to look at the incision that she had just been given by a thoracic surgeon who had a "bad day." I knew how long and ghastly the incision would look until it healed properly. Yen, being a beautiful Asian woman, would find little solace or comfort in knowing that eventually the scar would fade and be hardly noticeable at all. Yen has always looked so elegant and often wore open neck dresses that show her cleavage and clavicles.

Yen was home after only four days. Her mother came up from San Jose to help her convalesce. Her recovery was smooth and she was back at her job in a month or so.

The biopsy that almost caused my wife's demise came back from the pathologist as *"sarcoidosis."* At this point in time that was the only good news: no cancer or tuberculosis. Yen had pulmonary sarcoidosis. That is why she had a low-grade fever and the persistent cough. Without an adequate biopsy the diagnosis of sarcoidosis cannot be made. It would not be a definitive diagnosis on x-ray because it so much resembles tuberculosis and some forms of lymphatic malignancies. The treatment for sarcoid was for cortico-steroid tablets for two years. This was the regimen followed by Yen with good results.

Was this surgical complication to be considered an act of negligence? I inquired about this by consulting with three thoracic surgeons at three different hospitals that are the primary teaching hospitals of the two local medical schools (Stanford and University of California San Francisco). They reviewed the medical records and the operative notes that had been dictated shortly after the procedure was completed.

Much to my surprise the experts said that this was not an act of negligence. The consensus of opinion was unanimous: a lacerated blood vessel during the course of this procedure is considered to be a known, albeit rare, complication. Their conclusion was that the surgeon had an unfortunate complication and treated it in an appropriate and timely fashion. Since my wife was alive and well this opinion would be difficult to refute.

As a gynecologic surgeon I know full well that every procedure has a built in risk. Every surgeon is cognizant of the list of potential complications and the studied incidence or percentage of these adverse occurrences. Any invasive procedure from ear piercing and circumcision to organ transplant and Cesarean section can result in infection, hemorrhage, cardiovascular collapse and even death.

I asked the experts a question that weighed heavy on my head as a practicing physician, "What if my wife had died as a result of the lacerated pulmonary artery. Would you then have considered this as an act of negligence?" Again there was a unanimous "No."

They responded again by stating that the diagnosis and treatment were appropriate and this case would have to be classified only as a complication.

My tragic case, by contrast, that had occurred only eleven days before my wife's biopsy, was of a woman dying as a result of a complication from a surgical procedure. The Medical Board of California, spurred on by a well-known anti-abortion activist, labeled this case as "gross negligence." Then a year later they changed their minds, not because the science had changed but because of a change in political climate, and decided to call it "homicide." Thoracic surgeons have "complications" and physician abortion providers have "botched" abortions, leaving them open to charges of homicide or manslaughter.

There is an obvious double standard here. The demise of my patient was from a perforation of the uterus. This is a well-known complication. Any experienced abortion provider will admit to having had at least one. If he or she denies ever having perforated a uterus then I must conclude that they either have not performed too many second trimester abortions, or they are in denial, or just covering up with a sense of false pride.

The small perforation that I was responsible for was not diagnosed and therefore was not treated. Uterine perforations quite often go undetected. This is known to be so because many perforations are discovered later when the patient has a laparoscopy after the abortion for persistent pelvic pain, or for a sterilization procedure or to locate a missing fetal part. During this operation a uterine perforation may be noted that was not diagnosed at the time of the abortion procedure. Not all perforations invite intra-abdominal hemorrhage. Many perforations produce no unusual symptoms and therefore go undetected. When a uterine perforation produces pain or internal bleeding then close monitoring and intervention will take place.

In sad conclusion, I can state that perforation of the uterus during an abortion is not uncommon but it rarely results in a death. The same is probably true for laceration of the pulmonary artery during a diagnostic mediastinoscopy.

FELON

PROHIBITED ACTS WHILE IN CUSTODY

1. Killing.
2. Assaulting any person.
3. Fighting with another person.
4. Threatening another with bodily harm, or with any offense against his person or his property.
5. Extortion, blackmail, protection; demanding or receiving money or anything of value in return for protection against others, to avoid bodily harm, or under threat of informing.
6. Engaging in sexual acts with others.
7. Making sexual proposals or threats to another.
8. Indecent exposure.
9. Escape.
10. Attempting or planning escape.
11. Wearing a disguise or mask.
12. Setting a fire.
13. Destroying, altering, or damaging jail property, or the property of another person.
14. Stealing (theft).
15. Tampering with or blocking any locking device.
16. Adulteration of any food or drink.
17. Possession or introduction of an explosive of any ammunition.
18. Possession or introduction of a gun, firearm, weapon, sharpened instrument, knife, or unauthorized tool.
19. Possession, introduction, or use of any narcotic, narcotic paraphernalia, drugs, or intoxicants not prescribed for the individual by the medical staff.
20. Misuse of authorized medication.
21. Possession of money or currency unless specifically authorized.
22. Possession of property belonging to another person.
23. Loaning of property or anything of value for profit or increased return.
24. Possession of anything not authorized for retention or receipt by the inmate, and not issued to him through regular institutional channels.
25. Possessing any officer's or staff clothing.
26. Possessing unauthorized clothing.
27. Mutilating or altering clothing issued by the jail.
28. Rioting.
29. Encouraging others to riot.
30. Engaging in, or encouraging, a group demonstration.
31. Refusing to work, or to accept a program assignment.
32. Encouraging others to refuse to work or participate in work stoppage.
33. Refusing to obey an order of any staff member.
34. Violating a condition of furlough.
35. Unexcused absence from work, or an assignment.
36. Malingering, feigning an illness.
37. Failing to perform work as instructed by a supervisor.
38. Insolence towards a staff member.
39. Lying or providing a false statement to a staff member.
40. Conduct which disrupts or interferes with the security or orderly running of the institution.
41. Counterfeiting, forging, or unauthorized reproduction of any document, article, or identification, money, security, or official paper.
42. Participating in an unauthorized meeting or gathering.
43. Being in an unauthorized area.

RIGHTS

1. You have the right to expect that as human beings you will be treated respectfully, impartially and fairly by all personnel.
2. You have the right to be informed of the rules, procedures, and schedules concerning the operation of the institution.
3. You have the right to freedom of religious affiliation, and voluntary religious worship.
4. You have the right to health care, which includes nutritious meals, proper bedding and clothing, and a laundry schedule for cleanliness of the same, and opportunity to shower regularly, proper ventilation for warmth and fresh air, a regular exercise period, toilet articles and medical and dental treatment.
5. You have the right to visit and correspond with family members, and friends, and to receive mail at the facility rules and schedule.
6. You have the right to unrestricted and confidential access to the courts by correspondence.
7. You have the right to legal counsel from an attorney of your choice by interviews and correspondence.
8. With approval of the jail Commander you have the right to participate in the use of the law library reference materials to assist you in resolving legal problems.
9. You have the right to a wide range of reading material for educational purposes and for your own enjoyment. These materials may include magazines and newspapers sent from the publishers.
10. You have the right to participate in education, vocational training, and employment as far as resources are available, and in keeping with your interests, needs, and abilities.

RESPONSIBILITIES

1. You have the responsibility to treat others, both employees and inmates, in the same manner.
2. You have the responsibility to know and abide by them.
3. You have the responsibility to recognize and respect the rights of others in this regard.
4. It is your responsibility to not waste food, to follow the laundry and shower schedule, to maintain neat and clean living quarters, and to seek medical and dental care as you may need it.
5. It is your responsibility to conduct yourself honestly and fairly in your association with family, members, and friends and not violate the law.
6. You have the responsibility to present honestly and fairly your petitions, questions and problems to the court.
7. It is your responsibility to use the services of an attorney fairly and fairly.
8. It is your responsibility to use these resources in keeping with the procedures and schedule prescribed and to respect the rights of other inmates to the use of the materials.
9. It is your responsibility to seek and utilize such materials for your personal benefit, without depriving others of their equal rights to the use of this material.
10. You have the responsibility to take advantage of activities which may help you live a successful and law abiding life within the institution and in the community. You will be expected to abide by the regulations governing the use of such activities.

284

PROHIBITED ACTS WHILE IN CUSTODY (Cont'd)

44. Failure to follow safety or sanitation regulations.
45. Using any equipment or machinery contrary to instructions or posted safety standards.
46. Using any equipment or machinery which is not specifically authorized.
47. Failing to stand count.
48. Interfering with the taking of count.
49. Making intoxicants.
50. Being intoxicated.
51. Smoking.
52. Using abusive or obscene language.
53. Gambling.
54. Preparing or conducting a gambling pool.
55. Possession of gambling paraphernalia.
56. Being unsanitary or untidy, failing to keep one's person and one's quarters in accordance with posted standards.
57. Tattooing or self mutilation.
58. Unauthorized use of mail or telephone.
59. Unauthorized contacts with the public.
60. Correspondence or conduct with a visitor in violation of posted regulations.
61. Giving or offering any official or staff member a bribe, or anything of value.
62. Giving money or anything of value to, or accepting money or anything of value from, another inmate, a member of his family, or his friend.
63. Attempting to commit any of the above offences, aiding another person to commit any of the above offences, and above offences shall be considered the same as a commission of the offences itself.

JAIL VISITING INFORMATION

Riverside Jail Visiting Hours

Visiting hours vary.
For detailed visiting information contact your housing unit officer.

Banning Correctional Facility Visiting Hours

Visiting hours vary.
For detailed visiting information contact your housing unit officer.

Blythe Jail Visiting Hours

Sentenced males .... Sunday, 12:00-3:00 pm
Unsentenced males .... Sunday, 12:00-3:00 pm
All females .... Sunday, 12:00-3:00 pm

Indio Jail Visiting Hours

Sentenced males .... Sunday, 12:30-3:30 pm
                                            Wednesday, 7:00-8:00 pm
Unsentenced males .... Saturday, 12:30-3:30 pm
All females .... Sunday, 9:00-10:00 pm

Southwest Detention Center Visiting Hours

Visiting hours vary.
For detailed visiting information contact your housing unit officer.

RIVERSIDE COUNTY SHERIFF'S DEPT.
RIVERSIDE COUNTY JAIL
INMATE IDENTIFICATION CARD

BEDDING ISSUE/REC'D INITIAL _____

MATTRESS _____

BLANKET _____ SHEETS _____

TOWEL _____

THIS IDENTIFICATION CARD MUST BE SHOWN TO RECEIVE MEDICINE, COMMISSARY, AND AT THE TIME OF YOUR RELEASE

NAME _____

BOOKING NUMBER _____

DATE OF BOOKING _____

Loss of this identity card could result in delay in your release. If you lose or misplace this card, notify the housing officer immediately.

Chapter 31

Six In A Cell, One Bad Apple

My first three weeks in jail were spent in a six-man cell with a shower, a sink and a commode. There was a TV mounted on the wall that could be viewed from all of the six beds. I was on the medical floor of the county jail. My hypertension, glaucoma and being sixty-nine years old made me eligible for this consideration.

The four tablet medications taken daily for my hypertension and the three different eye drops for my glaucoma took five days to arrive from the local pharmacy that supplies the jailhouse.

Of the other five cellmates, two were insulin dependent diabetics; one had a seizure disorder and was on anti-epileptic medications. The other two were, I suspected, career criminals. One had a fracture of the tibia sustained from jumping out of a second story window. He was visiting his wife against the court ordered restraint. She called the police. When he saw the cops arriving he made it out of the back bedroom window on the second floor. Of course he was apprehended and brought to the hospital as a prisoner who had violated his parole and fractured his tibia. He was in constant pain from what I perceived as an ill-fitting cast on his leg. He was allowed Tylenol for the pain twice daily.

The last was also the least likeable. He was a womanizing, arrogant bully who had been beaten up in a jail cell brawl. He suffered a broken nose, dislocated mandible and a fracture of the left lower eye socket facial bone.

Michael was a 27-year-old American-born Hispanic. He was in the bed closest to the cell commode. He was awaiting sentencing for assault and battery. Michael tells me in a nonchalant manner that he is anticipating a life sentence because of the "three strikes" edict being enforced in California. His priors are more than three and are all assault with a deadly weapon or assault with attempted murder. The latter implies that you beat the hell out of someone and left them for dead but they recovered and suffered near fatal injuries.

Michael's latest victim was his brother-in-law who in a moment of anger slapped his sister's face. That was Michael's wife. To show his macho side to her he broke her brother's jaw and nose. Equally bad, by doing so, he committed another felony while on probation.

Michael is on the medical floor of the county jailhouse because a vicious inmate incarcerated in another jail facility beat him up in his cell. The assault weapon was a foot and knee according to Michael, who quipped that it was a "slam down" similar to a wrestling term that you might see on TV. But unlike professional wrestling this was without the phony acting. Michael smiled to show where several teeth had been knocked out and referred to his jailhouse beating as an "ass whipping."

When I asked Michael what happened to his brutal assailant he said, "Nothing happened, the big asshole is still in jail as far as I know." I inquired about the deputies on duty and if they asked him what had happened to him. He proudly told me that he simply replied, "I fell out of bed." The jailhouse has a "moral code" that one does not tell or squeal on a fellow inmate. It is actually a life or death code.

Michael married his 14-year-old girlfriend 12 years ago when he was 15 years old and a tenth grade drop-out. They have eight children, six boys and two girls, ages nine months to twelve years old. Another baby, *numero* nine, is due this year. In addition, Michael boasts of having two more children with a girlfriend. His wife, he says, knows of this and "treats them like one of her own." Michael claims that he has been in jail more than he has been at home during his short adult life. I suggested to him that his frequent incarcerations did not seem to be a very effective method of birth control. He frowned and informed me that he was a "good Catholic and did not believe in birth control." I did not pursue the topic of family planning or what it takes to be a good Catholic, nor did I divulge the fact that I was an abortion provider.

From my jailhouse observation of Michael, his gait and manner of speech evolve around his sexuality, violence and professed love for his wife and children. He has pursued the quest for *machismo* to the extreme with no regard or remorse for his numerous felonies and subsequent separations from his family.

Michael had been a truck driver in between incarcerations. He hauled a medical supply truck cross-country. He earned good money, "two to three grand a month." Medical supplies, he states are low risk items. "No one wants to highjack hospital gurneys or steal 1,000 catheters," Michael advised me with a forced laugh. We were viewing World Wrestling on TV. I suggested to Michael that his two favorite programs, the aforementioned and Jerry Springer, have something in common. The drama is staged. Michael's refusal to accept this opinion was bolstered by two other cellmates that were faithful Springer enthusiasts. Michael is convinced that the people that appear on the program with their self acclaimed sordid and trashy socio-sexual anecdotal narratives are there for the purpose of "coming clean, like a form of confession." I noted how serious Michael and his support duo were becoming so I attempted to inject some humor, "if I were having sex with a chicken, I would not want to confess that on national TV," I quipped. Not even a smile as they probably pondered that weird possibility. They were quick to rebut my comment that these people are receiving monetary compensation for making fools of themselves in public. Cellmate Jim proposed that they parade themselves on stage because they "become instant celebrities in their neighborhood."

Friendly inmate Jim then asked me why I did not enjoy the hit TV program "Third Rock from The Sun." I explained that I could not enjoy a sitcom even with a fine actor like John Lithgow because the laugh tract was overworked to the point of being insulting to me. A good comedy does not need to queue you to laugh after every few words. Jim argued that the laugh tract was designed to prompt the lower level intellect to laugh because most of the punch lines go over their head. I told him that I did not buy that. I suggested that the laugh tract is a guise so that the viewer will believe that everyone thinks the program is very funny and they become programmed to laugh along with the laugh tract.

Jim startled me by quipping with a rakish smirk, "There is the irony! That fact alone makes the laugh tract hilarious."

I observed Michael and Jim engrossed in a card game or conversation more or less oblivious to the sit-com on the TV and yet both emitted a robotic chuckle in unison with every laugh tract "ha, ha". They had no idea what they were chuckling about but were programmed into it.

There are so many sit-coms with laugh tracts not only viewed in jail but all over America by children and adults as well. Is this another facet of the "dumbing of America"? It's very scary to me.

Even scarier is how religion clouds the issues of reality and reasoning. Michael reads from the bible every night. He is barely audible as he spends 10 minutes or so with the New Testament secluded on his bed next to me. I wonder if his mind is concentrating on the bible or is he thinking about violence and revenge or violence and sex.

I asked Michael how he can put the bible back on his shelf and turn on to Jerry Springer and his trashy and ugly guests spewing out their sleazy, sordid and stupid perversions? After a three second pause he responded, "Hey these are my people." I knew that.

Microsoft's Bill Gates was doing a commercial on TV. I verified the fact that Mr. Gates was the richest man in the world and that his wealth exceeds most countries gross national product. After reading the New Testament for the night Michael, jokingly, said, "When I get out of here I'm going to kidnap that S.O.B. No one should have that much money." I informed Michael that Bill and Melinda Gates are major philanthropists to the poorest countries in the developing world and Microsoft has helped raise our economy to its highest level ever. Michael changed his plan and boldly declared that he will kidnap Bill Gate's wife Melinda instead.

Michael's wife will not be visiting him this Sunday. She will not find the time, according to Michael, because she attends church services twice on Sunday.

This highly inconsiderate individual loved to watch mindless sitcoms, wrestling and NASCAR races on TV. He loved the noise and turned up the volume to suit his moronic needs without regards to the rest of us who might be sleeping. He kept the TV on all night. Several times when I thought he was asleep I left my cot and shut the volume down. I had once turned the TV off only to have him turn it back on and curse me with jailhouse profanity. The TV stayed on until the breakfast trays arrived at 4:30 AM.

After his bedtime bible read, Michael changes channels on the TV (it is never off) to view Jerry Springer reruns. Every night as I tried to sleep I was subjected to Mr. Springer, his screaming human circus freaks, and the moronic audience punctuating every potential silence by yelling, "Jer-ry, Jer-ry, Jer-ry…" *ad infinitum*.

Bad as this was, the worst ordeal was not the TV but Michael pushing my shoulder with considerable force to awaken me from a much needed intermittent slumber. Michael would growl that my snoring was disturbing him. I told him that it was hard to believe that my snoring was louder than the Jerry Springer audience or the enthusiastic ringside announcer for World Federation Wrestling. He polled the other four cellmates and they unanimously agreed that my snoring was louder.

He went on to inform me that the next time my snoring bothered him he would shove a pair of socks or a bar of soap down my throat. That, I thought, would probably not occur. There was an element of macho jail talk involved here. Nevertheless I was more annoyed then intimidated. My lack of sleep and his closeness prompted me to send a written complaint to the Medical floor cops. Without using the name Michael or Miguel, I stated that "one of my cellmates", etc. It doesn't work well to tattle to the cops about an individual. Even the cops frown on that. Soon thereafter I was transferred to a single cell on the same floor.

"Roll it up, Steir," the militant deputy yelled over the cell speaker. I was ordered to gather up my meager belongings and bedding. The deputy escorted me down the hall and opened my new cell door. With a satirical tone he informed me, "Here is the honeymoon suite that you requested."

My new cell was small, consisting of a single size bed, a sink and a commode, but it initially left me with a feeling of joy and relief. I would now have some control of when I could sleep, watch TV, and read. On the other hand, I realized that I would have no one to talk to all day. It was not that the five cellmates that I left behind were stimulating conversationalists, it was still solitary confinement. Silence, however, I told myself, was decidedly better than sitcom reruns. I pondered with this mental double-edged sword and wondered if my hermit-like existence would be stimulating enough to compensate for the deliciousness of privacy and quietude. Soon it became apparent that isolation was more desirable than conversation that was for the most part worthless foam from the mouth and unrelenting noise from imbecilic TV shows.

I thought that for three more months I could endure some loneliness for the sake of serenity and sanity.

The loneliness for my wife was so much more overwhelming than living without the conversation of the other inmates that it paled by comparison. I missed her so much now that I was isolated that an old song, as I remembered it, became tattooed in my brain.

Nights are long since you've gone away
I think about you all through the day, my buddy
I miss your voice
the touch of your hand
I do hope that you understand
Your buddy, your buddy misses you

My son Philip, who shares my gallows humor, suggested that I would not tolerate isolation too long because I would be such boring company to myself. Alas, I never got the chance to find out.

CHAPTER 32

From Quietude to Noise from Hell

After about a week in my one-man cell, the cop on duty aroused me as he shouted over the intercom "roll it up and make it snappy." My immediate thought was that the judge had a change in heart and decided to send me home to serve out my sentence under house arrest. That would have been an appropriate gesture considering that the judge had indicated to my attorney that she did not plan to incarcerate me at the sentencing. She broke her promise under pressure from the family of the deceased and because of the power of the anti-choice people in the community.

This time I had to gather my bedding, plus two books to transport. I had no idea where I was going. Hoping beyond hope, I continued to speculate my leaving jail for home detention. The sheriff, I thought, doesn't need his staff to cater to the medical needs of an old spoiled physician. Besides I would be a legal and medical liability if I were to die or have a stroke and become gravely ill while incarcerated in solitary confinement.

As I rolled up the two blankets and bedding I recalled that I had acquired a second blanket in lieu of a pillow. Originally I had requested another blanket stating that I was cold at night. When the air conditioner was working it was usually too cold. The request for another blanket was apparently overused in jail. The medical authorities promptly denied my request. They suggested that I sleep in my bright orange jailhouse jumpsuit to keep warm. I was not cold. I just wanted a makeshift pillow.

I had, out of desperation, rolled the top end of the mattress up to simulate a pillow. That did not work too well because it was too firm and kept unrolling whenever I moved about. I sent in a new request after it became apparent that my snoring was infamous in my six-man cell. A known murderer had even threatened my life if I didn't stop snoring. I stated that without my head elevated my neck and shoulders ached, my snoring was inevitable and I had suffered with shortness of breath. My request was granted. Little things like an extra old woolen blanket can make jail life more tolerable.

I rolled up my two blankets and placed my toilet articles next to my two books. The brusque and grumpy cop with the crew cut returned to my cell and urged me to pick it all up and exit the cell. I placed the two rolled up blankets under my right arm. It just barely fit because the blankets were bulky and my arm is short.

The jail-issued cardboard box was full and I could not close the lid because of my two new books. I tucked the heavy box under my left arm. Now I still had my towel and sheets to contend with. I asked the deputy if I could make it out in two trips. I was hoping that he would volunteer to carry one of the three items. Forget it! He insisted that I place the linens and towel in my mouth and carry them doggy style. It worked. When we got to the elevator I held my parcels for about two minutes. My arms and jaws became tired so I placed my belongings on the floor beside me. When the elevator finally arrived I had to go through this humiliating schlep again. My summer employment as a bellhop during my college days came in handy fifty years later. I can remember placing the carrying string attached to a woman's hatbox as an item that was a natural for the mouth when the arms were full of suitcases.

We exited the elevator on the fourth floor. That meant that I was not going home. The basement is where inmates are admitted and released. My new neighborhood was going to be in the general jail population. I was going to be a genuine jailbird. I felt a sense of intimidation and shame. I had never dreamed that I would ever be an incarcerated felon. It was very surreal. There's no way to know the meaning of the phrase *out of body experience* until you have experienced it for yourself.

The cop on duty opened the main door of Day Room #2. The deputy on duty sat in a glass-enclosed booth that oversees the Pod where thirty-two inmates share sixteen cells and two shower stalls. From their booth the cops can automatically open and lock all the cell doors and call out to any or all of us through the intercom.

The brightly lit area, called a pod, was flooded with orange jump suits. There are eight cells on the upper landing and eight on the lower deck. The two floors connect by way of an open steel staircase. The large day room has a bare cement floor and six stainless steel tables and benches for four inmates per table. All the furniture is fastened to the floor. Nothing can be picked up and used as a weapon. There is a TV suspended from a ceiling mount. Its screen faces the day room so it cannot be viewed from the cells.

The TV power and volume can be controlled by the cops or by the inmates when they are out of their cells and in the day room. The day room also has a vending machine for candy, hairnets, cards, stamps, instant coffee packets, instant soup packages, chips of all flavor and a few toilet articles such as soap. Inmates are not allowed to carry cash so the vending machine card must have credit that has been fed into it by an external friend or family member via a money order. Very few inmates had such a luxury. Another vending machine dispensed soda drinks into your plastic glass. No cans or bottles are allowed in jail.

As I entered the pod the inmates stopped watching TV or playing cards and turned to stare at me. I knew they were thinking how old and frail looking I appeared. I thought that they must think that I am a white collar criminal because I am old, short, and balding and wear thick glasses. I tried not to make eye contact with them hoping that they would not notice me. I must have looked like an old beast of burden carrying all of my gear. The main door to the pod closed behind me. The cop on duty shouted over the PA "go to cell twenty-four." I looked around for a clue as to the whereabouts of this cell. Just then a tall and gaunt inmate approached me and without speaking took the bedding from between my teeth and the box that I held under my right arm. I followed him to cell 24. He placed the box and bedding on the cement floor. I thanked him for his kindness. "No problem Pop," he responded with a smile.

In my new cell there was a double-decked bunk bed. Also in my cell was a short and stocky middle aged Mexican. He introduced himself by nodding his head, pointing to his chest and quietly saying, "I Jose." I mimicked his polite introduction by shaking his hand and telling him that I was Bruce. Jose appeared to be in his mid-forties and he sported a thin mustache similar to the Mexican comedian, Cantinflas. I was to spend the next three months with Jose in a six by nine feet triangular shaped cell.

As I looked about the pie shaped cell I noticed that the upper deck bunk had been anchored to the wall incorrectly. The lower bunk had four and a half feet of space from the mattress to the frame of the upper bunk. The overhead of the upper bunk from mattress to ceiling was only about two feet. That is a significant difference in space for moving about. The inhabitant of the upper bunk cannot sit up or change sheets without great difficulty.

The cell has a stainless steel combined sink and commode unit. There are two metal shelves mounted to the wall just past the foot of the beds. That is for our toilet articles and reading material. The cell door is locked and can be opened electronically from the cop's lookout room just outside and above the pod. The upper part of the cell door is made of a window. I assumed that it is shatter proof. When the inmates or cops close the cell doors there is always a loud booming metallic noise. I think that is where the slang word "slammer" originated for a jailhouse.

There is a slit shaped glass window on the outside wall of the cell that measures about eight feet long and four inches high. The view of the distant purple brown hills is beautifully surreal, if not some sort of metaphor. The highest hill has a crucifix on the top with a road leading to it, and down below is the green tiled roof of the evil looking courthouse. Adjacent to its roof is a fenced off recreation area for the jail across the street. The rumor is that that is where you are sent if you give the cops any trouble. I was told that the facility is without air conditioning, is very crowded with several inmates in a cell and guarded by very grumpy marshals. Below the courthouse, I had learned first hand, is a long subterranean tunnel that leads from the courthouse to the jail across the street. Immediately after my surprise sentencing I was led through this tunnel in handcuffs to the jailhouse.

Several of the Hispanic inmates shouted out to Jose in Spanish that he should give the lower birth to the old man. Another inmate told me what they were saying to Jose so I knew what was going on. I denied this gallant gesture vigorously. I pointed to the upper bunk and told

Jose, *"por me"* and to be sure he comprehended I patted the lower bed and said *"no por me por usted."*

It became apparent that my level of Spanish was about the same as Jose's grasp of English. So for three months we grinned and bared the sound of Spanglish. In so doing we each learned many new words in the other's native tongue.

When our weekend lunch consisted of a bologna sandwich on cold and soggy white bread with mayonnaise, I told Jose that *"no bueno por perro"* he would smile and translate back to me "no good for dog."

It had also become apparent that that the upper bunk could not be made up with the bedding unless the thin mattress was moved out of the double decked frame. Jose showed me how to secure the small threadbare sheet on to the mattress jail-style. A single simple knot is placed in each of the four corners of the sheet. Then the sheet is placed on top of the mattress and the knots are tucked below to keep the sheet from sliding around.

I climbed the ladder with ease and placed the mattress on the upper bunk frame. Jose helped me place the sheet with the knotted ends under the mattress.

In order to get my body on to the bed I had to rotate my torso and right leg off the ladder. That maneuver meant that my left leg must remain on the ladder. There was no other way to do this given the small overhead that existed. This put a painful stress on my new left knee prosthesis. I was then able to swing my body around and up on to the mattress with difficulty and discomfort. The claustrophobic space plus this gymnastic feat convinced me quickly that this was not going to work. I decided that it would be better for me to sleep on the cell floor with my mattress. I pressed the cell's intercom button and asked the cop on duty if I could do so. I explained the problem to him and asked for permission to sleep on the floor. He replied with a simple, "I don't care where you sleep." I took that as a yes.

I tried sleeping that way for three nights. My feet were next to the commode and most of my torso and head were beneath the fixed metal desk. Soon after the first night I submitted a written request to be transferred to the next available cell with an open lower bunk.

On my fourth day in cell 24 with Jose, I received a call on the intercom from the cop on duty. She told me that my request for a lower bunk had been approved and that I was to move to the lower bunk. I inquired as to which lower bunk fearing that I already knew the answer. "Your cellmate will take the upper bunk and you will be in the lower one," she barked. "My cellmate had surgery for a bad back," I retorted to no avail. The cop shouted, "You are in jail mister and you will do as you're told." I persisted over the PA, "Taking away his bed is not my style. He has been in this cell for six months. Can you have a Spanish speaking person explain all this to my cellmate?" I waited for a response in vain. None came. I read the silence as a no.

Jose comforted my guilt by patting me on my back and uttering, "It's O.K., it's O.K., wow it's O.K." Jose took over the upper bunk. This time I helped him place the mattress and sheet up above. I had a Hispanic inmate explain this imposed swap to Jose as soon as I could.

Jose never complained about his sore back and confined space. I knew by his response that he had suffered worse hardships than this. Poor Jose had doomsday on his mind. He was awaiting trial and probable sentencing to a long stretch in prison.

He was arrested and incarcerated six months before my arrival. Jose had violated his probation. He had served six months in jail before having been charged with drunken disorderly conduct and assault. He was released with three years' probation. His violation this time was the same: drunken disorderly conduct. But now add: "firing an unregistered firearm in public and possession of one and a half kilo of cocaine." Jose claims that the cocaine was placed under his car seat by one of his two amigos that were in his car. They both fled to Mexico after Jose's arrest. Jose's Public Defender advised him that unless he pleads the charges down he could be facing as much as twenty-five years in prison followed by deportation to Mexico. When I heard this scenario the first thought that came to my mind is the same as you are thinking now. Why do they not just deport him now or after his sentencing and save the taxpayers some considerable expenditure for housing Jose for many years? It was explained to me later by his Public Defender that his criminal charges were local and not federal so the INS is not involved at this time.

I tried to imagine being Jose as I lied in my cell on the bed that I inadvertently confiscated from him.

Jose has a wife named Santana and they have six children: five *ninas* and one *nino*. He surely agonizes over what misfortunes he has brought on them by his craziness.

Jose is totally illiterate in Spanish and in English. He cannot read or write anything in any language. He never had the opportunity to spend even one day in school. His father, now deceased, forced Jose to care for the cows on their small farm near Cuernavaca.

As I daydream in my cell, I transport myself in my mind to a Mexican jail. Only Spanish is spoken here and that is the same with what I hear on the TV. I can barely understand what the inmates are saying or what the police are telling me to do or not to do. I understand little of the photographs that I view in the newspaper and cannot carry on a decent conversation with my cellmate. Fortunately, I fantasize that the jail confines a couple of other gringos. That allows me to play cards and exchange some conversation in English. I imagine how it must be to live one's life unable to write or read a love letter or record one's deepest thoughts. An illiterate person can think as clearly as you or I, but can only communicate their thoughts verbally.

Chapter 33

Written Up

One hot afternoon I awoke from a fitful slumber to see Jose lying on the cement floor of the cell clad only in his underwear. My first thought was that was a good way to stay cool. Jose had his head down between his forearms and he was crying softly. All I was able to do was pat him on his back, utter a few okays and hand him a piece of toilet paper to dry his eyes. I can only imagine the reason for this sudden breakdown.

Several days after the cops had me moved to the lower bunk I was summoned to leave my cell and go to the recreation area outside my pod. There I met with a Corporal Espinoza. The corporal introduced himself in an unusual friendly and polite manner. Espinoza was a middle-aged, overweight but buff looking Latino. He had a pleasant demeanor and wore his uniform with a neat appearance and sported a crewcut, not unlike a U.S. Marine. He explained that his job over the past twenty odd years was to investigate and to intervene in matters of jailhouse discipline. He wished to speak to me.

He proceeded to inform me that the cops had "written me up" because I had disobeyed their orders and subsequently they filed a complaint and forwarded it to him.

I asked, innocently, what order had I disobeyed. The corporal reached into his cop-shirt pocket and unfolded a sheet of paper. He read that I had refused to switch bunks with my cellmate. I responded to that by explaining that I had not refused to comply with their order but was strongly objecting to switching because it was not fair to Jose and such a plan was not my style.

To my surprise, the corporal agreed with me that such a move was not fair and that my reluctance to comply was normal conduct.

"However," he continued, "I must back up my staff when they file a complaint. I've been doing this for 28 years and I know that some of the deputies are too strict. You have the right to appeal this complaint before the Sheriff if you wish. Or you can accept the mildest form of punishment that I can give to you."

"And what would that be?" I inquired. Corporal Espinoza smiled and said; "We would add another year to your jail time" I smiled back hoping for some comedy relief. It came. "You will lose one week of commissary privileges, which means that your card will not be accepted by the vending machines. But because today is Saturday, he explained, that week will not begin until this coming Monday morning. So you have the weekend to buy and stock up on whatever you want."

Chapter 34

We are Praying for You

Two weeks into my incarceration the cops buzzed me in my cell early in the morning. "Steir," the cop shouted, "you have an eight o'clock visitor coming up." I had no idea who my visitor might be. I quickly put on my orange jumpsuit and washed my sleepy face. There is no problem in deciding what to wear when you are in jail.

The visiting area is down the corridor from the dayroom. That short solo walk requires that my hands be in my pockets. (Are they afraid I might otherwise punch myself?) There are six visiting booths. Each booth has a glass partition that separates the inmate from the visitor. There is a round stainless steel stool on each side of the glass. The stool is fastened to the cement floor. Each side has a wall-mounted telephone so conversation can take place. The cops can listen in if they wish. The deputy tells you when your fifty minutes is up. There is no opening in the glass partition for the passage of notes, photographs or contraband or for that matter a kiss or any contact at all. When a lawyer visits they have a separate room and may, with approval, pass legal papers to the client.

There is an elevator that opens up onto the visitor's side of the partitioned area. I am sitting on the cold stainless steel stool facing the elevator door waiting when out step several overweight women of various shades. I did not know them. Then a man reminiscent of Pat Boone emerged from the elevator. His buttoned down collar was buttoned and he carried a black leather bound book in his hand. I knew instinctively that he was cradling the Holy Bible. His fresh, wholesome looking face and Mormonesque smile told me that he is was my visitor. I have seen clones of him many times in front of abortion clinics. They inhabit the walkway and driveways in front of the abortion clinics. He (or she) usually carries an anti-abortion sign with a picture of a dead fetus. Sometimes they twirl a strand of rosary beads in their self-righteous hands.

I have seen the likes of him in Redding, Chico, Santa Rosa and Sacramento, Oakland and even in liberal San Francisco. They may curse me and inform me that I am going to hell or tell me something like "God loves you and he hopes you will stop killing babies." My retort was usually "God is a woman and she is pro-choice." They may wave their sign in front of me pretending not to be trying to hit me with it. But sometimes they did. I learned over the years not to grab the sign and destroy it because they will call the police and charge me with destroying personal property.

Often when I got out of the car at an abortion clinic I carried a drink: coffee or soda depending on the weather. If they tried to block my entrance to the clinic then whamo, they have a free drink in their passive aggressive face. They would then cry out "assault and battery" and call the authorities. The police arrive about ten minutes later and I defiantly tell them, "It was self-defense officer. I felt threatened by them and they blocked my path to my work place." My act, though, was not so courageous; I am wearing a bulletproof vest.

They believe in what they are doing and they get out of bed early in the morning to picket abortion clinics. They are well organized and well funded. Do I give them credit for what they believe in and what they do? Hell no! They could not care less about the women and their pregnancies. If they did, they would organize to address their real problems, which are largely financial. Like fundamentalist reactionaries across the globe, they are there to try to regain control of women. Not just control of her pregnancies or her body but the whole woman by shoving her right back into her place.

Allow me to attempt to read their minds and expose their twisted activism with you: " How dare she fornicate before marriage? What's more she sinfully enjoyed the sex. How dare she listen to her own heart and desires rather than listen to the dictates handed down through history? She got pregnant and now she is so evil she is going to kill her own baby. Only God can do that! Where is her morality? She is a whore! An irresponsible slut! College girls are having sex and doing drugs. Teenage girls are having sex instead of going to church. Next thing you know all these hussies are going to want birth control and sex education. And then what will become of civilization? God forbid!" What I am saying is that they are big time misogynists. That goes for the women picketers too.

I made eye contact with "Pat Boone" and motioned for him to sit down in cubicle number four in front of me. Pat picked up the telephone and introduced himself. "Hello, I am Troy Newman. I am a Christian and I am here to pray for you." My response was sincere. "Hello, I am Bruce Steir, I am a secular Jew and an inmate. Thank you for visiting me."

Troy went on to say, with that ever-present smile, "We are praying for you Bruce. Although we do not like what you do, we love you as a person and wish that you would save lives instead of killing God's children." I inquired as to whom he was representing and he told me that he was the coordinator for Operation Rescue in San Bernardino County. He told me that he lived in Lake Arrowhead, up in the mountains nearby. I told Troy that his people did a good job and were probably quite pleased that their efforts to have me charged with homicide were fruitful. "Here I am locked up in jail as my punishment. You anti-abortion folks won." Troy went on to assure me that Operation Rescue was not pleased that I had been incarcerated. "What we know of the case," he said, "It indicates that you were not aware that Sharon's life was in danger. We know that you did not intend to harm her or for her to suffer and die. Why would you? But abortion is a sin against God and both Sharon and you entered into an unholy alliance against God. Now he has punished both of you." I nodded my head in cynical agreement and agreed that Sharon had died and I was incarcerated and that could not be denied or argued.

The next theme of the conversation was already familiar to me. Troy told me that Jewish OB/GYN doctors seem to be quite prominent in the abortion business. He asked me why. "I think that is correct," I responded. "We are also busy in the business of social justice and for the rights of women to decide their reproductive fate. Yes, Jewish boys and girls study hard in school and forgo many pleasures and lost income to get accepted to medical school and the many years of postgraduate resident training. Jews are also prominent in the polio vaccine discovery business, heart transplant business, medical school professor business and Nobel Prize business."

Mr. Newman then told me that greed for an easy buck was foremost in the motivation of abortion providers. Now I was getting warmed up and a little annoyed. I was determined not to show my anger or annoyance to Pretty Boy Troy. My retorts were not difficult or metaphorical. Not like lines from a Shakespearian tragedy. I had walked this walk before and talked this talk before, but never before from the confines of a jailhouse.

I told Troy that almost all of the full time abortion providers that I knew do not get country club rich. From my personal experience I have received plenty of hugs and thank yous from abortion clients. Many more hugs from abortion clients then from the women who I assisted delivering their newborn babies. That is over a period of thirty years delivering thousands of wanted and some unwanted infants. Troy was listening with the same sardonic smile on his face that I had become accustomed to over the years. I reminded Troy that the vast majority of abortion clients that I see in freestanding outpatient clinics are MediCal recipients. (That is a welfare beneficiary's medical assistance in California lingo.) The state pays so very little for an outpatient abortion that if you calculate the overhead per client procedure the clinic may break even if they are fortunate. These women's clinics really have earned the right to be called non-profit organizations. Independent contractor abortion providers that travel to undermanned clinics, like me, typically earn between $30-40 per procedure. The number of abortion procedures performed per day varies greatly from as little as four to as many as forty in a day's work. This great hiatus in numbers is attributed to many factors: weather, the intensity of the picketing and the show rate of the clients scheduled. The latter was always lower near the beginning of the month because the state government folks in Sacramento are frequently tardy in mailing out the monthly Medi-Cal coupons. A June coupon will not fly in July.

I asked Troy if he knew why all these poor women go to these "butcher shop" clinics as his Operation Rescue people call them.

Troy did not answer or nod a gesture. He just continued to smile like a saint. I explained that the poor women on public assistance are not welcomed into the offices of the vast majority of private physicians. They simply refuse to accept the paltry remuneration by the state for services rendered. The reimbursement will not cover their office overhead or pay for their country club dues. You will not see too many Chicanos in the waiting rooms of private physicians who perform abortions in Palo Alto, Beverly Hills, Scottsdale, or the Hamptons. I chastised Troy for having the chutzpah to label abortion-providing clinics as "butcher shops" and also to accuse them of "racial genocide" for preying on poor women of color.

Troy then claimed that if abortion providers would devote their skills to provide care to families with good Christian morals and wholesome family values it would be better for America then to turn our skills to killing babies. He really said that! I could tell that Troy had become flustered and was losing the grasp of his argument against abortion. But he continued to look like Pat Boone nevertheless.

Troy pleaded his anti-abortion rhetoric by explaining that immoral and irresponsible women and men should have no place to turn in order to rid themselves of their unplanned pregnancy. This pregnancy is their sin and your coming to their rescue only adds to their social dysfunction. After awhile, he predicted, that without your help they would "see the light" the message would come home to help them.

He may as well have been saying that there ought to be no place in this world for forgiveness. Even an atheist like me knows this is not quite the line of argument he should pursue if he claims to follow the teachings of Jesus.

Nonetheless, he persisted in his misguided discussion. The leather bound bible that he carried was now the centerpiece to replace rationale conversation with the "wisdom of God's own written words." Troy read from a pre-saved page something about the wages of sin is death or something along that line.

His demeanor reminded me of the old movie "Rain." Walter Houston is the minister in a remote tropical paradise and he is preaching to a whore played by Joan Crawford. He is letting her know that she is heading to hell for her sins. Two scenes later he tries to seduce her and sermonize to her at the same time.

I ended the absurdity of this simplistic thinking by calling on one of my favorite pro-choice metaphors. I reached into my bright orange jumpsuit pocket and retrieved a small pencil with an oversized eraser.

Pens are not allowed in jail, only pencils. Pens are *verboten* because they can be used to create tattoos and pen graffiti is difficult to remove. I pointed to my eraser and told Troy that as long as there is a need for people to use erasers then there will be women having abortions.

Troy mentioned that if people took responsibility for their actions and did not blame society for their mistakes then they would not find themselves with an unplanned pregnancy. I reminded him that his organization, Operation Rescue, is not only anti-abortion they are also against sex education and contraceptive devices. I told him that these people are taking responsibility for their mistakes. An unplanned and unwanted pregnancy is a mistake corrected by a timely abortion. That is their "using the eraser." I asked Troy if he would prefer to see a high school teenager have a baby out of wedlock and drop out of school or have an abortion, (I was thinking about my sister) or a divorced single mother, a working mom, have a baby she doesn't want; or a how about a welfare woman and a crack addict with AIDS. Will one of your anti-abortion families adopt her baby?

Troy interrupted my sermon by reminding me that anti-abortion people (he calls them pro-life folks) are interested in installing Christian ethics back into American life. Then he reiterated the "family values" menu, which like Christian ethics never mentions slavery, the Inquisition, the Crusades or European imperialism. "We say prevention and you say cure." This time I interrupted him abruptly and explained that," we cure unwanted pregnancies with an abortion but I don't know where the prevention is on your part that you are claiming. You anti-abortion people are opposed to family planning and sex education too." His response was that of a politician. He completely evaded the issue. Instead he informed me that America is in grave peril because its people are moving away from God and his bible. I let that statement ride without comment.

Previous encounters with the anti-abortion people prepared me for Troy's next diatribe. "Have you Jewish abortionists thought about the unfortunate similarity of the Holocaust and the abortion business?" I reminded him with a tone of annoyance that that analogy has been thrown around ad nausea. It only demonstrates the insensitivity and stupidity of those that embrace such a moronic view of history. As for my personal perspective of Troy, I told him that I found his thinking irredeemable. "You are hopelessly lost in the quagmire of religion." I asked him how he could compare an eight-year-old child who is taking violin lessons and who kisses his mother goodnight to that of an unwanted embryo or fetus. "One is a living child that is brutally murdered by a bullet in the back of the head or gassed and cremated as compared to an unwanted mass of tissue that is voluntarily suctioned away."

Just then the cop called out over my telephone to inform me that time was up. Troy nodded and hung the phone up. I thanked him for his visit and invited him to return if he wished. Clasping my extended fingers below my chin, I bid him a Hindu farewell. That was preferable to a handshake that could not be given through a glass divider.

Nowhere in the bible does it advise believers to rudely point out the perceived sins of others, but it does give a directive to visit the infirmed and the imprisoned. Spending fifty minutes disagreeing with Troy Newman was better than being in my cell.

Chapter 35

Vending Machine Cuisine

(Notes from my Jailhouse Journal)

Today, like three days a week, it is another lockdown day. That means that I am in my small cell all day long except for meals for 20 minutes each, three times a day. Lockdown means the same as locked in. At Riverside County jail we had lockdown on Mondays, Tuesdays and Thursdays. Those are the days that inmates are removed from jail and taken away to prison to serve their sentences as dictated by the court. Transfers usually take place after midnight. When I inquired why there was such an arrangement, a fellow inmate with prior time served, informed me that a daytime transfer of a felon from jail was fraught with the danger of an inmate notifying family or friends about his impending trip to a state prison. The worry was that a possible hijacking of the police van and a rescue of the convicted person might occur. This seems far-fetched to me but it had happened I was assured. Why didn't the law enforcers just turn off the pay phones or make them off limit on jail transfer day? Jailhouse paranoia perhaps! But when I asked one of the marshals the reason for locking us down, his reply was a well-rehearsed standard brush-off, "because we can." This same crusty response was repeated to me when I asked one of the cops why the mail is delivered to our cells at 1:00 A.M. when we are asleep.

The air conditioning gave out. It is very hot outside as well as in my cell. As I lie here in my lower bunk, I cannot help but notice how protuberant my lower abdomen has become. I do not recall having a pot-tummy when I entered jail a horrible 67 days ago. There isn't a scale in my cell or in the pod but I surely must have put some pounds on and perhaps I have become bloated. I know why I have gained weight. We eat lots of starch: bread, spaghetti and mashed potatoes are frequently sharing the same plastic meal tray. The canned fruit salad is usually on top of the potatoes. An old-timer career criminal told me that the inmates who work in the jailhouse kitchen know which trays are going to our pod. Therefore these nasty criminals will joyfully sabotage the meals prepared for the "protective custody" inmates. The other criminals look down at us because we are reputably gay, baby bashers or wife beaters or sexual predators. Maybe all of the above! To these kitchen worker inmates we are all guilty until proven innocent.

Not all of my apparent weight gain is from the jailhouse meals. The extra pounds are also surely resulting from my midnight bedtime snack. Supper is served at 4:30 P.M. so I get hungry by 11:00 PM. In addition to satisfying my hunger, the vending machine offers something to do.

The vending machine in my pod requires a personal card with your name and picture on it. The machine does not take cash. Money is not allowed in jail. In fact when I entered the jailhouse everything I was wearing, all the contents of my pockets and any jewelry, was confiscated and is being held in security until my release. They would not allow me to keep my plain band of gold. (A marshal told me later that jewelry is not allowed, "Because it could be bartered for favors including sex.") I was allowed to keep only my eyeglasses.

The vending machine is operated with a plastic card that has cash value that must be added by someone on the outside mailing in a money order in your name. Very few inmates have any cash credit on their cards. Either family and friends have abandoned most of them or their support group has their own problems to deal with and do not have the luxury of sending money orders. Needless to say I was an easy touch for Cokes, coffee and candy bars. I must admit that I took care of those that I liked or felt sorry for. There were only a few who never asked me for any goodies from the vending machine. Perhaps their self-pride prevented them from asking or maybe they did not want to "beg" or feel obligated to me, an elderly "baby killer."

When we were not having a lockdown, we were allowed in the common area to watch TV, play cards, read, and use the vending machine. In the evening, when hunger gives way to the munchies, I was introduced to a special jailhouse snack.

It seemed that I was the only inmate with a useable vending machine card and with an interest in snacking before bedtime.

With only $4 worth of food we could concoct a feast for eight to ten inmates. The recipe consisted of three Top Ramen packets, two packages each of Doritos, corn chips and nachos. This was added to two or three hardboiled eggs that had been saved and hidden from a recent breakfast. These precious ingredients were then placed in a large plastic garbage bag and mashed together by hand. The contents were kneaded slowly and gently. This yummy mixture was then distributed to the lucky recipient's plastic glass. Hot water from a dispenser was then added. Voila! We had created our own signature "vending machine cuisine" and it tasted quite good, albeit quite salty.

On the nights we were in lockdown the vending machine cuisine was not available. Planning ahead, I would buy two Top Ramen and two Milkyways, one 2-course meal for me and the other for my cellmate, Jose.

In my best Spanish, which was superior to Jose's English, I asked him, *"como aqua caliente?"* That was the best I could muster to inquire how we could get hot water. His reply was simply, *"no problema para mi amigo."* He was right. At about midnight, a Hispanic inmate was given permission to leave his cell and provide hot water for the few lucky Top Ramen holders.

The good-natured cop allowed him to partially fill a clear plastic bag with hot water. The top of the bag was twisted tightly to render it sealed. Then the bag was laid on the floor directly in front of our cell door. The closed twisted end was then inserted through the small, half an inch opening under our cell door. Jose quickly grabbed the twisted end before it could unwind and then slowly slid the flattened hot water plastic bag under the door. This maneuver would then be repeated for the other one or two cells. The hot water Gunga Din man would be rewarded with vending machine coffee or candy. Not every nightshift cop was that willing to allow such shady hot water activity to take place on his or watch. After a while we all knew which cop we could count on for our midnight soup.

Today I am exercising my left knee. It is a ten-month old post-operative total knee replacement. Proper physical therapy is not available in jail. When I flex my knee up and down it emits a sound not unlike a bowl of Rice Krispies just having had milk poured on it.

When I stand over the commode to urinate into my stainless steel toilet bowl, I cannot see my penis or my toes as I always had in the past. Now I must lean my pot-tummy torso forward an inch or so in order to visualize my urinary stream. Every man who can see looks downward to follow his urinary stream. My energy is sapped. I feel sad and old. I miss my wife. (Although I may be old in years, seldom have I felt old until now.)

Some of the inmates call me Doc. Before they had learned that I was a physician they referred to me as Pop. Two of the inmates, both career criminals, called me Pops. To my ears this pluralized or possessive form of this noun takes on the sound of a low-class felon or a merchant seaman out of work. I disliked the title Pops but endured it. It is not worth getting upset or even discussing it with them. I knew that I would be out of here in seven weeks or so.

Four months' incarceration, by most sentencing standards, is "a walk in the park." This is such a short period of time as compared to the vast majority of the thirty-one inmates in my pod. Most of the other inmates are parole violators awaiting trial or sentencing for prison time.

I recently discovered that my pod was special. All of the inmates, including me, are in a category known as "protective custody." We are in jail and separated from the other jail population to protect us from violence. I was never told that I was being sent to a protective custody area. I am not certain why some of the inmates are in protective custody. Contrary to popular opinion, jailhouse manners dictate that you not ask, "Why are you here, what did they charge you with?" Questions such as these are a no-no and could open cans of worms no one is ready for. If an inmate wants to discuss why they are doing time, they will probably do so when they feel comfortable with you, if ever.

My pod has spouse abusers (a.k.a. bitch-beaters), child abusers (a.k.a. baby bashers), gays and sex offenders. Most of the sex offenders are parole violators with a repeat offense. Several inmates were pedophile sex offenders.

Robert, a nice looking and street-wise 22 year old told me that he and his live-in girlfriend had consensual sex with a 14-year-old girl who lived in their same apartment complex. He swears that he thought she was over eighteen. I did not believe him.

Robert was awaiting trial. His Public Defender (a.k.a. "public pretender" among the criminals) told him to plead guilty for a lighter sentence of 10 to 20 years.

Pleading guilty assures that that court and the DAs will win the case. The higher the batting average, the more likely it is that the voters will reelect them to office.

I was told that Riverside County DA's office has one of the highest conviction rates in the state. Their not-so-secret success boils down to a simple formula: "Overcharge the felon and he will plead down."

Michael, a middle-aged Italian American convicted felon, was awaiting sentencing. He saw me struggle with my spaghetti on several occasions. The only eating utensil given to inmates is a plastic spoon. Try eating pasta with only a spoon. Michael created a five-pronged fork from a spoon by slowly carving it out with a disposable safety razor that was skillfully removed from its plastic holder. In turn I presented him with several packets of instant coffee and a bag of Jolly Rancher candy. (I still have this spoon that I cherish as a jailhouse memento.)

For many years Michael had driven an ice cream vending vehicle about the streets of a small town in Riverside County without incident. One of his customers was, he says, a voluptuous and flirtatious fifteen year old. One day she approached his vehicle and told him that she only had a quarter but would love to have an ice cream.

He took the quarter, presented her with an Eskimo Pie and then made the mistake of dropping the two bits down her blouse. He told her that she could pay him back some other time. When she returned to her house her mother inquired as to where she had gotten the money for the ice cream. The teenager told her mother that he put his hand down her blouse and returned the quarter in that manner. She repeated that scenario in court after the mother had him indicted for sexual abuse with a minor.

Michael was sentenced to nine years and will probably serve five. For some reason I believed his version of the story. He is a family man with three children. I don't know for sure whether it's true in this case, but it just might be possible that on occasion judgments of guilt or innocence just might be driven by people's darkest fears rather than on the facts of the case.

I was in protective custody, not because of my pleading guilty to involuntary manslaughter, but because I was a serial baby killer (a.k.a. an abortion provider).

Protective custody seemed a bit paranoid to me. Who, I thought, would want to harm an old, diminutive, bespectacled doctor? Soon I realized that there were many inmates and cops who shared the same virulent attitude against abortion as did the recent California Attorney General.

I would have felt endangered to be incarcerated with the ilk of a Dan Lungren. He was the Republican who had lost the gubernatorial race to Gray Davis and is now once again in the US House of Representatives. He was anti-abortion and was man enough to admit so in a California campaign. Lungren was the self-appointed protector of women's unwanted embryos.

A private investigator, hired by my attorney, suggested that there was unconfirmed evidence that Lungren had connections with anti-abortion people on the Medical Board of California and that he had encouraged them to cooperate with the Operation Rescue people in Riverside County.

Their goal, which was successful, was to have my medical license revoked and to have me charged with homicide.

The reason that I was in jail was well known by the majority of the thirty-two inmates in my pod. The news about my sentencing was in the local newspapers and also in the *Los Angeles Times,* the *San Francisco Chronicle* and the *Sacramento Bee.* It was also on the local TV stations as part of the evening news. Yet only one inmate made any remark or reference as to why I was in jail and placed in protective custody.

One early morning at breakfast, I complained to my other three tablemates that the deputy had awakened me at 2:00 AM to deliver mail to my cell. One of the inmates, a tall and clean-cut 20-year-old Mormon, admonished me in a stern matter telling me that such an act was understandable and was part of my punishment. He went on to remind me, "You must remember that you killed a woman and her unborn baby, didn't you?"

This young anti-abortion inmate was awaiting trial and had been charged with child assault and torture. Gripped with anger, he had shaken his three-month-old son so vigorously that the baby suffered a cerebral hematoma from a ruptured blood vessel in the lower brain stem. The infant had undergone surgery for drainage and was semi-comatose ever since. The District Attorney's odd charge of torture is based on their belief that he derives pleasure from shaking the baby. The prosecution believes this because testimony revealed that he had shaken the baby on several occasions. He is facing 25 years if convicted. If the baby were to succumb to his brain damage, then daddy dearest would face 25 to life for homicide. The State, he said, will drop the charge of torture if he pleads guilty to child assault. That would be a mere seven years in prison. His family, including his wife, are very supportive of him and do not want him to plead guilty. They are going to testify that the child assault never happened but it was a just an accidental moment of bad luck. His defense lawyer wants the plea if he can get two years and anger management therapy.

Pleading guilty to a lesser charge is a way of settling a case without a costly trial for both the prosecution and the defendant. This also allows for a high conviction rate for the DAs office and few notices that this is usually accomplished by zealously overcharging the case. Many examples of all of this legal maneuvering, of course, are making me painfully aware that it is without regard to guilt or innocence.

I have been incarcerated and I am not guilty of committing a crime. But pleading guilty to involuntary manslaughter brands me forever as a convicted felon.

How horrible it must be for someone who is completely innocent to be sent to prison for a crime committed by another person. We now know that this happens more often than we would like to think. Forensic use of DNA evidence proves that the judicial system is sometimes too politically motivated and overly anxious to settle a case with little regard for justice.

To add another unjust insult to my incarceration and the enormous monetary expenditure for legal services, I had my Social Security benefits revoked while being in jail. Even my lawyer was surprised to learn that these earned and paid for entitlements are forfeited automatically. I was in county jail because of charges against me by the state and now the federal government decided to punish me too.

The monthly benefits are lost for any month that you are incarcerated for even one day of that month. So in theory, if I was jailed on May 31st and released on June 1st then I would lose two months of Social Security payments. I am fortunate to be married to a woman who works for a living. Pity the senior felon who counts on that social security check to help pay the mortgage, car payments, health insurance and provide food for his or her family. This is a federal law that should be challenged as being unjust. It's beyond unjust. It's theft, plain and simple.

Chapter 36

The Spousal Visit

Visiting hours at the jailhouse span throughout the day: 8:00 AM until 10:00 at night on Tuesday, Thursday and Sunday. The visit is for 50 minutes or until the cop tells you that time is up, which ever happens first. An inmate can have up to two visits on any visiting day providing there are enough slots open to accommodate everyone. Inmates are allowed only a total of two visits per week not counting attorney business. Visitors must arrive 20 minutes before the hour of their visit. The visitation appointment must be made by telephone and can only be scheduled for the next day. Getting through on the phone is very difficult and time consuming. Most complaints are about busy signals and being left on hold for fifteen minutes followed by a disconnect signal. Several visitors or would be visitors told me that the appointment makers were abrasive and curt.

On my wife's first visit she was unable to get through by phone on Saturday from our home in San Francisco. She wanted to set-up a visit for the next day, a Sunday. Yen caught an early Saturday afternoon flight to Ontario airport and a van to her hotel in Riverside. From her room she resumed her telephone calls in vain. Busy, busy signal for over one hour.

She could not get through and it was getting late in the day. Yen wisely decided to walk down to the jailhouse to make the appointment in person. It was only six blocks away.

When Yen arrived at the jailhouse visitor's window she requested an appointment for Sunday, the next day. The female uniformed deputy informed her without making eye contact that all appointments are made over the phone. Yen explained her inability to get through on the phone to do so. Yen pleaded, "I am here now in person in front of you, can't you please just give me an appointment with my husband for tomorrow?" The response was simply, "No, all appointments are made by phone." Not wanting to argue with such a robotic and rude individual with authority, Yen returned to the hotel. After two frustrating hours of calling she finally got through and set up her appointment for the next day. After her short visit with me she flew back to San Francisco.

On my 80th day of captivity in the Riverside jailhouse, Yen returned on a Saturday for a Sunday visit with me. I was very anxious to see her pretty face and to hear her voice, albeit over the visitor's phone. Although the glass partition separates us, preventing physical contact, seeing her close up provided me with a warm and loving feeling and helped me get through the rest of the day.

Another minor reason I was looking forward to Yen's visit was that my cellmate had the same hour for a visit as I did. Jose's wife, Santana, and his six-year-old daughter, Angelica, were coming to visit. Jose and I marched to the visiting area at 3:00 PM.

Soon afterward the elevator door opened and four women and a little girl emerged. None of them were my wife.

Perhaps the elevator stopped at other floors on the way up and there wasn't room for my wife. I became agitated after ten minutes because every inmate had a visitor on the other side of the glass window except me. I sat on my steel stool staring at the elevator door. Jose's wife could see that my visitor had not arrived. She asked Jose if my wife was Asian. He asked me and I answered *"Si"*.

Santana told Jose in Spanish that my wife arrived late and the cops would not let her onto the elevator to visit me. Jose's broken Spanglish got the message to me. Yen was very upset and was arguing with the uniformed authorities downstairs according to Jose's *esposa*.

I waved frantically to the surveillance camera overhead wanting to let the floor cops know what was happening downstairs. Over the P.A. I advised the cop that my wife had arrived late and was not being allowed to visit me. I pleaded with him to intercede on our behalf. The cop said that he would call downstairs and see what he could do. He told me to return to the dayroom in the meantime. Shortly afterward he buzzed me on the intercom to tell me what I already feared. He regretted that he had no power to interfere with the people down in the visiting reception area. The head sheriff has that authority but he is not around on Sunday. He went on to explain that my wife was ten minutes late and they will not let her visit you. I called my wife on her cell phone from the dayroom payphone. All calls from jail are collect. Yen was still downstairs. Her voice belied her anger and disappointment. I could sense that she had been crying. She reiterated what had occurred and she told me that she arrived ten minutes late, which was still ten minutes before the visiting time.

I never asked her why she was late. It did not matter. She would not be late on purpose. No different, in a sense, then my missing the diagnosis of a uterine perforation. It was not missed on purpose.

I told her that I loved her and that I would see her when I am released in five weeks. I suggested that she not return to visit me again but to be there when I am released.

Many sad, power-craving people who show pleasure with their sadistic demeanor inhabit this jailhouse and courthouse next door. Most of the cops are fairly decent people and perform their job in a civilized manner. Some of them exhibit little empathy for their prisoners. But I also met some cops that seemed to have stepped right out of the pages of history. They would have been excellent guards at the Nazi extermination camps. A different time, a different place, but some of them would enjoy beating and maybe even killing a few of the inmates if they could do so with impunity. Admittedly some of the criminals they deal with day in and day out could make a saint into a sadistic beast.

Chapter 37

Our Weekly Sarong Party

This is a brief run-down of the prisoners' schedule in Riverside County jail. Reliable sources (i.e., felons with long rap sheets) tell me that this schedule of activities is quite typical of other jails they have inhabited.

Monday, Tuesday and Thursday:

4:30 AM--"Chow time, chow time," Twenty minutes for breakfast. You must be dressed and out of your cell for a headcount.

5:00 AM--Back into your cell. Most inmates go back to sleep. Overhead cell light remains on all day and all night.

8:00 AM--"Pill call." Those that are prescribed medication line up outside their cells in the day room. The jail nurse dispenses medication through a small window with a shelf that opens into the day room. We queue up and identify ourselves to the grumpy nurse who then places the pills in our hand and watches us swallow with a gulp of water. Then back to our cells.

11:00 AM--"Chow time, chow time," 20 minutes for lunch then back to your cell.

1:00 PM--Electrically controlled cell doors are opened for us to have access to the day room. The TV is turned on. The 32 orange-clad inmates have the option of staying in their cells if they wish to. The day room has four round stainless steel tables that are attached to the bare concrete floor. Each table has four attached stools. There is no furniture to hurl, damage, or confiscate. In the day room we can watch a loud TV that is mounted to the ceiling on a metal bracket. Or, if we wish, we can chat, play cards, chess, dominoes, or read. It is usually the same five or so inmates that read the local newspaper. I received a *San*

Francisco Chronicle via subscription by my dear wife. It was usually four days en route but welcomed nevertheless. The entertainment section had advertisements for local strip joints and porno palaces with facial photos of the "star" performers. Several inmates vied for these pictures. My good friend Sheldon sent a subscription of *The New Republic* to me. This liberal weekly has no photos, cartoons or advertisements. I found out that in jail this magazine could be left out on a day room table without fear of it being borrowed.

Each pod of 16 cells for 32 inmates has two showers, two payphones for outgoing collect calls only, a soft drink machine and a vending machine that dispenses snacks and a variety of toiletries including hair nets for those in need.

4:30 PM--"Chow time, chow time," 20 minutes for dinner then back to the cell for lockdown until breakfast 12 hours later.

7:00 PM--"Pill call." If you were prescribed a sedative or an antidepressant or any medication to be taken at bedtime, well 7:00 PM is bedtime for the convenience of the jail's nurse. Some swallowed their pills and made an early night of it. Others, like myself, hid their pill in their hand, cheek, palate or gums and pretend they swallowed it by going through the motion. I was only caught faking it once in 113 nights. I would return to my cell immediately and remove my pill from behind my upper premolar and ingest it at my will around midnight.

11:00 PM--all bright overhead florescent lights in the cells are turned off but the security lights stay on always.

Midnight to 1:00 AM--Mail call. The deputy on duty delivers mail to each cell. Yes, mail call was usually after midnight. Although I was given the standard answer, "Because we can," by a cop when I asked, I learned that the actual reason for the mail delivery after midnight was to provide time during the day to read and, if need be, censor the incoming and outgoing mail.

Actually it takes the deputies most of the day in their spare time to read the mail and remove the stamps, envelope closure seal and return address labels. I was told that the stamp glue could be mixed with small amounts of drugs, like cocaine or heroin.

Most inmates rarely receive mail, if ever. Few of them write letters; some cannot write. I lie in bed eagerly awaiting my mail even though I am not thrilled about being awakened for it.

So Monday, Tuesday and Thursday are lockdown days from 4:30 PM to 4:30 AM. These days are long, boring and punishing. Ostensibly, that is what incarceration is about.

Wednesday, Friday, Saturday and Sunday the schedule is the same for the most part except that there is no lockdown after 8:00 PM. We are allowed into the day room until 11:00 PM or midnight. These evenings seem like treats. We seem elated.

Visiting hours are on Tuesday, Thursday and Sunday. We are allowed up to two 50-minute visitations per day, one in the morning and one in the afternoon or evening. Most of the inmates do not have visitors.

Recreation is a one-hour deal twice a week. Remarkably, only about a third of the inmates choose to participate.

Those men that choose not to walk single file to the gym are either depressed, lazy or prefer reruns of Hawaii 5-0 to an hour of "recreation."

The gymnasium is on the same floor as our pod. There is a half court basketball area that takes up 2/3 of a wooden floor gym. The remaining part has a chining bar and a ping-pong table. A deputy reads and watches us from a window-enclosed cage. His/her other functions are to tell us that they do not have any new ping-pong balls and the old cracked one will have to suffice and also to inform us when it is time to lineup and return to our cells.

There is an AA meeting one night per week and Protestant and Catholic lay services are held in a side room near the visitor's area once every two weeks. Being a devout, born-again atheist I did not inquire about Jewish services.

The Hispanic inmates make up about one-third of the pod. They stay pretty much to themselves when out of their cells. They converse in Spanish and play cards with great gusto. They have their own religious services everyday held under the steel stairwell. The TV is so loud that I wonder how they can worship and tolerate the noise. Why don't they turn the sound down?

They can lower the TV volume only on Hispanic day. There is a three-day rotation for control of the TV--White, Black, and Hispanic. It was all very democratic if not racist. When we had only two black inmates on board they still had their TV day.

One day while the Latinos were conducting their prayer services I became very annoyed with the TV noise turned up to full volume. Being short, I stood on my tiptoes to lower the sound. Several "old timers" instantly berated me. When I explained my righteous indignation they shouted me down promptly by yelling, "It's fucking white day." Democracy can only go so far. I should have demanded a Jewish day.

The regimented routine in jail does not make the days, hours or weeks go faster. Everyday is like a bad toothache that cannot be ignored. The mental pain of incarceration is there and will not go away. There are light moments of joviality, even camaraderie and sad goodbyes when a nice person is leaving jail for a long prison sentence. But for the very most part being in jail is humiliating, boring, noisy, and unhealthy and should be avoided if at all possible.

Saturday morning is the Big Sarong Party. The event takes up about two hours of our valuable time. It is a humiliating but mildly enjoyable happening because it breaks the monotony of the cell.

We strip our bunk bed of the two sheets and bundle them up with our towel, underwear, socks, and orange jumpsuit. There is no pillowcase because we do not have pillows. My guess is that a pillow is not issued for two reasons: 1) sanitation 2) it is a possible quiet homicide weapon.

The cops hustle us out of our cells. We line up in front of our cell doors. They call roll. We are all wearing a sarong. The wrap is our olive-drab woolen blanket that is folded and tucked in around our waist. It is itchy and looks foolish. Otherwise we are wearing nothing else. The blanket extends from the waist to my ankles and I have a difficult time keeping it from sliding down. My Mexican cellmate, Jose, shows me the proper way to fashion a blanket into a sarong.

The purpose of the Sarong Party is to get us out of our cells, provide fresh clothing and bedding and to search our cells for contraband.

Perhaps we might be smuggling in semi-automatic weapons or vodka, or cigarettes, or porn stars, or boxes of chocolate bon-bons! They know that we do not possess such illegal items but each week for security purposes the cops purge our cells and confiscate whatever they deem contraband.

Mostly they are looking for hidden oranges or bananas, a daily fruit treat, which could be squirreled away to make a fruit wine. An extra towel or a pair of socks might be discovered and confiscated. I had complained about being cold at night and requested an extra blanket. Being old and feeble the nurse ok'd my solicitation. My intent was to use the extra blanket as a pillow. Sleeping flat and on my side was most uncomfortable for my neck.

I then made the mistake of leaving the extra blanket on my bed and the alert cops took possession of it. When I asked the cops why they took my extra blanket away they of course replied, "Because we can."

Next, the cop of the day shouts, "take off your blanket, now unfold your blanket, now hold your blanket in front of you, now shake your blanket, now turn around and face your cell with your blanket in front of you."

We 32 felons look like nude, transvestite fan-dancers. On command, we turn around again and face our fully clothed uniformed captors.

"Now wrap the blanket around you once again," he commands like a Marine Corps drill sergeant. "Pick up your used laundry and pass out of the day room in a single file." He orders us to place the various used laundry articles into large plastic bags that are held by the cops. We march out, hands behind our back, as is required. I keep hoping that my sarong remains securely fastened. We are ushered into a side room down the hall that is used for AA meetings and religious services.

In this room are twelve or so bright blue plastic chairs. Twenty of us stand showing off our olive drab or West Point gray woolen army surplus blankets--I mean sarongs. Out of respect for my age several inmates offer me their chair. I thank them and continue to stand by the window.

The four-inch slit of a window allows me a peek of the street four stories below. It is so interesting to view a new street having grown tired of the view of the street from my cell window where I hardly ever see a person. I can see people walking alone and couples crossing the street holding hands. No one is wearing an orange jumpsuit or walking with leg shackles. I noticed that consciously. Such a weird and sad feeling suddenly comes over me, so I turn away from the window. I cannot imagine how some of the inmates who are going off to prison for many years must feel.

The younger rowdy guys are looking at women walking down the tree-lined streets that are also lined with shops. Some of the inmates make vulgar sexist remarks. Mostly, though, we are quiet during the 45 minutes that we are there.

We are then marched back to our cells where we receive our fresh laundry. The cops always asked me, "What size Doc?" referring to the orange jumpsuit. At first I would reply "Medium will do," and they would throw a rolled up large one for me to catch like a well-thrown forward pass. They would laugh and say, "Here, grow into this one." Later, during my short confinement, I told them that "any size will do." That of course took their fun away.

In my cell I notice that, in addition to my extra blanket, a small plastic bag that I had on my shelf had disappeared. I had saved it to be a holder for my bar of soap. I complain to my cellmate, who doesn't understand English, that the cops probably thought that I was going to use the plastic bag to commit suicide or homicide.

Chapter 38

My Hospital Visit as a Felon

In September 1999 I had a total knee replacement. My damaged, 68-year-old left knee had fallen ill to erosion, tears and resultant arthritis that produced more pain as time went by. The final blow to my lame knee occurred while skiing at Squaw Valley. I made a right turn and my knee went straight ahead or so it seemed. This was the incentive for surgical intervention. During the postoperative period I attended physical therapy three times a week at Kaiser Permanente in San Francisco. I also swam laps twice a week in the Olympic size pool at the University of San Francisco.

But eight months later a surprise jail sentence was imposed on me and I was whisked away to jail in handcuffs as if I suddenly were a dangerous criminal.

Incarceration meant the end of physical therapy. Recreation time for my jailhouse pod was one hour twice a week in a closed jail gym —not nearly enough, but it was a welcomed break in the week.

Available recreation was basketball and ping-pong. I could not shoot or slam-dunk with the "brothers" but I did play table tennis and was able to beat most of my fellow inmates. The ping-pong ball usually had a dent or a slit that made the game technically awkward. My summertime experience was that it was always too hot in the gym and all the participants perspired heavily.

There are only two showers in our pod. We were allowed a total time of 20 minutes for all 32 of us to shower before we were back in our cells. Who would get to shower was always uncertain and chaotic. Like school kids we would shout out "first shower" or "second shower" on the way to the gym or sometimes on the way back. It was understood that the shower would be one to two minutes long per man.

My total knee replacement seemed to feel tighter and I noted a loss of some extension and flexion. My new knee was in need of physical therapy. I was able to perform some exercises in my cell but was not able to do this often enough to make a notable difference. Most disturbing of all was that for the first time the knee made a crackling noise that was emitted from the knee when I exercised it in my cell bed.

I thought it wise to put in a request for a visit to a local orthopedic surgeon. In order to obtain such a visit I needed to fill out and submit a request slip and present it to the nurse during pill call. The request form for a visit with a nurse or physician is called a "blue kite." Blue because that is the color of the request slip, and kite, I think, is because after it is submitted it flies away as in "go fly a kite." But I pestered and persisted until finally an appointment was made for me to visit an orthopedic physician. It took a full six and a half weeks for the kite to fly, far too long for anyone to wait for needed medical attention.

Pill call was twice a day. The nurse came by the pod and dispensed medication that was ordered by the jail doctor. Each time I asked the nurse about my requested appointment. The nurse's response was always the same: "Your appointment has been forwarded on to the authorities." After a month had gone by since my blue kite was submitted, the response changed to, "Your appointment will be this month." Well I figured out that this was July 19th and there are 31 days in July so my appointment must be in the next 12 days. The actual date remains a secret until the guard informs me in my cell via the intercom that I should get dressed and stand outside my cell door. Getting dressed is easy and deciding what to wear is no problem. It's one of many decisions that has already been made for me: the orange jump suit will do just fine for the occasion. The actual date for my medical appointment must be kept a secret for fear that a planned terrorist attack on the police van might take place during its trip to the county hospital.

If they had told me the exact date and time of my appointment at the County Hospital, I would have notified my wife in San Francisco. She in turn would put into action a planned commando raid in Riverside County. Suffice that I had only two more months to serve in captivity; I would try a daring escape in broad daylight. My petite, soft-spoken wife who abhors violence (being a war refugee from Vietnam) would not only hijack the van, free all seven inmates, subdue the two armed cops and assist my escape by climbing up the rope ladder to board a chopper hovering above. We would then fly to the landing pad adjacent to the Beverly Wilshire Hotel. After checking in I would have my shackles removed from my hands, waist and ankles and then take off that awful orange jumpsuit. What would I do after that? I never fantasized further other then changing my identity and joining the *Mosad (Israeli secret service)*.

The first notification I had of my impending doctor appointment was at 3:00 A.M. on July 26th. I had managed to fall back to sleep after being awakened at 1:30 A.M. by the cop on duty. He knocked on my cell door to announce that I had mail: three letters, a *New Republic* magazine and my *San Francisco Chronicle*. I felt quietly grateful, realizing that that is more mail then most inmates receive in a year. By this stage in the incarceration I found myself mulling over the same thoughts. For example, I again reflected on the fact that the *New Republic* is especially practical to receive when behind bars. There are no pictures or advertising contained within so if you leave it outside your cell on one of the pod tables or on top of the vending machine, no one will steal it. Long-winded left wing essays and editorials condemning the Florida voting in the national elections is not a jail favorite even for those inmates that can read.

At 3:00 A.M. the intercom in my cell blasted out, "Stein, pill call now, you're going to court." I knew that I was Steir but Stein would have to be me especially since my cellmate was Jose Quezada. I also knew that I was not going to court because I had already pleaded guilty and was serving out my sentence. I figured out that they were going to give me my morning pills now instead of the usual 8:00 A.M. pill call because I would be away from my cell at that time.

Following that early morning medication I had the usual 4:30 A.M. breakfast with my other fellow inmates. I was summoned out my cell at 5:30 A.M. I would not return for 11 hours.

I was ushered down the hall to the jail elevator that would take me to the basement floor and to the transportation area. There I was lined up against a wall with five other inmates from other parts of the jail. We were then stripped searched. Totally nude, we are ordered to bend over and spread our gluteal cheeks to enable the deputies to view our anal opening. This is followed by the mandatory order to "cough real hard." This is done ostensibly to suddenly increase the intra-abdominal pressure. (This is the moment that an AK47 will slide out of the rectum that I thought to be so cleverly concealed!) The humiliation is easy to forget but I still wonder today what the cops would suspect that we would smuggle *OUT* of jail! Oh, sure! I want to sneak my pencil out to write my experiences at the hospital on the trouser leg of my jumpsuit, but not badly enough to hide it where they were looking for contraband.

After redressing we were handcuffed and shackled around the waist and the chain was secured with a large Master lock at the lower back. I was then placed alone in a holding cell for over an hour. My boredom turned into an itch on my nose. The waist chain prevents the fingers from reaching your face so I rubbed my nose against my knee as best I could.

At 7:00 A.M. we were lined up against a wall again and the cops had our ankles clamped with handcuffs attached to an eighteen-inch chain. We were then marched to an unmarked Ford van. I was placed in a cage in the back behind the rear seats.

The cage size was half the size of the van's width and contained a metallic seat. Another cage was behind the driver's seat. There was a female inmate inside this partitioned area. She was of course separated to prevent malicious groping by the male inmates (and cops?). I am isolated because I am a notorious baby killer in protective custody. The van left with seven inmates and two deputies at 7:30 A.M. This was my first time out of the jailhouse in two months to the day.

Fifteen bumpy minutes later we arrived at what appeared to be a very new and large County Hospital out in the desert in a remote and barren suburb, far away from the town center. It was still early morning when we arrived and by the looks of the almost empty parking lot, very few outpatients had arrived as yet. Police vehicles had their own parking lot. This was not a big surprise to me. With so many jails scattered around Riverside County and untold thousands of inmates that had been convicted or were awaiting trial or sentencing, more than a few in number would be needing medical appointments on an everyday basis.

We were removed from the van and lined up to march single file to the outpatient building. Our orange clad jumpsuits seemed brighter in the glow of the early morning sun. I would have preferred being invisible at that moment. As we trudged along slowly with our fettered arms and legs I was at once so humiliated that the pain in my ankles from the chain abrading against my sockless skin was becoming bearable.

On our march to the back entrance of the hospital clinic we passed an outdoor garden area set-aside for smokers. I made eye contact with one of the smokers, a middle-aged Latina woman. She must have pondered, as I did, the question, "What the hell did that little old man do to end up on a chain gang?"

The five-story medical center had one floor set-aside just for the jail and prison inmates. Riverside County knew how to plan for the future.

Three other inmates from other jail facilities with orthopedic problems waited with me in an examining room. One, a 25-year-old black male had broken three metacarpal bones in his right hand (between the wrist and the knuckles). He sustained this injury from a strong right hook into a cement wall in his apartment. This self-destructive rage was brought on because he had violated his parole and knew that the cops were coming to arrest him and put him back in prison. The sad looking felon had berated his ex-girl friend for having a new man in her life. She had a court order for him to not see her or even telephone her.

He wore an aluminum cast along with handcuffs. A young and tired looking resident came in and interviewed him after looking at his x-ray on the wall mounted view box. He told him that he was scheduling him for surgery. When asked when that would be the resident simply replied "soon." This was in keeping with jail medicine. The last thing the hospital wants is a hostage to be taken and the prisoner freed. That may sound far-fetched and maybe even somewhat paranoid. There are career criminals who would plan and execute such an escape if they had the necessary information.

A nurse assistant asked me about my orthopedic problem. I explained that my total knee replacement had left me with limited flexion and extension since my incarceration almost three months ago. She ordered an x-ray. She did not ask me why I was in jail. She escorted me down the hall to a marshal who complied with her order to remove my ankle shackles for the exam. After the chain was removed I felt the soreness and saw the skin abrasions around my ankles but I did not complain to anyone. I tried to console myself by asking, whether Steve McQueen would kvetch about such a small problem?

An hour later a young resident with a Jewish sounding name came to see me. He flexed my knee and acknowledged the existence of this amusing sound that emanated from my artificial knee. He flexed my knee several times before informing me that my x-rays looked very normal and that the prosthetic was in place. He even went so far as to say that it looked better than most knee replacements he had seen. I inquired of him as to his being a resident physician. I omitted the word "just" having been one some time long ago. He took no offense and reassured me that an attending orthopedic physician had viewed my x-rays too. The resident's advice was reasonable, pragmatic and anticipated. He suggested that I exercise my knee as best that I could in my cell and that I should return to my pre-incarceration physical therapy and swimming and biking after my release. I told him that I was going to be released in about a month. He did not ask me why I was in jail.

Deputy Gutierrez escorted me to a room at the far end of the detention floor. The deputy opened the locked door. The room had two beds. One was made up with mattress, pillow and blanket. The other bed was void of all the aforementioned and was only a bare metal frame.

The deputy pointed to the bed at the far end of the room and said, "See that bed with the blanket and pillow? Don't touch it. See the empty bed without a mattress? You can sit on it, lie on it or whatever, but don't touch the other bed." Then he left me alone.

I was very sleepy and wanted to lie down and put my head on a real pillow. It had been a very long time since I'd slept on a pillow. Back in my cell I used a rolled up blanket to substitute for a pillow. Maybe pillows conjure up fears of homicidal suffocation or maybe they are difficult to be sanitized or maybe it is just part of the punishment meted out.

I noticed that there was a surveillance camera in the corner of the ceiling. I therefore resisted the temptation to place my head on this most inviting clean soft pillow. I did not want to give Deputy Gutierrez the pleasure of "writing me up" and disciplining me.

The hospital room was clean, cool and large in comparison to my cell back at the jailhouse. There was a shower in the room too. I wished that I had a towel so I could have a hot shower. The room was too cool and there wasn't a thermostat to control the temperature. Another deputy brought me my sack lunch. It was always the same food; fairly nutritious but not delicious. The meal consisted of cold and damp white bread with a slice of bologna and a square of American cheese. Sometimes they threw in a packet of mustard or mayonnaise. To accompany this sandwich was a package of peanut butter cookies from Planters and a small container of reduced fat milk. After I finished my lunch I placed the wrappers and empty milk carton back into the paper sack and wrapped it in toilet paper. I used this beehive size concoction as my pillow. I sat in a chair and grabbed a nap with my head on my "pillow" resting on the metal bed frame. This was more comfortable than the floor.

In the late afternoon I was escorted out of the hospital room and joined up with the other six inmates. Once again we were stripped searched. At last we were ready to leave. On the way to the elevator we had to walk single file, cuffed and ankles shackled, wearing our bright orange jumpsuits, through a large and crowded waiting room filled mostly with mothers and children.

As we slowly trudged through a carpeted center aisle of the waiting room I noticed that the people were politely averting their eyes as much as possible without being too obvious. One little dark-haired boy, perhaps three or four years old was standing next to the center passage way. He made eye contact with me. He was smiling at me so I smiled back. His mother was instinctively protective and rushed to pick up her little son and placed him on her lap as I passed by. I felt a sudden lump in my throat. To momma I must have looked like the escaped and fettered elderly convict wandering about the marshes in Dickens's *Great Expectations*.

An indescribable feeling cut through me at that moment. For the first time in my life I experienced what it must be like to be instantly held in low regard by others, regardless of who I am as a person. In that split-second I realized I now was regarded by strangers as valueless, an undesirable element of society, someone to be shunned and it left me very sad. Aside from the constant noise in jail, that was the worst moment of my incarceration.

Only a few years prior to that, I could have been walking through that waiting room wearing a crisp white coat over a green scrub suit with the emblematic stethoscope dangling over my shoulders. The paging system would be calling out, "Doctor Steir, you are wanted in surgery," and people would listen in deference to everything I had to say. It was a great lesson to be made aware of the extent to which I had benefited from being the recipient of the unusual amount of respect that is regularly paid to people in my profession, not because of who we are as individual people but simply because of the medical profession itself. The memory seemed such a strange juxtaposition with the current setting.

When our single file caravan reached the police van it was at least 100° or perhaps 105°F outside. The desert wind added to the discomfort. From my three years at the Marine Corps Base at Twenty Nine Palms I remembered the sensation of my nostril hairs feeling curled when I took in a deep breath. Sometimes the temperature there would hit 118°F.

The cops, again, directed me to the cage in the rear of the van. The senior deputy was a bottle blonde woman whose uniform was far too tight for her. I felt comfortable enough to ask her why I was placed in the isolated rear cage. I told her that I understood why the female prisoner was separated from the men, but why was I? She hesitated and looked around and then told me that I was being protected from the other inmates. "They may not like you for the reason you are in jail."

Back at the pod I looked about and realized that my other 31 fellow inmates were all in protective custody too. We are alas, the prisoners that are regarded as contemptible even by the other prisoners: gays, baby bashers, wife beaters, men who have committed sexual assault, and me, a baby killer. We are locked up together here, being protected from one another as inmates. Some of them are murderers, repeat offenders and career criminals awaiting trial or sentencing. While others of us are just victims of circumstance.

About the Author

Bruce Steir is a retired physician living in San Francisco. He was raised in Miami Beach, Florida and received his undergraduate studies at the University of Florida and then attended medical school at the University of Miami.

After completing his internship and residency training in Obstetrics and Gynecology he served five years as a medical officer in the US Air Force where he helped to pioneer "fathers-in-the-delivery-room" in military hospitals.

During his 12 years in private practice in Seattle, Washington he became Board Certified in OB/GYN and was the recipient of the Margaret Sanger Award from the Planned Parenthood Federation of America for his contribution to the advancement of voluntary family planning. He opened and operated the first outpatient Alternative Birthing Center in Seattle.

Returning again to the military, he served as a Commander in the US Navy attached to the US Marine Corps at Camp Pendleton, California.

The author then received his Masters in Public Health from the University of California in Berkeley. He served as a consultant and trainer in Contraceptive Technology and Reproductive Health in Egypt and Russia.

Before his involuntary retirement he served as Medical Director and full time abortion provider for the Women's Health Specialists in Northern California.

Printed in the United States
118539LV00001B/253/P